Chrétien de Troyes:

Inventor of the Modern Novel

AMS PRESS
NEW YORK

Chrétien de Troyes:

Inventor of the Modern Novel

by

Foster Erwin Guyer

Bookman Associates : New York

Library of Congress Cataloging in Publication Data

Guyer, Foster Erwin, 1884-
   Chrétien de Troyes.

   Reprint of the 1957 ed.
   1. Chrestien de Troyes, 12th cent.--Influence.
2. Romances--History and criticism. 3. Fiction--
History and criticism. I. Title.
[PQ1448.G77 1972]   841'.1   73-168215
ISBN 0-404-02965-5

Reprinted with permission of Twayne Publishers, Inc.
From the edition of 1957, New York
First AMS edition published in 1972
Manufactured in the United States of America

International Standard Book Number: 0-404-02965-5

AMS PRESS INC.
NEW YORK, N. Y.   10003

Preface

The purpose of this book is to attempt to restore to his proper historical position of high distinction the inventor of the novel, Chrétien de Troyes, a French author of the twelfth century. This great innovator has been mistreated, probably, by fate and the literary critics more than any other great genius in all the history of the world. His accomplishment is one of the greatest ever known in the history of literature.

There is no person living in the civilized countries of Europe or America, who has had a high school education, who does not know something of the great stories that Chrétien wrote; and only a small percentage of all these people ever heard his name. He collected the material and composed the stories that deal with the knights of King Arthur's Court. School children throughout our country learn about these stories. Every college in the country teaches them. King Arthur's name has appeared in the moving picture theaters. These great stories still survive. Nine centuries have not put an end to them, nor will time ever destroy or obliterate them.

Chrétien de Troyes not only wrote these undying stories; he was the first writer of our Christian era to give a prominent role to women, the first to introduce a love story into a literary work written in French. He developed the metaphorical style that characterizes the love known as courtly love. He combined love with adventure and chivalry. He created characters of great nobility, of courteous manners, of invincible strength, undaunted courage and highly superior skill at arms. The finest ideals of chivalry appear in his works. He did more to establish the charm and the influence of chivalry than any other. He thus gave the highest conception of nobility of character to the society of his day and of all the world in all time. Out of the chivalry that he pictures in his great poems high ideals entered the hearts and minds of fierce and brutal knights and gradually developed there into the compelling sentiment of "noblesse oblige," finest element in the social consciousness and ideals of European aristocracy, even outliving the days of nobility's usefulness.

Chrétien de Troyes created a new form of literature at a time when no models existed in his own language. Crude epics were written in French with little adornment in style. The romances that Chrétien wrote—the first form in which the novels of the Christian era appear—are so different in style and content that the national epics were of no influence in the creation of the novel or romance, which was the work of a single great genius with no predecessors. Chrétien fashioned this new form by means of adapting the structure and material of Virgil's *Aeneid* and innumerable suggestions from the works of Ovid to the needs and taste of his own age and country. In those authors, and to a far lesser degree in Horace and Statius, he found artistic inspiration and a new figurative style. He adopted Virgil's method of connecting great events, great purposes, adventure, love, courage, high ideals, and noble character with the life and experiences of a single hero. Ovid was of tremendous help to him in forming his style and in furnishing material and splendid suggestions for thrilling episodes and even ground plots. This great store of artistic form and material was revamped by a great innovator and amalgamated with material drawn from popular stories and realistic descriptions of all the life and color about him with a mingling of marvelous elements drawn from the Classics, from native lore and native superstitions supplemented by his own marvelous imagination applied artfully to take his readers out of the stultifying boredom that filled much of their lives.

The church fathers, especially Saint Benedict and Saint Augustine, whose example was followed by many churchmen, preached against the reading of the Classical Latin Authors—Ovid in particular—warned against the wickedness of Ovid's writings, and tried to prohibit the knowledge of his works. His books did not appear in school lists until the twelfth century. Although Ovid was known by the beginning of the tenth century his popularity dates from the twelfth century. When once an interest in his works was created, his popularity became immense.

His great influence is first to be seen in the imitation of his manner of treating love as it appears in his *Art of Love,* his *Cure for Love,* the love epistles some of which are called *Heroides,* the *Amores,* lyric love poems, and the *Metamorphoses.* This interest in Ovid and the adoption of his metaphorical style in treating of love and his analysis of the passion began with the translations of his *Art of Love*—although slight indications of acquaintance with love sickness and the power of Love appear in early poems of the Provençal troubadours—and the first translation of this work was made by Chrétien de Troyes, who adapted the Ovidian precepts to Medieval needs and tastes; perhaps we should say to his own needs and that he created a new taste in France. He started a vogue that lasted into the seventeenth century.

Virgil had always been used in schools and offered a rich source of inspiration to European authors who quoted him profusely. Chrétien not only found his model for the general outline of his romances in Virgil but his descriptions of fighting and military strategy as it appears in his works were based largely on the *Aeneid* and imitated from that great classical masterpiece.

An attempt is made here to show in considerable detail such sources of Chrétien's works as can be discovered and to indicate how he adapted his source material to form the great stories that have delighted centuries of readers and served ever since their creation, directly or indirectly, as models for those idealistic and love elements that have appeared in the romantic type of literature.

The influence of Chrétien is outlined as it has persisted down to contemporary times directly and indirectly in an unbroken chain. Certain important works that show the tradition clearly are treated with a necessary rapidity and immense numbers of other works that might be mentioned or given important consideration have been arbitrarily omitted. A full and complete treatment of such works would run into encyclopaedic proportions and consequent tediousness.

Chrétien had a strong and direct influence in Provence and in France. He, also, had some influence on Italian writers. Early Italian literature owes much to the Provençal authors, whom it imitated extensively. In turn, the Italian authors had a very strong influence on English literature. Here lies the main source of the tradition. Except for a slight expedition into Spanish literature, works in other languages are neglected.

There is no intention, in the pages of this book, to compare Chrétien de Troyes to the great geniuses of the literary world such as Homer, Virgil, Dante, and Shakespeare. Chrétien's greatness lies in his historical importance as creator of an amazingly new literature and the forerunner and fountainhead of the idealistic novel.

Whatever Celtic material may have found its way into these stories, the transmission is as yet unexplained, the amalgamation is still obscure, the main themes do not seem to me to be derived from the Celtic stories that we know today. For these reasons the Celtic side of the problem of Chrétien's sources is left aside for other scholars to pursue.

Contents

			Page
Chapter	I.	Introductory	1
Chapter	II.	William of England	12
Chapter	III.	Erec and Enide	17
Chapter	IV.	The Translations from Ovid	41
Chapter	V.	Tristan and Isolt	55
Chapter	VI.	Cligès	62
Chapter	VII.	Lancelot	79
Chapter	VIII.	Yvain	89
Chapter	IX.	Perceval	111
Chapter	X.	Romances of Antiquity	116
Chapter	XI.	Provençal Literature	123
Chapter	XII.	Imitators of Chrétien	136
Chapter	XIII.	Influences of the Romances in Italy and Spain	149
Chapter	XIV.	Chaucer and Shakespeare	162
Chapter	XV.	Seventeenth Century French Novels	171
Chapter	XVI.	Corneille	185
Chapter	XVII.	Racine	188
Chapter XVIII.		Manon Lescaut	195
Chapter	XIX.	Rousseau	199
Chapter	XX.	Sir Walter Scott	204
Chapter	XXI.	Victor Hugo	211
Chapter	XXII.	Alexandre Dumas	222
Chapter XXIII.		Théophile Gautier	226
Chapter XXIV.		Honore de Balzac	229
Chapter	XXV.	Tennyson	232
Chapter XXVI.		Rostand	234
Conclusion			240
Index			243

CHAPTER I

Introductory

In 1137 the most beautiful woman in the world, at that time, came to Paris to become the Queen of Louis le Jeune, the seventh of the Louis. This glamorous girl of fifteen was the granddaughter of a Provençal duke, the first of the famous lyric poets of Provence, William the Ninth of Aquitania. Her name was Eleanor. She was a person of great energy and tremendous ambition. Heiress to vast lands in Southern France, imbued with the advanced ideas of a more cultured society to the south, accustomed to the courteous and flattering subservience of poets and nobles, rich, powerful, adored for her beauty, she intended, with a purpose that brooked no restraint, to establish and maintain an important place for women in her court and in the polite society of her country. She was a tremendous worldly force by the side of the sacred authority of the Holy Virgin, whose worship raised woman to a position of moral superiority. Social and legal importance came to many women when their lordly husbands joined the crusades and left their lands and property in the control of their wives. Although the status of women has never risen to equality with that of men even today in the whole world and though it lagged for centuries even in the most advanced civilizations, the improvement in woman's social position in France led to a role in literature in the twelfth century that is conspicuously absent even in the first half of that century. Whatever the inevitable tendency in her improved social standing might have accomplished in bringing about a change in literature that would have given a place to feminine characters, the importance of the innovation produced by Chrétien de Troyes in giving woman a role of equal elevation to that of the male, at that time, is a literary accomplishment of very great importance. This Chrétien was one of the admirers of Eleanor, the new Queen.

Chrétien was born in Troyes. There he studied Latin and read the grand stories of a civilization long past and a literature that had no survivors. The glowing embers of classical art had turned to ashes, dead and cold long since.

These stories that had come from a pagan world a thousand years back in a dim and mythical past, describing events then far back in an historical past and heroes guarded or harassed by otherworld figures, gods of superhuman powers lending their magical control, the inescapable decrees of fate, and their own supernatural struggles, ambitions and hatreds to human events and human emotions, these stories entered the receptive mind of this youth, flooded it with glorious music, gleaming light of esthetic joy and imaginative ecstasy, awakening an explosive force of creative compulsion and the desire to produce literary art of his own, to rival the grand inventions and artistic masterpieces of classical antiquity, but to put his own works in medieval garb and give them a contemporary meaning.

He never ceased to pore over his favorite Latin authors. He knew all of Ovid. Ovid taught him style and inspired the new form of love treatment that became the metaphorical description of the symptoms and effects of love in the system of courtly love. Virgil's *Aeneid* was his model. It offered the plan for structure, the nobility of characters and their lofty purpose, the conflict of love and duty, high adventure, and warfare. Horace contributed the theory of literary craftsmanship, a deep sense of pride in artistic creation, confidence in the immortality of great art, and a few suggestions for direct use in literary productions. Statius was also well-known to Chrétien as well as other classical material in whatever form it may have come to him.

This was the source of inspiration. From the great masters of classical Latin literature he learned to write, how to develop a new style, how to form a plot, how to create noble and courageous heroes, how to describe military strategy, conflict in battle and in personal combat, and to describe personal character, physical traits of personal appearance, and love in its awkward and timid beginning, in its pain and suffering, and in its patient enduring.

This deep appreciation of the great classics, this understanding of literary values, this impelling desire to emulate his great masters, this feeling that France and the French language should have the great honor of leading the world in literary achievement fired his youthful ambition. A great assurance of his own ability to accomplish this purpose for country and for self grew in his mind, fortified his marvelous inborn talent, and encouraged his creative genius.

All this inner fire, the compelling force and urgent need to create and to excel was accompanied by a facile skill in narration, in riming, and in turning elegant rhythmic verse. His cleverness in the stylistic manipulation of his language amazed and delighted two centuries of followers and imitators, who never hoped to equal his masterful technique.

Chrétien was also a keen observer of the color, form and movement of all the materials and the life around him.

As a child he lived in a great commercial city where merchandise was brought to great fairs that lasted through a large part of every year. He saw knights and courtiers in attendance at an important court, under powerful rulers famous for their generosity and their energy in making Troyes a beautiful and convenient center of trade and culture.

Everything this youth looked upon had its impact on his consciousness.

Suffering and misfortune he noted and often described. Poverty awakened his pity. He observed cruelty and ruthlessness. His work portrays them. Deceit and thieving also are described in terms that prove acquaintance with such baseness.

We know nothing of Chrétien's parents or even relatives. We might have reason to fear that he was an orphan. No record shows that he ever owned any property. Yet he expresses scorn of rustics, of low-born people, even of merchants. He has great respect for nobility and praises and grants worth only to men of noble birth. Heredity is an important theme for Chrétien. Valor and adeptness in the use of arms, bravery and prowess in combat are described as inborn. Cowardice is unknown by any of his heroes and shown by only a few of their foes. His attitude is always assurance and confidence in his own ability and fame.

His admiration, his joy in the contemplation of wealth and adornment seem to be the result of lacking them personally rather than experienced possession of riches and finery. He saw bright armor sparkling in the sunlight. In the stalls of the markets he saw silk, satin and velvet, expensive furs, ermine, sable and variegated, cloth of silver, cloth of gold, utensils of copper and gold. He saw tournaments, men and horses killed in clouds of dust; fair ladies watching. All these things and many more he observed with the eye of an artist. He retained vivid impressions and knew how to describe them so well that a clear background of reality serves as a solid framework for exciting stories of bravery, love and phantasy, mingled with the weird and the impossible.

This obscure youth, of whose family we know nothing, appears to have worked out his own course of life, to have lived in a world of his own imagining, beautified by love of letters, an appreciation and comprehension of art scarcely known or felt by his contemporaries, made happy and endurable by hope and ambition and by a keen zest and delight in everyday experiences. With the artistic eye he saw kaleidoscopic variety and vivid charm in all the events of life and the daily movement of teeming activity in a world of glittering wealth, ruthless knights, greedy merchants and desperate crowds of toilers breaking their backs, living in poverty and filth, compelled by fate to slave for a society of more fortunate people heedless of the wretches trampled beneath their selfish and merciless weight.

He saw thick-walled castles, from which knights came forth, incased in protective armor, attended by their squires and followers, bent on depredation, spurred by anger or greed, to plunder, burn or seize property guarded with equal determination, lust for power, or selfish grasping pride of possession.

He saw victorious knights returning with prisoners, who might be inhumanly tortured or thrown into deep wet dungeon cells to rot, starve, and fight off rats.

He saw bands of armed ruffians, errant and idle, now that a petty war was over, roaming over the highways in search of plunder.

Often a knight watched, like a beast of prey, in his castle, to issue forth and strike down a weaker victim passing by the dangerous retreat.

All this fury and rapaciousness appears in Chrétien's works, but from among these monstrous and ferocious humans, who furnish a realistic background for Chrétien's fine stories of love and adventure, the author lifts up idealized figures whose nobility, generosity and unselfish kindness are matched only by their superhuman courage.

The century in which Chrétien lived is one of the most interesting and remarkable in the history of the world; and Chrétien de Troyes mirrors most of the startling accomplishments of that era. Its quickening impulses, the youthful vigor and the fresh charm of its glorious advent resemble the delight of springtime's joyous arrival, fresh green beauty, and gladdening warmth after the deathlike chill of winter. The twelfth century was, in fact, a renaissance period. The upsurge of civilization, after a century or so of groping, followed the Dark Ages when all French culture reached a point so low that ignorance, violence, and bestiality covered and drowned every despairing hope, every glimmer of decency, confidence, or moral aspiration. Education was non-existent—except momentarily at the court of Charlemagne. Only a few monks could read or write. For centuries no literary work of even the slightest merit was written.

The first form of literature worthy the name was the national epic, which began to be written early in the twelfth century. The best known of these epics was *The Song of Roland* written after the turn of the century and containing allusions to the First Crusade. This poem has a few stirring lines written in a crude style. It reveals the first love of the fatherland, pride in the glory of France and high praise of bravery in battle. The epics depict the violent passions of cruelty, greed, and hatred and describe the mass fighting of armies defending the king against the Saracens or against some great lord or the quarrels between nobles. There were no love themes in the early epics. Women rarely appear and then they have scarcely any feminine traits or charm. Sometimes they fight like men in defense of a castle. The style in which these epics of the first half of the twelfth century were written is crude and unadorned. These epics were written in French and give evidence of a language that had developed some refinement but they offered no real literary aid or influence for Chrétien. Other uninspired forms of writing, such as lives of saints, were of no use to Chrétien as models.

In architecture, however, the Gothic style had its purest and most charming development in the twelfth century. The high walls, tall pointed arches, elaborate carving and lacy stone openwork of lofty towers and spires displayed a graceful artistry.

There were some great teachers in that age who are still famed in the history of Education. Bernard de Chartres and Abelard were great men and inspiring teachers.

Libraries were growing and furnishing many copies of a large number of Latin works by the best authors of antiquity. These Latin masterpieces were studied with a fervor that has never been excelled. John of Salisbury and Peter of Blois were the two greatest scholars of the century. They had a deep love of the classics, read them with unbounded joy and cited them voluminously in works that they wrote in Latin.

Social groups flourished at Paris and in some of the smaller courts of France especially at Troyes. Eleanor and her daughters fostered the arts and supported poets and artists at their courts.

Chivalry was established. Its code demanded the worship of God, defense of the weak, especially of women. It postulated nobility of character, respect for women and courtesy to all. The church fostered chivalry and tried to prevent internal warfare, while preaching the crusades.

The ideal of chivalry was rarely exemplified in real life. It appeared highly developed and finely portrayed in the works of the great poet Chrétien de Troyes.

Charity or generosity was regarded as the greatest of all virtues. It has prominent examples in the fame of Alexander the Great and in the twelfth century, especially in the courts whose capital was the city of Troyes—Thibaut during the youth of Chrétien and Henry during his manhood.

Chrétien was, at an early period in his life, a professional story-teller. No doubt, he moved about, and in all probability he made his way to Paris, and adding the name of his native city to his own, called himself Chrétien de Troyes.

Excluding the epic, fiction is usually divided into the two classes of romances and novels. Novels are more recent and are supposed to describe real life. Romances are supposed to deal with something legendary or something unreal. The stories of King Arthur are called romances. Many people think of the prose romances that describe impossible combats with giants and magicians, and the valor of invincible knights that defeat opponents by the thousands singlehandedly. There was, also, a metrical romance, which preceded the prose romances. The first of these versified romances were stories about knightly heroes who were connected with the court of King Arthur. These first romances were written by an author of tremendous historical importance because he was the inventor of modern fiction. His name was Chrétien de Troyes, and he lived in France in the twelfth century.

The origin of our modern novel has been placed by many scholars in England and in the eighteenth century; but there were novels in seventeenth century France that were intended to describe real life. Madame de Lafayette's *Princesse de Clèves* is such a work. Scarron's *Roman Comique* is not too far removed from early English novels. There were the interminal novels of Honoré d'Urfé, of which the best known is *Astrée,* and of Madeleine de Scudéry, known especially for her *Clélie,* which contains the famous Map of Love. Those novels were preceded by pastoral romances and these by romances of chivalry.

When much of the miscomprehension regarding the work of Chrétien de Troyes is removed, his romances will not appear so different from the novel. In fact his works are extremely modern in many respects. They tower above the fictional works of five centuries, through which Chrétien's influence streams, to bridge a wide gap and to assume his true importance as the distant precursor and to claim with insistence the title of inventor of the novel of the Christian era.

There is almost nothing of the legendary in Chrétien's works. King Arthur is a literary creation of the Welsh author Geoffrey of Monmouth who wrote the *Historia Regum Britanniae.* This literary figure is based on a more or less legendary leader of the Welsh. In Chrétien's romances or versified novels King Arthur is a virtual figurehead. The heroes of these stories are knights who are attached to his court. Nothing else about these romances is legendary. They represent the life of Chrétien's time in a remarkably realistic manner. They also have a romantic trend which wanders deeply into the ultra-heroic, the exotic, the unreal, the weird, and the impossible. This romantic escape from stark realism, which appears in abundance in Chrétien's works, as well as in the life of the age, is mingled with reality, in order to take the readers of the twelfth century out of the boring humdrum and the gloomy oppression of harsh and uncomfortable living and to relieve the cruelty and danger of their existence with glamor and noble sentiments.

Men could not venture on the highways unless armed and clad in protective armor. They moved about in groups for mutual protection from robber barons and ruffians living on what they could secure by force of arms. Merchants traveled in terror at the risk of complete ruin, when their merchandise was taken from them on the roads. Many a man, even of noble birth, found himself suddenly imprisoned in a dark dungeon, lying on damp and rotting straw, attended by snakes and rats, living on bread and water or entirely forgotten to starve and go mad in the gloom.

In wild terror he explored the moist and filthy walls, and often fell through a craftily placed hole to land in unheard screaming on spikes fifty feet or more below or to be dashed on rocks and washed away by a roaring torrent racing down a steep declivity. Women spent hours alone in cold and dimly lighted castles and there in silent discomfort without entertainment or diversion, day after day, how eagerly they read the golden and diamond studded novels of Chrétien de Troyes, that took them into realms of joy and enchantment, filled their hearts with vicarious love, their minds with noble thoughts and exciting interest, teeming with deeds of valor performed by chivalrous knights of impeccable virtue, displaying the charm of physical beauty, courteous conduct, and indomitable courage!

Two centuries of followers and imitators in all of civilized Europe praised Chrétien to the skies, proclaimed him their master, and used his works as a quarry for material and artistic inspiration; and through them his inventive genius still transmits much to the present in literature, in social attitudes and ideals and on the cinematographic screen. Every child in school reads about the heroes of his great romances, every student in high school, college and university has, in a degree, familiarity with his creations in some form. Many of these children and older students never heard the name of the original author of the stories of King Arthur and his knights, which still delight them and will never cease to please the Christian world.

The great originality of Chrétien de Troyes has been obscured by a theory of chronology advanced by scholars who could not believe that he could have produced stories of such excellence and of a novelty so pronounced spontaneously. It seemed to those scholars that some gradual development some transitional evolution must have paved the way for the creation of the superior art that Chrétien displayed. There are three romances of importance that several scholars have attempted to date; and they have placed them chronologically before Chrétien's romances. In the first place this arrangement was suggested merely for the reason that it was likely that translations of Classical Latin works would precede original romances. This theory seems logical enough. All three of the romances in question were translations with adaptations; and they have been called romances of antiquity. They are in chronological order without dispute at present: the *Roman de Thèbes* translated with variations on the part of the translator from the *Thebaid* of the Latin poet Statius, *Eneas* translated from Virgil's *Aeneid* with considerable additions and variations, and the *Roman de Troie* much longer than the other two and relating with extensive variations the story of the siege of Troy. These three romances have been considered precursors that pointed the way for Chrétien and other authors of the period. Later scholars accepted this view as established and attempted to strengthen the theory by means of parallel passages with identical rimes and wording. This method is only one of comparison; and it cannot establish the priority of any of the romances.

The same scholars who nonchalantly advanced this logical theory also applied it to Chrétien's own works, declared that his own list of his earlier works at the beginning of *Cligès*, the second of his longer works that remain to us, were not given there in chronological order; but that his translations from Ovid no doubt served him in the development of his style and composition and preceded *Erec and Enide*, which is the only one of his romances listed there that has been preserved. [There is no proof of this theory nor even a tiny scrap of evidence to prove any of this theoretic chronology either of Chrétien's own works or of the order of the other romances with relation to those of Chrétien. There is a great abundance of unassailable evidence to prove both that Chrétien's *Erec* preceded his translations of Ovid and that all of the romances that he completed and that have come down to us—and excepting only *Perceval* which was unfinished and so different from the other romances as to be of special interest only because it seems to have inaugurated the romances that treat of the search for the Holy Grail—preceded all three of the romances of antiquity. Sufficient proof of these statements will be given below.

It should be of great interest to readers to know what were the sources of inspiration for this great writer, who was the first to compose novels, to write novels whose creation was so spontaneous and original that it is one of the literary wonders of the world, novels whose influence direct and indirect is relatively greater than any other during our whole Christian era. Chrétien took popular tales such as the *Three-Day Tournament,* the story of Gyges ring, of Solomon's Wife, native French material, and folk tales widespread through the world at the time when he wrote. A great deal of the realistic description was due to Chrétien's observation of the life around him. Geoffrey of Monmouth contributed the literary figure of King Arthur and that of Queen Guenevere as well as some other names and one whole episode in which King Arthur kills a giant, the feat being performed by Yvain in Chrétien's *Chevalier au Lion* or *Yvain.*

Chrétien's great masters were Virgil and Ovid. Virgil's *Aeneid* was Chrétien's model for the general plan of his romances. This Classical Latin work and the poems of Ovid provided a vast amount of material and models for Chrétien's style. Ovid inspired an entirely new style and method of analyzing and describing love, its symptoms and its effects. Horace and Statius made contributions.

It was Chrétien's creative imagination that took materials and suggestions from numerous sources, adapted them to his needs and the taste of his age, and combined them in new and brilliant masterpieces.

CHAPTER II

William of England

The first of Chrétien's works, as far as we know, was a tale of adventure. He followed the suggestion of the Latin poet Horace that an author make use of familiar material. A great poet, according to Horace, in his *Art of Poetry,* can take a well-known story and make of it a work of art so fine that another may "sweat and toil in vain" in the same attempt. Chrétien based his tale on the legend of Saint Eustache and the familiar folk theme of the Man Sorely Tried by Fate.

Although this is a slight effort in comparison with Chrétien's later works, written in simple, straightforward style, it is a remarkable achievement for the time. It presents an entirely new form of literature only a step away from the full-fledged romance, predecessor of our modern novel.

A very pious king named William, is the hero of this tale entitled *William of England.* King William had visions, in which it seemed to him that God commanded him to relinquish his throne, to dispose of all his worldly goods, and to depart from his home and kingdom.

Filled with deep grief over the enforced parting from his dearly loved wife, he follows the command from Heaven. His mental anguish, however, cannot be concealed from his devoted wife in spite of his firm determination to keep his secret carefully guarded. And although the Queen expects to give birth to a child in the near future, she will not be left alone.

Man and wife set out, therefore, and travel on foot into a wild country near the shore of the sea. There in a rocky cave the Queen gives birth to twin baby boys, attended in her ordeal only by her distracted and worried husband, trembling with the terror of such a fearful risk. He tears away one of his coattails for each of the infants. They have no other covering for their tender bodies. The parents have no food for themselves. Mother and father are assailed by almost unendurable hunger. They even think of devouring their offspring; and refrain from such pitiable cannibalism only with heroic determination.

Soon some merchants arrive and snatch the Queen from her husband and carry her away in their boat. The heartbroken King is left to care for his two infants. In despair, he thinks he will try to get to a place where some food may be found for the babies. He carries one of them to an empty boat that he has discovered on the shore. When he returns to get the second child, he sees a wolf running away with the coattail in which the baby is wrapped. He pursues the wolf in vain. When, finally, he is obliged to abandon the chase and return to the boat, he finds that it is gone and he has lost his other child. Now all four members of the unhappy family are separated, except that the two boys, brought up by merchants, are neighbors. The wolf had dropped the baby it had stolen, unharmed; and a merchant had taken it.

The King himself now becomes a merchant and carries on trading for a while.

Chrétien's habit is to bring a family separated by misfortune or misunderstanding back together. The rest of this tale describes the adventures of the various members of the King's family until they are finally reunited.

This story has an underlying idea that is one of Chrétien's firm convictions; namely, that heredity is more important than environment and that noble birth usually guarantees nobility of character, courage, and skill in the use of warlike weapons. The King remains dignified and regal even though living as a merchant, which in Chrétien's opinion is a degrading profession. The Queen attracts the attention, respect and even the affection of a nobleman, who marries her. The Queen outwardly accepts this solution of her life's problem but remains loyal to her former husband and ever chaste.

The boys cannot endure the unreformed manners of the merchant folk who are their foster parents. Therefore, while still in their youth, they run away from their home, take service with a nobleman and soon display their naturally courteous behavior and inborn superiority in hunting and in the use of arms, so that they are adopted by the nobleman until such time as the King remounts his throne and the whole family is reunited.

Chrétien's knowledge of the classics is shown by a passage mentioning covetousness, Tantalus, and his unassuaged thirst suggested by Horace in his *Satires* and also a remarkable description of a ship caught in a terrible storm at sea imitated from passages in the works of the Latin poet Ovid:[1]

> The wind begins to rage,
> And stirs up a heavy sea
> Sailors shout: "Hard a port."
> But the waves tear with violence.
> They strike and pound the ship.
> Now the sides begin to crack
> And the beams nearly break.
> The sea, so smooth and flat before,
> Now is nothing but mountains and vales.
> The waves climb so high with deep valleys between
> That the ship tosses and helplessly
> Mounts and descends on the swell.
> The day grows dark as night
> And spreads misfortune over all.
> The sky and the air are black.
> The swollen sea expands
> And now it visibly contracts.
> Despair overcomes the captain of the ship
> When he sees the terrible might of the winds.
> Attacking the air and the sea
> Whirling, thundering, destroying.

---

[1] Tristia I, 1 and 2, 25 ff.; *Metamorphoses* XI 496 ff., 516 f., 523 ff.

He loses control of the ship
And lets it aimlessly rock.
The waves toss it back and forth.
A game of tennis they seem to play.
The waves float it up to the clouds
Then down in a gaping abyss.
The winds grow more and more angry;
With violence they rend and tear
Every rope and every sail.
The canvas is torn to shreds,
The mast is broken too.
Anguish and fear seize the crew
Everyone prays fervently to God.
And they all raise their voice and shriek:
"Saint Nicolas come to our aid.
Pray God to grant us mercy.
Beg him to have pity on our souls
And bring peace among the waring winds
That torment us unjustly.
Each other they fight but us they kill.
Displaying their power on the sea,
The winds quite clearly appear
To act like the great lords of the land.
Whoever their discord may injure,
They will never suffer at all.
Sad witnesses of their outrage,
Which gives them only delight,
We it is who will be destroyed.
Thus the winds wage their war
Just as the barons of the earth,
Who, for the joy it brings them,
Burn and destroy the land.
Thus we, poor weak creatures,
Pay for the wars of the noble lords.

Truly one may rightly compare
The winds to the barons; the sea to the land;
For the barons harm the land
Just as the winds disturb the sea.

CHAPTER III

Erec and Enide

The simple tale of *William of England* is not at all typical of the real romances that Chrétien created. It might be regarded as a timid and youthful testing of his ability. It was followed, as far as our knowledge goes, by a romance still lacking the full development of his refined style and his typical manner of analyzing and describing the effects of love. This first romance, still to be regarded as a youthful work, is *Erec et Enide*. In spite of its less perfect style and the fact that it is not a courtly romance like the later ones, its simple charm, its greater naturalness and the appealing hero and heroine make it the most enjoyable for the modern reader.

In *Erec et Enide* Chrétien has created the structure of a romance according to his desire and understanding. The plan was supplied by Virgil in his *Aeneid* and consisted of a number of adventures experienced by a single individual. The destiny of Aeneas is the chain on which his adventures are strung. In Chrétien the adventures are held together by the love story of the hero. This was the structure of the early romances of Chrétien's imitators and followers. There might be more than one hero; but the romance is concerned with the adventure of single individuals as opposed to the mass fighting described in the epics. In the grail stories the love element is largely subordinated and sacrificed to that of the search for the holy vessel.

Just as the *Aeneid* has twelve books, *Erec et Enide* has a dozen episodes. Aeneas was looked upon as a model hero, a man of great fortitude, high ideals, and praiseworthy character. Erec, as well as all the heroes of Chrétien's romances, are the very finest examples of chivalry, and therefore represent ideal conceptions of manhood. The *Aeneid* has the typical plot of classical stories, which take a hero to a distant land, through difficult and dangerous adventures, where the reward of valor is the love of a fair lady. This is the situation in Chrétien's romances.

In the *Aeneid,* the hero is caught in the struggle between love and duty, and fate decrees that he must give up Dido, whom he dearly loves, to fulfill his great destiny and found a new nation in Italy. But Chrétien, like his contemporaries, disapproved of this faithless abandonment of the loved woman. The Dido story of the fourth book of Virgil's *Aeneid* is the initial source of Chrétien's *Erec et Enide* and furnishes the chief conception of the central plot, which represents a knight winning a wife in a distant land, a period of uxoriousness wherein all thoughts of personal glory and manly pursuits are sacrificed to dalliance with the object of an ardent love. Just as Aeneas was awakened from his sloth by Mercury, messenger from the gods, Erec, too, is awakened and devotes himself to further adventures of great difficulty attended by grave danger.

Aeneas wins the love of Lavinia, later, in Italy. Chrétien, however, unites these two women in the person of Enide and thus avoids the faithless betrayal of which Aeneas was guilty.

The complete break between Aeneas and Dido becomes, in Chrétien's story just a quarrel between husband and wife—a severe one but one that is finally resolved with a complete reconciliation and the same ardent love as before. A careful study of Chrétien's works reveals many similar adaptations and often surprising changes and even weird distortions of the material that he takes from his sources of inspiration. He gathers in an immense number of suggestions from the classics and fits them into his story in an amazing mosaic with an application so at variance from their original use by the authors of antiquity that they completely evade the notice of the casual reader. They have also evaded the attention of scholars. There are two reasons why previous scholars have not noted the great influence of the classics on Chrétien's works. One is the belief, held by a great number of students of Chrétien, that his romances were adaptations of Celtic material.

This view is known as the Celtic Hypothesis, still cherished by a great many Arthurian scholars, who have patiently and conscientiously sacrificed precious years and the strength of their fine intellects in a vain effort to discover single Celtic sources for Chrétien's romances, which not only have no similarity to any Celtic story written before his time, but also never have single sources. Rather, each romance has a number of sources amalgamated in a story of great originality. The second reason is that, until recently, Chrétien has been regarded as a relatively ignorant man, whereas, in fact, he was a profound student of classical Latin literature.

Lavinia, herself, does not play a prominent role in Virgil's epic. Latinus, her father, had refused her hand to many suitors, preferring to await some great prince from a foreign land. Aeneas was such a man, a great hero descended from an important line of kings and destined to found a great nation. Amata, Latinus' queen, favored the suit of Turnus, a neighboring king, who, for this reason considered his marriage to Lavinia assured. He would not give up his claim to Lavinia's hand; and a great war ensued, which was finally settled by a single combat between Aeneas and Turnus, resulting in victory for Aeneas, after Turnus' sword broke in his hand. This whole situation with numerous special details served Chrétien in *Erec et Enide* and in a later romance entitled *Cligès*.

In *Erec et Enide*, Enide's father, a nobleman had refused the hand of his daughter to numerous suitors, reserving her, like Latinus, for some great hero of noble race, who might arrive from a distant land. Chrétien did not use the war between Aeneas and Turnus in *Erec et Enide* but he did use it in *Cligès*. The incident of the broken sword occurs, however, in a combat between Erec and Guivret le Petit, later, in *Erec et Enide*. Chrétien often used his source material repeatedly in the same or in more than one romance, often splitting the material into fragments to be diversely employed.

This romance is written by a confident poet. The days of story-telling may not be over; but the gleam of interest in his listener's eyes and the easy grace with which he spins out a tale in words that ripple and sing like a racing stream adorned with the gleaming foam and the exquisite coloring of happy stylistic gems, like the mingling of the water's green with the white to make rich sapphire rings that wind their loveliness around your pulsing heart, assure him of his present power and fame through time's unending span. He makes his claim to all that fame in words like those that Horace wrote, in the *Art of Poetry,* and in his *Odes.*

In an ode on his own works—the thirtieth selection in the third book of his *Odes*—Horace wrote that he had created a monument more lasting than bronze and more sublime than the regal elevation of the pyramids, which the innumerable succession of the years would never be able to destroy, that his fame would never die, and that his praises would ring as long as the priest should ascend the Capitol with the vestal virgin. Chrétien himself saw how long the fame of Horace's poetry had lasted, and he proclaimed that his own work would endure as long as the Christian religion.

In the opening lines Chrétien called his first romance a "very fine conjuncture" or combining of various sources of material, using familiar stories to form a new one, according to the recommendation of Horace in the *Art of Poetry,* and one that could not be equalled by others making a similar attempt.

King Arthur is holding court, in the early spring, at Cardigan. For thrilling entertainment, he orders a hunt for the White Stag. This is no ordinary chase; for, according to the custom, whoever kills the White Stag may and must kiss the most beautiful lady at the court—a dangerous act because there are many fair ladies at the court and brave and powerful knights who will be sure to claim the first place in this beauty contest, each for his own lady-love. For the sake of peace a miracle must and will occur.

In order to set the stage for the necessary miracle, the author, who plans his plot with care, keeps the best knight of all the court out of the hunt and has this knight, whose name, of course, is

Erec, merely ride out to watch the hunt from a convenient spot; and Erec is unarmed. He encounters the Queen, who, accompanied by a pretty maiden, is also going to watch. As the three stop in a clearing near a road, a knight approaches in the company of his damsel and preceded by a dwarf, who carries a leather lash. The Queen desires to learn the name of the knight. So she commands her attendant maiden to ask the knight to bring his damsel to the Queen and make himself and the lady known. But the ugly and irritable dwarf shouts to the maiden that she must not approach the knight. The maiden pays no attention to the dwarf or his arrogant words; but as she continues to advance the dwarf strikes her with his whip and raises an ugly welt on her hand, that she raises to protect her face.

At the Queen's request, Erec now makes the same attempt, but with no more success. He returns with an angry welt raised by the dwarf's stinging lash. Being unarmed Erec does not dare to punish the dwarf on account of the fully armed and arrogant knight who had permitted his impudent dwarf to commit such an outrage.

Since there is no time for Erec to return to Cardigan for his arms, he follows the knight all day; and at night they enter a town filled with a throng of visitors. Only with difficulty can Erec find a lodging. At last he is welcomed by a poor nobleman, a proud and worthy man though the victim of adversity.

It is not poverty, however, that explains the lack of the courtly element in this romance. It is, rather, the date of its composition. Chrétien never adopted the Provençal worship of woman as the representative of God on earth. Chrétien's contribution to courtly love is in the analysis of the symptoms and the effects of love, developed on the model of Ovid's treatment of love, as a disease, warfare or torment inflicted by Cupid or by the loved woman herself when, in arrogant acceptance of her lover's subservience and assumption of tyrannical power over an enslaved lover, she takes over the function of the god of love. Chrétien also developed, in imitation of Ovid, a metaphorical style, which became one element of courtly love in later literature, with Chrétien himself the master craftsman imitated by his contemporaries and followers. It will be helpful to the reader to have a chronological list of the important romances and tales of this period. The following dates are intended to be only approximate but recent scholarship has definitely determined their relative order:

Chrétien's, *William of England,* before 1150;
Chrétien's, *Erec et Enide,* about 1150;
Wace's, *Brut,* 1155;
Chrétien's translations of Ovid including *Philomena* and his *Tristan,* 1150-1160;
Chrétien's, *Cligès,* about 1160;
Chrétien's, *Lancelot,* 1164-65;
Chrétien's, *Yvain,* 1166-67;
Chrétien's, *Perceval* (not finished), 1170-75;
    Roman de Thèbes, after 1167;
    Eneas, after 1167;
    Lais, of Marie de France after 1170;
Gautier d' Arras', *Ille et Galeron,* finished 1175-84;
Gautier d' Arras', *Eracle,* finished after 1180;
Benoît de Sainte-More's, *Roman de Troie,* after 1184.

The omission of courtly love from the first romance is evident from the first meeting of Erec and Enide, who is the daughter of a poor nobleman. It is no less evident throughout the story.

Enide appears in ragged clothing; and she attends to Erec's horse, leading it to the stable, feeding and currying it. Although her beauty shines through her tatters and in her lovely face, no arrow was shot from Cupid's bow, no wounding glance from the fair maiden's eyes nor from those of the handsome guest. These two examples of nature's purest art, paragons of the human species, will, of course, be married; but there is no indication of trembling, sighing, sleeplessness or loss of appetite on the part of either. Neither grows pale or thin. There is no timid hesitation, no love monologues in which the lovers hope, doubt, and worry.

All these metaphorical descriptions of love await Chrétien's later manner, after he has translated Ovid's *Art of Love;* and then, and always thereafter, he treats love metaphorically in a new style adapted from his study of Ovid.

Erec asks why so many people have flooded this town; and he learns that, on the next day, a prize is to be awarded to the most beautiful woman. His own damsel's claim to the prize, which is a sparrowhawk, will be defended against all challengers by the arrogant knight whom Erec has been following all day with the intention of somehow avenging the insult to himself and to Queen Guenivere. This knight, whose name is Yder, has won the prize of beauty for his damsel in two successive years. If he wins again this year he will retain the prize and the contest will be over. Thus the motive of a beauty contest is reduplicated.

Meanwhile at King Arthur's court, the King himself has killed the White Stag and he will kiss the most beautiful lady. Queen Guenivere persuades the King to wait, for three days, the return of Erec before bestowing the kiss. In this way, one episode is set within another, providing a strong element of suspense. This procedure is common in the structure of Chrétien's romances.

Erec now has a fine chance to try to get his revenge; that is, to enter the beauty contest. Here was Enide, the most beautiful girl he had ever seen. At this point in the story we have to assume that he was strongly attracted by Enide. At any rate, a father could give his daughter in marriage. The daughter was not supposed to have much to say about it. Erec was the son of a powerful and famous king named Lac. Even a king would be glad to give his daughter to such a man. So when Erec offered to champion Enide as the lady most worthy of the sparrowhawk and promised to marry her if he were successful in the combat, the nobleman was glad to give his consent and to lend Erec arms for the tournament.

A large crowd was gathered to watch the event. Their comments before and during the fight add to the story by giving additional praise of the beauty of the ladies, the strength and comeliness of the knights, the fierceness of the fight; and they add an element of excitement as they exclaim over the blows, the wounds, and the danger that each contestant incurs as he risks his life in the deadly struggle. This interest of friends and of observers of the incidents in his stories is an important feature of Chrétien's technique and is to be found in all of his romances.

As must be expected, Erec wins after a difficult fight; and the sparrowhawk is awarded to Enide.

As the vanquished knight, and in return for his life, that Erec spares, Yder is in honor bound to go to Cardigan with his damsel and the spiteful dwarf to surrender himself to the will of Queen Guenivere. As these three approach Cardigan, they are espied from the castle and the Queen and several others mount to the higher windows in the castle wall, from which vantage point Guenivere recognized the knight in the distance. They wonder whether the knight is coming to report victory or defeat; they worry over the fate of Erec; and they are filled with delight and eager impatience for Erec's return when they learn from Yder that Erec will arrive the next day bringing with him the most beautiful maiden that Yder ever saw in all his life. The Queen is thrilled over her premonition that Erec's adventure might have a solution for the serious problem of observing the custom of the White Stag and the kiss that is to be given to the most beautiful lady at the court.

Erec insists on taking Enide, in the dress she was wearing, to the court at Cardigan to be adorned for their wedding there by Queen Guenivere. He promises to send later for Enide's parents and to give them two castles in his father's kingdom.

The poet describes the scene as Enide leaves her home. Mother and father weep and Enide too. Love of parents for their child, a child's love for home and nurture cause emotion that cannot be controlled.

Now the young couple leave for Cardigan. The new emotion of love of youth for youth dispels the sadness of the parting. Each gazes hungrily and their eyes tell each other of their love. A love scene, natural and charming, delights the reader. No artificiality in the style such as we have in the late development of courtly love appears. There is no enumeration of the symptoms and effects of love.

We do, however, have here an indication of the source of the personal portraits that are so common in Chrétien's romances and in later ones. As gentle love fills his heart, Erec admires the laughing eyes, clear white forehead, nose, mouth and the whole face of his lovely companion. His gaze flows over Enide's whole body, chin, throat and bosom, arms, hands and softly molded sides and hips. This passage must be joined to the later description of the scene in their bridal chamber when loving gazes continue to observe all the charms of personal beauty; and they each give its due to each member or feature.

Here is a beginning of portraiture in the stories of the twelfth century. Since we have opened this parenthesis, in the belief that the reader will be interested in this explanation of Chrétien's literary technique and its origin, we must turn now to a more complete example of personal portraiture which appears in *Philomena.* When this passage is united to the description of Enide's beauty in *Erec et Enide,* the classical source will become evident. Before beginning his portraiture, still mindful of Horace, his mentor, promising to apply all his understanding and ability, he directs us to a classical source of inspiration by asserting that neither the art nor language of Plato, Homer, or Cato could tell the beauty of this maiden. This statement mirrors Ovid, in the eighth book of his *Metamorphoses,* who wrote that if he had received from Apollo a hundred mouths and a hundred voices, all gifts of the muses, he still could not give an adequate description— not of beauty, to be sure, but of grief.

In Philomena's portrait, *each* part of the body is taken in turn. The forehead is smooth and white, the eyes are bright and clear like jewels, the nose is high, long, and straight. Roses and lilies are mingled in the complexion, the mouth is smiling, the lips full and vermilion. Her breath is sweet. Her teeth are small, white, and set close together. Her chin, throat, and bosom are whiter than ermine. The breasts are like two small apples, the hands are long, slender, and white; the body is slender and her hips are set low. Chrétien adds an extended description of Philomena's mental ability and accomplishments.

Such elements of beauty are common in the classics; but they are new in medieval literature; and Chrétien learned to use them especially from Virgil and Ovid. We know that Virgil's *Aeneid* was the source of Chrétien's essential plot in *Erec et Enide*. We know that the story of Lavinia had a direct influence on Chrétien's romance and for that reason it is evident enough that Virgil's description of Lavinia, wherein he compares her complexion to the whiteness of ivory tinged with vermilion and also to mingled roses and lilies is imitated in the portrait of Enide. Describing Enide, Chrétien wrote:

> More than the lily's flower
> Her forehead and her face were clear and white,
> And like a miracle over the white
> Her whole face was illumined,
> By a gift that Nature gave,
> With a fresh vermilion color.

Chrétien mentions Narcissus and his story in Ovid's *Metamorphoses*. He compares Cligès, in the romance having that title, to Narcissus when he gives a detailed portrait of his hero. Narcissus, as described by Ovid, has eyes as bright as stars—just like Enide—hair like Apollo, neck like ivory, a charming mouth, a complexion white as snow but tinged with rosy coloring. The final and definite proof that Chrétien went especially to Ovid to learn about portraiture is to be found in the *Amores* where Ovid describes Corinne, who stands revealed, just as Enide appears on her wedding night. Ovid explains, "What shoulders! What arms! Perfect throat, faultless breast, soft white skin, divine form, fresh young legs! But why stop over *each* of her charms?" Ovid stops at this point to leave more for the imagination and Chrétien imitates this spicy trait. In the first book of the *Metamorphoses* Daphne is described as she races before the pursuing Apollo.

She has eyes like stars, an attractive mouth, fingers, hands, arms; and what is covered by the clothing seems in imagination still more beautiful. In *Cligès* Chrétien says of Soredamor that he would like to tell about the charms hidden under her clothing.

Here then are the models that Chrétien used to introduce the first examples of portraiture into early French literature. The listing of one feature or part of the body after another, the touch of raciness added by suggesting something that is not told and especially the suggestion that *each* part is mentioned or not mentioned gives away the secret since Chrétien speaks of giving *each member* its due.

The intellectual acquirements also come from Ovid, as well as Philomena's sweet breath. They are to be found in the third book of the *Art of Love*.

When they arrived at Cardigan, Erec was welcomed with great joy, for everyone at the court is very fond of him. Enide is greatly admired on account of her marvelous beauty. The King himself comes forward to help her alight from her horse. The Queen takes Enide at once, following Erec's request, to her apartments, there to have her clothed in a rich and beautiful gown ornamented at the neck and wrists with precious jewels set in gold and lined with ermine. Over the gown is placed a lovely mantle also lined with ermine, having golden tassles and sparkling jewels. She wears a golden belt and a thread of fine gold is woven through her hair; but her hair is more radiant than the gold.

The Queen takes Enide to the great ball of the castle. The room is full of knights from many parts of King Arthur's realm.

> When the pretty girl, a stranger,
> Sees all the knights encircling her,
> Gazing in wonder at her beauty,
> She bows her head in modesty.
> No wonder confusion rises in her breast
> And tinges her face with rosy light.
> Embarrassment becomes the lovely girl
> Making her more charming still.

Seeing her embarrassment, King Arthur takes the timid girl gently by the hand and makes her sit beside him. The Queen is quite contented and takes great satisfaction over the prowess of Erec, who has won such a wonderfully beautiful wife in a distant land and brought her to the court to solve the dangerous problem of the kiss that now may be bestowed without contention or objection; for clearly Enide surpasses in beauty all the ladies assembled at the court. How fortunate was the delay, awaiting Erec's return!

The King and all the court agree that Enide's beauty is greater than any at the court, or in all the world, though one should search through all the land even to the point "where Heaven meets the earth."

Then comes an elaborate wedding, with a tremendous crowd of guests. The wealth and generosity of the King are indicated by the numbers, by the gifts, and the entertainment. Any one who wishes may come to enjoy the banqueting and be served anything he desires.

A tournament is held, in which Erec distinguishes himself so much that he is considered the best of all the knights. This enhancement of Erec's strength and prowess serves as a contrast to the period of uxoriousness that is to follow after Erec has taken Enide to his father's kingdom. There he lies in dalliance and idle adoration of the wife he loves so passionately that he is never seen any more at tournaments or in any manly sport or activity outside of the nuptial chamber. The idle voluptuous life of Eneas held in the charming toils of Dido's love, forgetful of his duty, his own great destiny, and the grand designs of fate that have destined him for heroic deeds and the founding of Rome, was broken by the will of the gods; and his awakening from slothfulness was accomplished by Mercury, the messenger of the gods.

There were no gods in the medieval conception of life. Chrétien could look upon the influence of supernatural forces only as allegorical, to be replaced in his works by the influence of the world, of one's friends, or by the conscience of the individual. So in *Erec et Enide* the awakening is brought about by the gossip of the court, the slander of detractors, and the sorrow of his friends, finally communicated to him directly by the distress of his wife, who heard the evil rumors about her and deplored the public shame, of which her dear husband seemed to be entirely oblivious. She takes the blame upon herself and weeps to think that she had ruined her husband's reputation and held him captive by her love.

Once as she weeps in the early morning, gazing at the manly beauty of the one she loves so dearly, sleeping by her side, and she leaning over him, some tears fall on his chest and awaken Erec from his slumber.

She talks softly to herself, deploring the situation, taking the blame, and saying that her husband is most unfortunate. Erec hears some of her words; and asks for an explanation. Enide is sorry now that she ever said a word or allowed her husband to know how she is grieving. She fears Erec's anger and, at first denies that she had spoken at all. But Erec insists that she explain her words and her sorrow. Enide is compelled to admit that she regrets the shame that has fallen on Erec and that her own pride has suffered.

"You are right," says Erec, "and those who blame me are right."

Erec is deeply hurt by his wife's lack of confidence in him. He feels that her love is not as great as he had thought, since she seems to doubt his valor and side with those who condemn him and believe that he is less valiant than before.

Erec's anger is strengthened by the prick of his own conscience and a deep wound in his own pride. He makes a sudden decision to test himself, to prove his own courage to himself, to others, and to his wife. He will test his wife's love and loyalty too. She must accompany him on a long, arduous, and dangerous venture of knight errantry that will end in death or vindication. This trial will solve the problem of their love and their trust in each other.

Erec commands Enide to ride ahead of him and never to speak one word to him. Adventures are soon encountered. Various robber knights appear on the road; and Erec seems to be deep in thought. Enide fears that he has not seen approaching danger. So in spite of Erec's command and repeated remonstrances, berating and scolding, each time Enide warns him, in spite of her fear of his anger. Erec defeats all those who attack him and orders Enide to drive the horses that he takes from his enemies. Enide loyally submits to all the harshness and watches over her lord and the horses while Erec sleeps.

All this severity recalls the well-known Griselda story, in which a wife is cruelly tortured by her husband until her loyalty and submission prove her to be an ideal wife, whom the husband now rewards with tender love. However brutal it may seem to force a woman to endure all the hardships, the mental anguish, and the dangers of such a trip and such a testing, the story was thrilling for Chrétien's readers and the situation was often repeated in the romances.

After defeating eight knights on the road, Erec sleeps in the open while Enide guards the horses and watches tenderly over her lord, reproaching herself the while for the unfortunate words she spoke in pride and in disloyalty to her husband. Almost despairingly she deprecates her previous sorrow and weeping, so insignificant now in the midst of mortal danger, anguished fears of the perils that lie ahead, and worry lest she never regain the love of the man she honors in her heart, adores and admires for all his strength and bravery. Why did she arouse her husband's wrath and precipitate this bitter quarrel? How can she now prove her confidence, her constant loyalty, her ardent faith in this man, who is her sole joy and comfort?

Opening another parenthesis here and interrupting our story, it is important for the reader who wishes to understand the progress of Chrétien's art, the development of the romance, and the literary trend of the century, to note the charming and loyal humility of the heroine in this first of all the romances and compare Enide with the arrogant ladies who subject the heroes of the later romances to the pain and suffering of love's torment. Here the male is sovereign, later he becomes the docile slave of love and of the loved lady. Literary influences and the chronology of twelfth century romances, as well as other forms of literature, hinge on this situation and the style in which the romances are written. Chrétien is the creator of the romance. All the other authors of romances follow him.

In the morning the two travelers approach a town. They look somewhat rumpled after their night without a comfortable lodging. A squire, carrying food, meets them. He is a practical fellow, who understands the advantage of courtesy at the right moment and offers welcome nourishment to people whose appetite is sharpened by the crisp morning air. Gratefully they accept this generosity; and we have the pleasant and somewhat homely scene of picnicking on a white cloth spread over the greensward. Many such attractive pictures out-of-doors or of interiors—such, for instance, as the merrily crackling open fire in the home of Enide's indigent parents—are rapidly sketched by our author's facile pen.

This little interlude is introductory to an episode in which a popular tale is used, which appears, in one form, in the Old French poem, *Pèlerinage de Charlemagne à Jérusalem,* wherein a nobleman or king hears of a person reputed or described as handsomer than he or superior to him in some way; and he goes to see for himself, to make his own comparison or match his strength against the other.

Erec, evidencing the remarkable generosity of a great and worthy personality, according to the ideal of Chrétien and his time, rewards the squire's kindness by the gift of one of the eight horses he has won by combat at arms. And riding back, now, to the castle of the noble knight whom he serves, the squire is seen by the lord of the castle, who asks him how he gained possession of such a fine steed. The squire describes the handsome man who had given him the horse; and, when urged by his master, gives his opinion that Erec is handsomer than his lord. The squire also mentions the beautiful Enide. The lord of the castle, ruler of the land, whose name is Count Galoain, goes to see Erec at his lodging in the town. He wants to see the fair lady too; and therein lies great danger of death for Erec, the loss of her loved husband for Enide, and captivity for her person. Count Galoain intends to snatch Erec's bride from him and kill Erec, if he resists the will of this arrogant count, who exemplifies realistically the true manners and ruthless covetousness of the typical knight, so at variance from the ideal of chivalry and the noble-minded heroes of Chrétien's romances.

As a bit of character portrayal, surprising at this early date in the history of Christian literature, that appears often in personal traits, this brutal and arrogant count, puffed up with vanity, is depicted as a stupid man, on whom Enide plays a trick to save herself and her husband's life.

The Count offers Enide comfort, luxury, and social position if she will become his wife and abandon Erec; and if she refuses and clings to her husband, she will see him killed in her presence. Enide judges the count to be a fool; and she suggests a plan that she claims will be much better, more suitable for his reputation and hers. In the morning the count should have Enide carried away by force. Erec will rush to her defense and then he can be destroyed with no loss of her good reputation or his. The Count agrees; but Enide arouses Erec early in the morning, reveals the dangerous situation, and husband and wife leave before the arrival of the Count and his men. Erec gives all the horses to his host in payment for his lodging.

Erec and Enide still are not safe. They are pursued by the count and a large force of armed men. The count and his seneschal both overtake Erec but they have outstripped the others, so that Erec is able to kill the seneschal and severely wound the count.

Frequently Chrétien describes a knight as ruthless and brutal but after combat showing remorse, a decided change of heart, or a great and lasting friendship for the knight who has defeated him, thereby winning his admiration. Here again is stark realism re-

lieved by the finer instincts of men, which Chrétien wished to
exalt in his efforts to raise the standards of life and conduct
through idealization of the best qualities in men and women—an
ideal and ambition of the Church and a mark of the twelfth
century in general in its striving toward a rebirth of culture, art,
and morality.

We have a similar indication of diversity in personality and
character in the next episode. Erec and Enide pass a lofty castle
from a tower of which Guivret le Petit, a knight of small stature
but of great courage, espies an armed knight; and Guivret rushes
out on a rapid charger to attack Erec. Guivret is a powerful lord.
He owns wide lands. He is ruthless. To punish a neighbor who
has angered him he will march forth with a large army, attack
his neighbor, burn all his property, and lay waste his land. In his
fight with Erec, he is defeated when his sword breaks in his hand,
just as happened to Turnus when fighting with Aeneas in Virgil's
epic. But now Guivret is filled with admiration for Erec, vows
a life-long friendship, and later in the story comes to Erec's
assistance and helps him recover from almost fatal wounds. Thus
Chrétien shows an ability and an interest in character portrayal
that is remarkable. Any description of personal character, otherwise, in literature has to wait, in France, until the advent of the
classical school. Personified abstractions are considered an approach to characterization as they appear in morality plays in
the fifteenth century. Even in classical literature, where man is
portrayed in the universal manner with the purpose of creating
characters that will appear truthful throughout the whole span
of human life, types are portrayed, unvarying in their attitudes
and actions. For variety, in the characterization of individuals
who act with unpredictable impulses and inconsistencies, we have
to wait for the Romantic School of the nineteenth century. Chrétien
thus appears amazingly modern in his technique.

To describe Guivret's descent from his castle and rapid advance
to attack Erec, the speed and noise of his career is couched in an
elaborate figure of speech:

> The knight comes racing down
> From his castle on the hill.
> Mounted on a mighty steed.
>
> And making a most terrible din,
> It pulverizes beneath its hoofs
> And turns the stones to meal,
> Just as a millstone crushes grain.
> In every direction, flying wide,
> Bright red and blazing sparks
> Fly from all four feet
> That seem to be on fire.
>
> Enide is terrified:
>
> Enide hears the frightful din.
> In fear she nearly falls,
> Helpless and in a faint.
> Weakness spreads through every vein
> As though all her blood were drained.
> Her face becomes as pale
> As though she really were a corpse.
> Dread fear is in her mind.
> She dares not warn her lord;
> He had told her not to speak.
>
> She tries in vain to speak
> And moves her tongue to utter words;
> But her voice cannot come forth.
> Fear closes her chattering teeth;
> And shuts all sound within her mouth.

There follows the first of the famous monologues that appear in Chrétien's works, usually love monologues, in which the person in love debates with himself or herself the probability or improbability of a return of affection from the loved one. Worry and fear alternate with wavering hopes and longing. The monologue is imitated from Ovid where it appears in the *Heroides,* the *Amores* and the *Metamorphoses*. In this monologue Enide wavers between her inclination to warn Erec of approaching danger and her fear of doing so on account of his wrath, his scoldings and his threats. Incidently Chrétien cleverly indicates Erec's gradually fading anger and growing confidence in Enide's love. At one point he tempers his threats with a mental reservation that he may change his mind.

Erec is sorely wounded in the fight with Guivret. Still he refuses to rest and will not accept Guivret's invitation to stay with him until his wounds are healed. Here and later in this story we find the same tragic theme of excessive valor, that characterizes the Old French epics.

There follows an incident that is repeated again in *Perceval*. King Arthur moves his whole court out into the country and supplies tents for all the knights and ladies in a sort of glorified picnic and hunting expedition such as delighted Francis the First in the prosperous days of the early sixteenth century. And it happens that Erec passes by the rich and marvelous encampment. An opportunity is also afforded to introduce a little humor furnished by Kay, the King's seneschal, an exceedingly rash and bold man but not an adept at arms. He is always trying to attempt personal combats in Chrétien's works, but is always easily defeated.

Gawain, King Arthur's nephew and a great knight never allowed by Chrétien to be defeated though he constantly appears in Chrétien's romances, has left his horse tied to a tree and his lance and shield on another. Kay takes the horse, shield and lance for a little private sport, pleased to gallop about. Encountering Erec and seeing how grievously he is wounded, Kay urges Erec to come to the camp to rest and receive medical care. With stubborn intention of continuing his ordeal even to the breaking point, Erec refuses. Kay now strives to compel Erec to accompany him; and finally he rides away to wheel and attack with the lance. Since Kay wears no armor, Erec strikes him only with the butt end of his lance; but the shield is driven against Kay's face. The shield cuts Kay; and he is thrown violently to the ground. Erec teasingly takes the horse; but when earnestly entreated by Kay, who now confesses that the horse belongs to Gawain, he allows the unhappy seneschal to return the borrowed animal.

On Kay's return to the camp, where he tells of the sorely wounded knight, whom he has not recognized, the King, always kind, generous, and courteous, begs Gawain to ride out and attempt to bring the unknown knight to the camp.

This gives Chrétien a chance to depict two characters that are in sharp contrast. Kay is vehement and irascible, envious of others, conceited, anxious to win glory, tricky, always trying to be the first to engage in a combat but always defeated. He is vengeful and mean. In *Perceval* he slaps a young girl's face and kicks a jester into an open fire.

Gawain, on the other hand, is exactly the opposite, always courteous, even-tempered, elegant in language and manners and an invincible knight. Here again is interesting character sketching unequalled in French literature for several centuries. Moreover we have in the two characters a remarkable antithesis—a surprisingly early example of a literary form so highly developed by Shakespeare, Swift, Victor Hugo and others.

In spite of all his charm, Gawain cannot persuade Erec to enter the camp. Thereupon he sends a messenger to King Arthur and asks him to move the whole camp so that it will lie across the route that Erec and Enide are following. The King is willing to perform this remarkable act of courtesy so far beyond imaginable human amenableness, but indicative of the lofty idealism of our author and his desire to lift polite conduct to the highest possible level, setting standards in the ethereal realms of imagination.

Erec stays in King Arthur's camp only one night. He receives superior medical attention verging on the magical so that his wounds are much less painful.

The next episode is a conjuncture within a conjuncture. This is typical of Chrétien's manner in building his plot. Perhaps it would be better to say that he weaves his plot. Just as a weaver selects his brilliant yarns, or silken threads and watches the warp grow on the woof in pleasing patterns that warm his heart or the painter feels the joy of the colors that delight his soul and so charm our admiring gaze that the chords of our inner consciousness vibrate with ecstasy, so Chrétien found delight in themes, figures, and motives that gleamed in ancient verse with a glow of artistry that not only was non-existent in anything he could read in French but so wondrous that he wanted to take them and handle them with the tingling and thrilling touch of the sculptor as he moulds voluptuous forms of splendor or delicate beauty. He used his favorite themes and motives over and over and wove them together or entwined them with the threads of popular tales and his own imagining in patterns whose newness and originality disguise and mask the source of his material.

This section combines a fight against giants with the motive of the Pyramus and Thisbe story that Chrétien also often used in *Lancelot* and in *Yvain*. The story of Polyphemus may have contributed a suggestion. Virgil gives another. In *Yvain* there is the hero's combat with a giant named Harpin of the Mountain. This whole episode, which is not dissimilar to the one in *Erec,* is unquestionably based on one in the Latin *Historia Regum Britanniae* of Geoffrey of Monmouth, where, in the tenth book King Arthur fights with a Spanish giant on Mount Saint-Michel.

Riding through a forest, Erec hears a damsel crying in distress. He spurs on; and soon he sees the lady weeping. She tells him that two cruel giants have taken her lover away. They have stripped him and tied him on a horse. They, no doubt, will kill him in some horrible manner.

Having left Enide behind, Erec overtakes them and sees the naked knight bleeding from cuts the giants have opened as they beat him. Erec boldly attacks them, wounding one in the eye, just as Ulysses wounded the giant Polyphemus. The wound proves fatal; and the other giant is killed in a manner learned from Virgil. In the ninth book of the *Aeneid* Turnus encounters Pandarus and splits his head apart so that it falls away from the shoulders in two equal halves. If Chrétien has Erec defeat two giants, it is, no doubt, partly to enhance his hero's valor at this point, which may be regarded as a climax in the cruel testing to which Erec has subjected himself and Enide. The solution of the quarrel between man and wife will follow quickly after the fight with these two giants. A second reason is that Chrétien wishes to use two methods of securing a victory. A third reason may be that Virgil, in the ninth book of his epic, to which we have already referred, describes two gigantic brothers in battle on the Trojan side. Both are killed; and one of them is Pandarus, whose head was split in half.

Exaggeration, at this point, is not surprising; and tremendous exaggeration we certainly have. If the brains are spilled out of Pandarus' head, the body of the second giant is split in two halves and the bowels are spilled on the ground. This second giant had rushed, in a rage, to avenge his comrade just as Pandarus tried to avenge the death of his brother.

These giants had been armed with clubs; and Erec had not come out of the fight unscathed. In fact, his wounds are opened and he falls in a swoon as he makes his way back to Enide who has been waiting in terror and still regretting her spoken reproaches that had angered her husband and led to so much danger and suffering.

Erec appears to be dead and Enide believes that he is dead. Now, like Thisbe in the story of Pyramus and Thisbe, she draws her husband's sword and would have killed herself if a count had not arrived in time to prevent her.

Another element undoubtedly out of Virgil's *Aeneid* is Enide's invocation of Death, upon whom she calls to take her and end her wordly existence. Dido also invokes Death after the loss of her beloved Aeneas.

Still one more thread is woven into this episode. It comes from the tenth book of the *Aeneid* where Mezentius laments the death of his son, blames himself for the tragedy, reproaches himself for living on and resolves to die immediately. So Enide is filled with a similar remorse and in language closely resembling Virgil's takes all the blame, reproaches herself for living after Erec is dead and tries to take measures to end her life at once.

The Count takes Erec to his castle, where he is placed on a bier. Now the Count talks of marrying Enide; and Erec hears her refusal even though she believes him to be dead. He hears her wish only to follow him in death. She will not be comforted. She will not eat at the Count's demand. In anger, now, the Count slaps her. Then Erec, revived by anger, arises from his bier, kills the Count with a mighty blow that spills his blood and mingled brains, terrifying all who are present; for they think a ghost has risen with supernatural power.

Erec recovers his horse and arms; and taking Enide up with him on the horse, he rides away entirely unmolested.

Now Erec knows that Enide loves him truly. He forgives her for the words that hurt him and angered him. All his confidence in the fullness of her love is restored:

> He kisses her and comforts her.
> He clasps her to his loving heart,
> Holding her close, calls her his darling.
> "Have no fear or worry," he says,
> "For now I love you more than ever.
> Again I trust you and believe
> That you love me with a perfect love.
> Your every wish or least command
> Henceforth will ever be obeyed."

Now we are told, in words borrowed from Virgil in the fourth book of the *Aeneid,* that news (rumor) travels faster than anything. So, the news comes to Guivret le Petit, who has sworn undying friendship to Erec. He hears of a sorely wounded knight who has died in a forest and that he was accompanied by a most beautiful lady, that Count Oringle had taken that lady to his castle and planned to marry her against her will. Guivret thinks that the knight might be Erec and the lady Enide. He, therefore, sets out with a large following to rescue the lady and recover the body of his friend.

Most unfortunately Guivret encounters Erec on the way; and, not recognizing him, attacks and wounds Erec. When he discovers

Erec's identity, however, he takes him to a castle nearby where his sisters, skilled in the art of healing, cure Erec and make him strong and well again; but only to attempt a new adventure.

He comes to the castle of the King Evrain, where there is a garden surrounded by an impenetrable wall of air, no doubt suggested by a similar wall of air in the stories of Virgil the Magician. Within the enclosure a knight is held by a lady, not in slothful dalliance, but in that manner that Circe held men captive; here, however, without degrading the male. Whoever enters the garden by a small entrance, is no more able to get out than one could find his way out of the Labyrinth of Crete. Just as those who entered the labyrinth were compelled to fight the Minotaur with certainty of death, so those knights who enter the garden must fight with a powerful, undefeated knight, the heads of whose victims are displayed on a row of spikes.

Erec succeeds in defeating this formidable opponent and instead of freeing victims delivered as an enforced tribute, frees the monster—here a knight—who has been an involuntary prisoner, in accordance with Chrétien's favorite manner of distorting and changing, in weird or comic style, a well-known theme or story.

This adventure was called the Joy of the court; for there was great joy when the captive knight was freed and Erec blows a horn, as required, that dispels the wall of air just as the walls of Jericho came tumbling down at the sound of the horn.

Erec thus accomplishes a final adventure in which he is successful and comes out strong rather than weakened almost to the point of death.

Not long after Erec's return to King Arthur's court, his father died and Erec succeeded to the throne. Chrétien describes the crowning of Erec in considerable detail.

CHAPTER IV

The Translations from Ovid

The production of *Erec and Enide* is an event in the literary history of the world, whose importance cannot be exaggerated. Out of almost nothing a great form of literature was spontaneously created and the novel, which delights the modern world most, was born.

Descartes, the great French thinker of the seventeenth century, believed and proceeded to prove that all the textbooks and all the teaching in the schools of his day were wrong. Chrétien de Troyes may have seen some flaws in Medieval methods of instruction, but he found inspiration in the learning he acquired in school that blossomed into the romances of chivalry, that spread their glamor and their glorious light of idealism, of manly valor, of courteous manners, and of worshipping love of man for woman over all the centuries of our Christian world since the day of their creation down into our own era; not only to add to our joy in the appreciation of human aspirations, but to contribute much that is fundamental in present day literature.

Latin was the language of the schools in Chrétien's time. That part of his schooling that he loved and that is important to us was rhetoric; and the chief texts that were used for teaching rhetoric were Virgil and Ovid. Virgil and Ovid were Chrétien's masters. His knowledge of those two Latin authors is thorough.

Most of the writers who lived in France in the twelfth century wrote in Latin. They were scholars well versed in classical Latin literature. They had a great love of those ancient masters and filled their books with quotations from them. In spite of their ardent admiration of the Latin classics, however, they did not know how to use them for any original contribution to the history of literature.

In the midst of this scholarly and literary world of slavish imitators there suddenly appeared a great creative genius who knew how to use the materials that lay at hand, to take them into his skillful hands and weld them into literary forms that bridged the long gap of the centuries. These new forms were amazingly original.

Literary figures and literary style are basically the same throughout the ages. It is the individual flavor, the freshness of thought and the emotional inspiration that put the life and sparkle or the rich glow of art that delights or deeply moves into those set patterns. Chrétien took over many classical Latin figures of speech almost intact. He did, however, vary them some and created many of his own modeled on those of his masters.

Chrétien delved into the works of antiquity for great blocks that serve as themes or motives, he gathered threads of beauty and golden dust that he scattered in gleaming adornment all through his works. Whatever he took, nevertheless, he fashioned anew and combined in a form of literature, which, though even in its main structure it resembles the works of antiquity, is highly original.

Love entered these stories to give them a fragrance and a charm that was new in Northern French art. Love as it appears in *Erec and Enide* is delightful and natural. Later Chrétien was inspired to make his treatment of love more elaborate. In order to do this and to create a new style in the description of love, he turned to Ovid's *Art of Love;* and Ovid became his authority and model.

It may be futile to speculate on Chrétien's reason for translating Ovid's *Art of Love* into French. Nevertheless a certain number of ideas force themselves upon us. Since it seems likely that Chrétien depended on a patron, who would pay to have such a work translated? The answer seems clear and sure. Eleanor of Aquitania, the Queen of France. Her grandfather, William IX of Aquitania, knew Ovid and made a slight and timid use of Ovidian love doctrine in some of his poems. A few other poets of Provence also knew and borrowed slightly from Ovid. Chrétien's development of a feminine character in Enide of *Erec and Enide* must have interested Eleanor intensely since it was an amazing literary enhancement of woman; and the importance of women in society and in literature was what the Queen ardently desired. In this connection it should be noted that Chrétien's *Cligès* shows an exact geographical setting and knowledge of the location of English towns, quite in contrast with the vague and unexplainable itineraries of the personages in the other romances, that seems to prove that Chrétien was in England. And how could that have happened unless Eleanor had taken him there or called him to her court after she became the Queen of Henry II?

Unfortunately Chrétien's *Art of Love* is lost and we know nothing about the form in which it appeared. We do know that it must have followed *Erec et Enide* and we know that Chrétien's later style in treating love is based directly on Ovid's *Art of Love* supplemented by borrowing from and imitating the *Heroides* (love letters by famous characters in Classical Latin literature), the *Amores* (love lyrics), and the *Metamorphoses.*

Ovid's *Art of Love* is a light-hearted and humorous work purporting to indicate the way in which love may be won and retained. The love here described is extra-marital. It causes a great deal of suffering; and the male lover is represented as tiring of love unless the loved lady is voluntarily cruel and unpredictably uncooperative, refusing her love at moments when the lover is most ardent. Frustration is supposed to strengthen the passion.

Ovid calls himself the teacher of love. He first indicates ways and means of meeting attractive women. When the lady has been discovered and Cupid's arrows have been shot through glances and furtive touches have supplemented the appeal of the eyes, it is well to cultivate the acquaintance of the loved lady's personal maid. If you first win the maid's friendship and affection she can help you by sly suggestions as she combs her mistress' hair and attends her with other ministrations night and morning.

Love is described as sweet torment. Cupid's arrows wound the heart and create a fire that is painful and consuming. The victims sigh. They weep. They lose their appetites and cannot eat. They become pale and emaciated. At night they turn and toss in their beds, unable to sleep at all. At the sight of the loved one they tremble. They dare not tell their love. In spite of all this suffering on account of this disease, they do not wish to be cured. In long meditations or mental monologues, they waver between hope and despair. Only a return of affection can cure the pain.

Sometimes the lover is spoken of as a prisoner bound in the chains of love; or, as a soldier under the command of Love. In the service of Love hardship, pain and distress exhaust and discourage the faithful. The lover must yield to the loved lady's every whim. He must be an obedient slave. Neither shame nor suffering should be avoided. He cites Milanion suffering and toiling under the cruelty of Atlanta, the mighty Hercules dressed as a woman and docilely obeying every command of his mistress, the god Apollo tending sheep for the sake of love. Unrequited love often leads to madness and suicide.

Ovid's treatise is divided into three parts. The first tells how to win the love of a woman; the second, how to hold the love once gained. The third is to instruct women in the art of winning the love of men.

The *Art of Love* is followed by Ovid's *Cure for Love*. If the efforts to win the loved lady are all in vain and the love sickness threatens the health and perhaps even the life of the lover a cure may be impossible. The disease may prove fatal. Ovid is the doctor but doctors often lose their patients. The most important is to eradicate the ill before its roots have struck down too deep into the heart. A flight to a distant land may help. Another method is to turn the lady's charms into faults. If she is small call her a runt; if she is tall call her an ogress; if she is delightfully plump call her fat.

Whether Chrétien made a fairly accurate translation of Ovid's *Art of Love* or whether he expanded it into a romance we cannot know. The importance of this lost work is the undeniable fact that it marks a dividing point in Chrétien's literary career and gives invaluable evidence to help in the chronological study of twelfth century romances. It places *Erec and Enide* much earlier than any romance that shows the Ovidian type of love because the translation of Ovid's *Art of Love* lays all the ground work for the metaphorical style that appears first in Chrétien's works, which were imitated by other writers of love romances in France, that characterizes courtly love so famous in later Provençal lyrics wherein Chrétien is extensively imitated, which influenced the *dolce stil nuovo* in Italy, the love poetry of Dante and many other Italian writers. The romances of several centuries continued their style, in which love is treated in the poetry and novels of the seventeenth century, in love discussions at courts in twelfth century France, mirrored in the *De Amore* of Andreus Capellanus, and in similar discussions in the French *salons* of the seventeenth century. Even our modern literature retains much of this style in treating trembling and sighing lovers, who pass sleepless nights and suffer all the pain as well as the joy of love.

At the beginning of *Cligès* five earlier works are listed, apparently in their true chronological order. *Erec and Enide* is the first. *William of England* is not mentioned. It is quite possible that other earlier works are not mentioned either. The second of those listed is the *Art of Love*. Next comes the *Shoulder Bite*, also lost, considered by scholars to be an adaptation of the classsical story of Pelops and his ivory shoulder.

Chrétien refers to a story of Tristan, of Isolt and King Marc which is probably the first romance concerning Tristan and Isolt.

Finally he lists his adaptation of Ovid's story of Philomela in the sixth book of the *Metamorphoses*. This forceful tale, that has been published under the title of *Philomena,* which is the form that Chrétien gives to the name of this Ovidian character, was most fortunately discovered by the great French student of Medieval literature, Gaston Paris. He found it embedded in a curious and a very long work entitled the *Moralized Ovid,* written by a well-known but extremely stupid author of the fourteenth century named Chrétien Legouais, praised by Eustache Deschamps as an important writer. He translated the stories of Ovid's *Metamorphoses* and drew a moral from each of these entirely un-moral tales. When Legouais came to the story of Philomela he substituted Chrétien de Troyes' adaptation.

Chrétien expanded Ovid's short tale to nearly fifteen hundred lines, in his usual manner, by inventing questions and answers that he cleverly wove into long conversations in a natural and pleasing style. There are detailed descriptions, psychological analyses of motives and mental attitudes, a long explanation and discussion of the nature and tyranny of love, comparisons and numerous other figures of speech, as well as repetitions in the nature of variations and orchestrations of his themes.

In Ovid's story in the *Metamorphoses* Philomela, a maiden of great beauty, was the younger daughter of Pandion King of Athens. The older daughter, named Progne was given in mar-riage to Tereus, King of Thrace.

Furies attended this inauspicious marriage and prepared the marital bed for later misfortune. A horrible ill-omened owl fell dead on the roof and lay above the bridal chamber, portending a horrible fate, as the course of events reveals in the story. In-stead of the Furies, unnamed by Ovid in this story, Chrétien, no doubt in order to vary his source a little, substituted one Fury, Tisiphone by name, and one of the fates, Atropos. Chrétien may or may not have known the names of all three Furies. Tisiphone was well-known to him. He had been deeply impressed by two descriptions of this monster. One occurs in Ovid's story

of Pyramus and Thisbe, which Chrétien used repeatedly in his
romances. There he read that Juno descended to the frightful
realm of Pluto, King of Hell and god of the dead; and called
upon the avenging goddesses to destroy the palace of Cadmus,
to drive Ino, his daughter, crazy and her husband, Athamas to
madness and crime. Tisiphone obeys the command. Hanging
about the horrible face of this monster is a tangled mass of snakes.
Like a belt around her waist she wears a knotted cord of serpents.
Blood drips from her foul mantle. Her torch has been dipped
in blood. She arrives in the very bedroom of the unfortunate
pair. The loathsome Fury snatches two writhing vipers from
the hissing tangle that hangs in twisting horror from her head
and hurls them on the naked breasts of the defenceless victims,
into whose veins poison enters from the cruel fangs. Driven
insane, the father snatches his son from his wife's arms and
dashes him to pieces against a wall.

Chrétien had read about Tisiphone at the very beginning of
Statius' *Thebaid* which was a source for a considerable part of
Cligès. Oedipus, there, invokes Tisiphone and says that she was
present at his own incestuous marriage with his mother. Tisiphone is described. Her eyes are blood-red; and above them a
hundred vipers raise their terrifying heads. Her flesh is swollen
by black and poisonous blood. A belt of snakes secures her
hairy mantle; and a fiery vapor pours from her mouth, spreading
all around hunger, fever, disease and death. This is a particularly
interesting source because Atropos, the fate that cuts the thread
of men's lives, is joined in this work to Tisiphone and explains
why Chrétien used the name in *Philomena*. Incidentally, we have
here one of a hundred pieces of evidence large and small that
help in establishing the chronological order of twelfth century
romances. Atropos does not appear in the Old French *Roman
de Thèbes*. This shows us that Chrétien used Statius' work as
a source in this instance. It is no less true that he turned to Statius
whenever he made use of the material of his classical story.
It will be evident in a later chapter that the Old French *Thèbes*

borrowed directly from *Yvain,* next to the last of Chrétien's known romances. Since it is known to be the first of three romances, the others being *Eneas* and the *Roman de Troie,* all of which scholars have dated earlier than Chrétien's romances, we can confidently reverse the theory and date all three of these romances that deal with classical material later than Chrétien's works.

Chrétien, no doubt, realized that one dead owl on a roof would not appear adequate to his readers; and accordinlgy he increased the evil omens by a varied collection of owls and hoarse-voiced imps of hell all of which raise a tremendous din above the palace.

Tereus, who was a tyrant and a felon, took his wife back to Thrace. A son, named Ithis was born to them, only to add eventually to their misfortunes.

After a separation of five years Progne was anxious to see her younger sister; and she persuaded Tereus to go to Athens and see whether he could bring Philomena to Thrace for a visit.

On arriving in Athens, Tereus makes the request of Pandion to allow him to take Philomena back to Thrace to visit her sister. He promises to bring her back to Athens soon. While he is making the request Philomena enters the room.

Her beauty captivates him: flesh clear as the lily's pure and glistening white but gently tinged with mingled coloring of the rose, eyes like sparkling jewels gleaming softly with a light that charms and melts the heart of the stricken Tereus, divine forms that awaken yearning love.

Now Tereus burns with a fire of passion so intense that all of his being trembles and the god of love drives and compels his will. Nothing can restrain him now. Base lust controls his every thought and all his wily deeds. He uses all his persuasive art; and Philomena also pleads.

The reluctant father's mind is filled with worry; his heart with anguished fear.

He bows his head upon his hand,
In deep annoyance over this.
And well he might be thus annoyed.
But an answer to their pleas he still must make.
He says "Dear children well you know
That all I own in all the world
I gladly would bestow and you may take
And use in any way you wish.
Still I am sure that if you only knew
How much any daughter's presence means,
You never would demand of me
The sacrifice that now you ask of me.
In deep despair I'd ever be
If even for a day my daughter were away.
Just like a crutch and guiding staff
I need her now and always will
For the few short years I still may live."

His daughter's loving care keeps him alive; without her constant help and comforting hands he would quickly die. Tereus, in taking her away, would shorten Pandion's life.

This refusal casts Tereus into despair. The pain of love grows swiftly stronger. He sighs, thus showing the first symptom of the love disease. He feels weak. He loses the power of speech. He laments. Madness seems to destroy his reason.

So Myrrha tried to speak; but her voice failed her. Lamenting and weeping is common to all who fall in love in Ovid's poems. Madness assails many but the best source is Medea's monologue in the seventh book of the *Metamorphoses*. Her reason turns to madness. This is a favorite monologue that Chrétien uses more than once; and it is an important source for a portion of *Cligès*. When we discuss that romance we shall return with enthusiasm to Medea and her monologue.

A meditation on love follows. It resembles the love monologue so highly developed by Chrétien and modeled on similar monologues in Ovid's work, except that, here, in contrast with the usual type in which the victim of the love sickness meditates, it is the author himself who asks questions and answers them. The first question is whether a person conquered and totally defeated by love can become the winner and secure the victory. Since Tereus is finally successful in his scheming and his ardent desire to satisfy his mad lustfulness, the author seems to be looking ahead to a later development of his plot.

The doctrine comes out of Ovid. In the ninth elegy of *Amores,* Book I, love is compared to warfare. Both love and war are uncertain. This uncertainty is underlined by Chrétien, who declares that Love is lighter and more agile than the wind, and therefore, false and undependable. He is generous with his promises but fickle and miserly in keeping them. Many who have been sorely afflicted by the pains of love bear witness to the deceit and faithlessness of love. Moreover Love tortures his own followers mercilessly.

All this uncertainty, fickleness and the suffering that Love causes those who serve him faithfully is exemplified in the *Heroides* or *Epistles* written in anguish by Penelope languishing while Ulysses delays his return, by Phyllis complaining because Demophoon fails to return on the promised date, by Briseis writing to Achilles, by Aenone addressing faithless Paris who has deserted her for Helen of Troy, Hypsipyle of Lemnos whom Jason abandoned, Dido from whose love a glorious fate drove Aeneas to great deeds of glory, and by others. The theory is lyrically expressed in *Amores* I, the ninth elegy and the ninth elegy of the second book of the *Amores.* Ovid says that those who are conquered in war or in love often rise up to win and those who were considered invulnerable fall in defeat. Love is lighter and swifter, therefore more false, than his wings whose speed outstrips the wind. The hardships of love are indicated: the lover must be inured to long watches, lying on the ground before his mistress' door, to long marches on which he must willingly follow the loved woman to the ends of the earth, enduring torrential storms or snow and bitter cold. The suffering lover calls out to Love asking why he can never rest in comfort, why he should be reduced to nothing but skin and bones, why he, the most loyal of Cupid's followers, should be so pierced with his master's shafts that his body is more filled with arrows that the quiver of his tormenter. In spite of all his wounds and the constant fire, that consumes his heart the poet declares that he will never desert Cupid's army nor ever wish an end of the sweet torment of love. The love of a young girl is too sweet a pain.

The doctrine is also to be found in Ovid's *Art of Love*. We have already noted Ovid's insistence, in that work, that the lover must slavishly obey every whim and command of his mistress and gladly endure any humiliation or labor in her service.

Chrétien says the medicine of love increases it and strengthens it so that like a tree its roots go deeper and become stronger. In the *Cure for Love* Ovid says that one must not let the love sickness get strongly rooted. It must be torn out in its early stages. Tereus would be wise to tear this budding love from his heart and sail away home to Thrace without Philomena; or better still he never should have come to Athens. Now the medicine for love is a return of affection. The loved one alone can provide any relief of the suffering. So in the *Heroides* Aenone writes that only Paris can put an end to her suffering, Phaedra appeals in like manner to Hyppolytus and Hermione declares that she will surely die unless Arestes becomes her husband. In the *Metamorphoses* Byblis writes to Caunus to tell of her desperate suffering and to implore his aid. She has struggled alone against this malady. Her health, her life depends on him. He alone can save her from despair and death.

In despair Tereus thinks that he is becoming crazy. He contemplates slaughtering the whole city in the night. Reason prevails, however, over madness; and he resorts to persuasion. Now he is successful and wins the consent of Pandion.

The impatient lover has to wait for the next day to dawn before he can set sail. He must pass a whole night in Athens.

And what a night! He cannot close his eyes in sleep. All night long he tosses and turns. He twists and writhes. During a night that seems endless he takes every possible position on a comfortless bed.

The principal source of such restlessness at night when one is suffering from love sickness, Chrétien's favorite source and one that he uses repeatedly, is the second elegy of the *Amores*. In this lyric outburst, the poet in the throes of the love malady cries out:

> "Who can tell me why my bed is so hard, why my cover continually falls to the floor, why the night seems so long, and why I toss my weary bones in every direction?"

On the following day Tereus is able to sail away with Philomena; and carry out his evil purpose. He takes Philomena to a house in a wood; and there after destroying her virginity, he cuts out her tongue and puts her under the guard of two women.

Instead of saying in straightforward manner that Tereus takes Philomena to a house in the woods, Chrétien uses a periphrase in anticipation of later niceties of the sort, but really a very pretty one:

> He takes her to a lonely house,
> Impatient in his mad attempt.
> No town was near on any side;
> Nor field nor meadow there about,
> Nor any road nor any path.

It is quite amusing to note that the fourteenth century poet was not satisfied and that he inserted two lines of his own to explain the situation and thereby attached his own signature:

> The house was in a wood.
> So says Chrétien Legouais.

Honest Legouais wanted his readers to understand. He wanted to put his own name in evidence in this modest manner; but the strangest result was nearly achieved by modern scholars, who attempted to blot his name from the memory of men by claiming that Chrétien de Troyes had named himself at this point. The flatness of these two lines in a very smooth and pretty passage gives away their identity. Our Chrétien would never have written them nor would he have entered his name in such an awkward place. Chrétien Legouais is named on several manuscripts.

Tereus arrives home in Thrace with tears in his eyes and falsely reports the death of Philomena.

Progne mourns her sister. She calls on Death complaining because it does not come quickly. This invocation is similar to the one noted in *Erec et Enide* and reminiscent of Dido's plea. In order that the soul of her unburied sister might be taken from the body, Progne makes an elaborate sacrifice to Pluto. Although the details are undoubtedly Chrétien's the classical influence is evident; and Progne's resolve to celebrate Philomena's death annually recalls Aeneas' promise to celebrate the death of his father, Anchises, each year, as we read in the fifth book of the *Aeneid*.

In personifying Death Chrétien remembers passages in Horace's *Odes*. In the first book and the third ode the Latin poet speaks of the inevitableness of death which advances more rapidly than formerly. All of us must die. In the fourth ode Horace says:

"Pale Death knocks impartially at the hovel of paupers and the palaces of kings."

It is interesting to connect this passage from Horace with the Medieval Dance of Death, represented in Church plays and by painters and sculptors. One of the most famous examples formerly appeared on the walls of the Cemetery of the Innocents in Paris. It was made famous in modern times by the paintings of Holbein. This Horacian passage may even be the original source of the idea, in this dance, of death being no respecter of persons. At any rate students of the Dance of Death should investigate the importance of Horace in this conception.

The location in which Philomena was imprisoned and the cruel actions of Tereus were revealed to Progne by a tapestry that her sister wove and managed to send to Progne. Progne rescued Philomena and the two sister's took a horrible vengeance on Tereus by serving his son's body at the table and hurling the boy's bleeding head at his father.

CHAPTER V

Tristan and Isolt

Although Chrétien's version of *Tristan and Isolt* is lost and we know nothing about it, many scholars believe that it was the first romance dealing with those two famous lovers that have been made widely known by Wagner's great opera and by Joseph Bédier's modern French version of the story.

The origin of this story is unknown. Some scholars think that was originally a Celtic story. The name, Tristan, seems to be Pictish, the scene is laid in Cornwall; but there seems to be no real evidence of any extensive Celtic influence or any Celtic source for the main features or plot of *Tristan and Isolt* as we know it today. It cannot be definitely denied, to be sure, that some of the trickery may have derived from Celtic stories; neither is it at all necessary to believe that it is so. Tristan's voyage in a rudderless boat in search of healing could be a Celtic trait borrowed from the stories of saints that visit marvelous islands.

There are Old Irish stories of a crude and sad beauty that are vaguely similar, because of a tragic love situation, to *Tristan and Isolt.*

From among the Festivals, Navigations, Combats, Massacres, Captures of Fortresses, Cattle Raids and Abductions which make up the bulk of Old Irish literature, there is no more charming and appealing story than the tragic tale of Deirdre.

On account of a prophesy that Deirdre would bring great suffering and distress to the men of Ulster, the warriors of the land would have killed her while she was still an infant. But King Conor saved her and had her brought up away from the court, intending to marry this most beautiful of all Irish maidens himself. Conor waited for her to become a woman; but he waited too long. Thoughts of love and marriage developed in her imagination. Like many a maiden she dreamed of happiness with a man who would conform to a vague ideal, until one day, while she was watching the skinning of a calf, in the winter, she noticed the blood on the snow. A black raven came and dipped his beak in the blood. And the colors seemed to represent black hair on a man whose snow-white body and face was illumined by the blush of health and vigor. She turned to Levorcham, a witch, who was her only companion; and she said to her:

"I shall never marry a man that does not have hair as black as the raven's feathers, a body as white as snow and cheeks red like the blood on the snow."

"I know that man," said the witch. "His name is Naisi. His cry is loud and it fills the air so full of music that even the placid cows are happy and their milk flows much faster."

Down from the mountain came this handsome Naisi; and when Deirdre saw him, love filled her heart. She was able to escape and join him on the plain. She passed by him with tempting allure and soft glances.

"Wondrous fair is the young heifer that runs by me," said Naisi.

Then she spoke to the handsome man who pleased her fancy so much and asked him what young heifers could do without a male.

"Your bull is the greatest bull in all of Ulster. It is King Conor," answered Naisi.

"But the king is old," she replied. "I need a young bull; and I prefer you."

Naisi feared the prophesy and the trouble that might come to him and to the men of Ulster; and so he tried to evade her. Thereupon this enterprising and self-willed girl rushed upon Naisi, seized him by both ears and threatened him with shame and mockery if he did not take her away with him. Naisi was persuaded; and then misfortune began for both of them.

They had to flee from the wrath of Conor. Naisi with many loyal kinsmen, their wives and servants went into exile, lived by hunting and fishing. He and his followers were continually fighting and trying to avoid the ambuscades of Conor. Finally Naisi was killed in battle and Deirdre fell into the hands of Conor. She hated Conor because of her husband; and she showed such scorn and dislike that Conor gave her to one she hated even more, to Eogan the very man who had killed Naisi. So the life of this lovely girl, who had suffered so much for love ended in despair. She dashed her head against a rock and killed herself.

This forceful tale of tragic love with its deep emotional appeal has been compared by some scholars to *Tristan and Isolt.*

Another Irish story that has seemed to some scholars to resemble the Tristan story sufficiently to have been a possible model is the *Wooing of Etain.*

In a former existence Etain had been the wife of Midir, king of the fairies of Bri-Leith. This union had ended through the magic arts of a jealous lover named Fuamnach.

Now, by a metempsychosis, she is living as a human, married to King Eochaid of Ireland. Midir had appeared to her mysteriously several times before her marriage and again after she had become the Queen. He wished to take her back to fairyland; but she refused to go with Midir unless Eochaid would consent.

So Midir called on Eochaid one day and played a game of chess with him. The stakes were fifty horses. The shrewd fairy king allowed Eochaid to win. A second game was played with the winner having the privilege of naming the stakes after the game was finished. Eochaid won again and required Midir to perform several difficult feats. A third game was proposed and the stupid Eochaid overconfident because of previous victories agreed to the same stakes. This time, however, Midir won. Midir asked for a kiss from Etain and put both of his hands on the Queen. Eochaid asked for a month's delay; and on the appointed day he had the palace filled with guards. Midir escaped with Etain, nevertheless, as two swans.

Eochaid was able, however, by the aid of magic to regain his wife after a struggle of several years.

A third story is somewhat more like *Tristan and Isolt*. In the *Elopement of Diarmaid and Grainne*, the hero was, like Tristan, remarkable for his strength and agility. He won the love of Grainne, who like Isolt was the wife of the hero's uncle, Firm MacUmail, a great chieftian. The two lovers, like Tristan and Isolt, lived for a time, in a forest. Diarmaid was in the habit of sleeping somewhat removed from Grainne; and he placed a stone between them while they were asleep. One is reminded of the sword that King Marc saw lying between Tristan and Isolt when he came upon them while they were sleeping in the forest.

The love of Grainne for Diarmaid is represented as irresistible on account of a mark on his body called a love-spot. Any woman who saw the love-spot was compelled by its effect to fall in love with Diarmaid.

There is one small trait that is found in the story of the *Elopement of Diarmaid and Grainne* and also in the Tristan story. No one can be sure, however, that this trait was present in early versions of the Irish story.

Grainne persistently teased Diarmaid because he refrained from any intimate contact with her. One day as she walked beside him she stepped in a pool and water was splashed high on her thigh; and she declared that the water was more courageous than Diarmaid. Water splashed up under the skirts of Isolt of the White Hands as she was riding with her brother Kaherdin. She jokingly remarked that Tristan, now married to her, had never been so bold as the drops of water.

The question of chronology which has not been solved and perhaps will never be answered makes extremely doubtful the possibility of any influence from this Irish story, even if other difficulties, such as the strangeness of the language and the establishment of any contact on the part of French authors of the twelfth century, with Irish sources, could by any possible chance be removed. Although the story goes all the way back to the ninth century, it exists today only in fragments and those fragments that contain the vague similarities that we have mentioned appear only in redactions too late to serve in this connection.

In its essence *Tristan and Isolt,* as we know the story, is the struggle of a vassal to remain loyal to his suzerain in spite of an overwhelming and irresistible love for his overlord's wife; and this situation is eminently French. The style, structure, and general picture of life is clearly French. There is a story of Tristan's parents—another similarity to the French stories of the time, the situation arising in some of the Old French epics. We have the relationship and affection of the hero's uncle for the sister's son that is common in French stories of the time.

Tristan was an orphan brought up and educated by loyal subjects of his father. He became strong and skillful in the use of arms and a great hunter. He learned to sing and play the harp so beautifully that he recalls Orpheus of Classical lore. He has a bow that never misses its mark, thereby recalling Cephalus of Classical mythology, whose javelin never erred. In addition both Tristan and Cephalus possessed remarkable dogs.

Just as Tristan was becoming a strong youth he was kidnapped by Norwegian merchants and carried away from home on a boat. A violent storm blew up and the merchants feared that the tempest was due to the fact that they had seized the boy unjustly. They, therefore, set Tristan ashore on the rocky coast of Cornwall. He reached King Marc's court, was quickly identified and won the deep affection of his uncle.

Much of the material from which various episodes of this romance were constructed is classical. The most obvious of the classical themes that have been woven into this story are those of Jason and the Golden Fleece, the Minotaur, Theseus, and Medea whose knowledge of magic is shown by Isolt's mother who mixed the potion whose potency unites Tristan and Isolt in love that can never die. Isolt has Medea's knowledge of herbs and her ability to cure.

Tristan became a knight and killed Morgan the enemy who had killed Tristan's father. Soon thereafter the gigantic Morholt appeared at the court and demanded the tribute of young men and maidens that the king of Ireland demanded regularly. Like Theseus who killed the Minotaur, Tristan killed Morholt, thus freeing Mark from the tribute as in the classical story.

This adaptation of the Theseus story is linked with that of Jason and the Golden Fleece. Tristan is sent on what would seem to be an impossible adventure in search of a golden-haired princess. Tristan defeats a dragon and thereby wins the golden-haired Isolt. Isolt cures him of wounds received in the fight with the dragon. Like Medea, in Ovid's story in the seventh book of the *Metamorphoses* she wavers between her admiration for Tristan and her hatred of him as an enemy; for Morholt had been her uncle. Isolt saves Tristan from great danger in a hostile country and returns with him to the court of King Marc for whom Tristan has won the beautiful princess. On the boat, however, they both drink a potion brewed by Isolt's mother and intended to assure the unending love of Marc and Isolt. The result is the uncontrollable love of these two young people that can never end. Through the strength of duty in the feudal system and Tristan's love for his uncle and his loyalty to his overlord, Tristan takes Isolt to Marc's court where she becomes the Queen; but they are continually drawn together in a secret love that by clever trickery and constant vigilance is concealed from Marc in spite of suspicions voiced by enemies and repeated traps and ambuscades in the attempt to prove the guilt of the lovers to the King.

Finally Tristan and Isolt flee to the forest to follow a difficult and dangerous life hunted by the enraged king, after Tristan had saved Isolt from a group of lepers, to whom the jealous king had abandoned her.

King Marc came upon the two lovers asleep in the wood but when he saw the sword that Tristan had placed between them he believed in Isolt's innocence. He took her back; but Tristan was exiled.

In one of his adventures Tristan won a bride, named Isolt of the White Hands, in a distant land. Tristan could not love this second Isolt on account of the first.

Finally physical wounds and love wounds combined brought Tristan close to death. He wanted to see Isolt before he died. She was the only one who could cure him. This incident recalls the Ovidian love doctrine so highly developed by Chrétien wherein the loved person is the only doctor who can cure the love malady. Returning to the Theseus theme again, white sails are to signal the arrival of Isolt; but Isolt of the White Hands learned of her rival's approach and treacherously informed Tristan that the sails on the ship were black. Isolt therefore arrived only to find Tristan dead, killed by the shock of the false report.

CHAPTER VI

Cligès

Chrétien began this romance with the statement that all the honor and glory in arms and in literature, which used to be held by the Greeks and the Romans, had now come to France. If such honor in the realm of literature was in France then it was certainly upheld by Chrétien de Troyes; and this confident poet hopes that France will always maintain its supremacy.

Cligès delighted the readers of his day and of centuries to come, in France, more than any other romance. It has the most complete analysis and description of love in its beginning of any of Chrétien's works.

Cligès begins with the story of the hero's parents. Alexander, son of the King of Greece and Soredamor, the niece of King Arthur and the sister of Gawain. These two lovers could stand as models for all time. Alexander was handsome, skilled in the use of arms, first among all the knights of the world. He had a spirit of adventure unsurpassed by any man that ever lived.

Soredamor was a maiden of striking beauty. Not only was she golden-haired; she was made for love. As her name implies she was gilded with love; and the romance itself is gilded with Ovidian love and metaphors.

The poet's mind, as he starts to write this romance, teems with classical suggestions—the strands that he must weave into the woof of his own invention, but glorious threads of inspiration for a work of art that will thrill the hearts of men who read and especially of women, who live a life of monotony and boredom in dark and gloomy castles, little more than servants of their brutal husbands.

He is going to send a young man from Greece to England, almost at the other end of the world. So this youth resembles Jason and he will sail on a venturous ship—a medieval Argonaut. He spurns the sloth that held Aeneas in Carthage. He had heard of King Arthur's court and his knights. With thoughts of those great knights, whose fame had spread all over the world and whose names would ring through history, undying, his heart was set on living with them and vying with them. He knew that his father would object, that he would want to keep his son in Greece where he would soon rule over that country and Constantinople. So he asked his father to grant him a boon. Thus Phaeton, desirous of driving the chariot of the sun, first obtained a boon from Apollo, his father. Rashly the god gave his promise to his son; and the promise of a god must be inviolate. The personages of Chrétien's romances resemble the gods of ancient mythology. They perform the deeds of demigods. They act with all the august majesty of the Greek and Roman gods. Alexander's father grants the boon as rashly as Apollo, for can he not grant anything that anyone might ask? Like Apollo he regrets his promise when Alexander asks for ships and men and treasure to go to England. He tries to dissuade the bold young man in vain. Treasure he will give in fabulous amount for a man must always be generous. In words similar to those of Horace in the first book of his *Satires* the King condemns covetousness and stinginess.

Chrétien has planned his story in advance. He is going to use a portion of Statius' *Thebaid* and the story of the brothers, Eteocles and Polynices, whose rivalry caused so much suffering and tragedy in the Latin poem. Chrétien however, will vary the material that he takes from Statius. He wants his hero to be justified in his claim on the throne. He therefore has Alexander several years older than Alis and so the rightful heir to the throne.

Sailing for many days, Alexander arrived in England, reached King Arthur's court and distinguished himself in tournaments and was dubbed a knight by the king. He was much liked by all at the court and became a favorite of the King and Queen.

King Arthur desired to go to Brittany and during his absence he left the realm under the rule of Count Angrès of Windsor, to keep the country safe and peaceful until his return. The King and the barons had great confidence in Count Angrès, but their trust was misplaced as will appear. This situation and the consequent war that Arthur is obliged to wage in order to wrest the power from the treacherous Angrès and punish him for his treason is based on the revolt of Mordred against Arthur as told by Geoffrey of Monmouth in his *Historia Regum Britanniae*.

On King Arthur's ship, Gawain is sailing. Soredamor, his sister, is there and also Alexander.

Here the love of these two charming young people begins. The youth is handsome, noble in every thought and gesture. Soredamor stands near. Sunlight caresses the rippling gold of her hair that gleams and sparkles at its touch. And the wind softly waves her streaming locks and outlines her loveliness, sculptured beneath the clinging folds of her garments. Each one casts furtive glances at the other and each glance bears a shaft from Cupid's bow. Both tremble and grow pale before the Queen's discerning eye. The Queen would have guessed their love, as she later did, if it were not for the waves that playfully rock and toss the ship. The Queen is deceived, thinking that the young couple are seasick. Chrétien delights in a bit of humor, here tucked into an incorrect diagnosis of an illness. For the lovers are very ill with a sickness that will give them pain by day and by night until love itself, known and comforting, can soothe their feverish hearts.

Chrétien is going to strive, as Horace commands, to use all his ability and all his knowledge of Ovid's teaching to construct a tale of love as it first buds and blossoms in human hearts. The ground pattern will be planned with the aid of the second elegy in Ovid's *Amores*.

In this love lyric Ovid cries out:

"Who can tell me why my bed seems so hard and why the covers ceaselessly slip to the floor? Why have I passed a whole night without sleep and a night that has seemed interminable? Why must I turn my weary limbs in every direction in painful twisting? Is it love? I surely would have known it. Is tricky Cupid laying an ambush with the design of taking me by surprise? In fact, Love has pierced my heart with his sharp arrows; and the cruel tyrant has established his power over my heart. Shall I yield to him or shall I give new strength to the flame of love by resistance? I yield!" Between the question and the answer there could be a long experience and much pain and suffering. Chrétien widens the gap, to slip in there a large portion of his story, which is developed mainly in two long monologues by Soredamor and one by Alexander. This development is built up in large part by the use of Ovidian suggestions and the stories from the *Metamorphoses* of Pomona (Book XIV), Narcissus (Book III), Medea (Book VII), and Pyramus and Thisbe (Book IV).

Pomona's name is due to her interest in growing fruit. She is named for the goddess of fruit trees. Soredamor means gilded with love. Both Pomona and Soredamor shunned numerous suitors who swarmed about them. Neither would have anything to do with love. Both fall in love, nevertheless, and yield to love. A similarity in the two texts seems to show that Chrétien was thinking of Pomona, who scornfully rejects love, when he tells of Soredamor's disdain for love, in spite of her name.

In the poem that first inspired Chrétien, Ovid explains what would happen to him if he were disdainful of love and would not yield to the power of the god of love. One who resists is treated with greater cruelty and tyranny. A burden becomes light for one who has learned to bear it. Parenthetically one should remember that Ovid calls himself the teacher of love and Soredamor says that she has learned much of love. She has been in school and learned through stern teaching. A flame dies down when a brand is left quiet, says Ovid; agitation makes it burn faster. Young oxen who revolt against the yoke are beaten much more than older ones who have learned to wear it. Ovid declares himself the victim of Love. He holds out his hands in sign of complete subjection and asks only to obey. Love is his master and he is Love's slave. All this information about love, the punishment that the recalcitrant must endure, and the final and complete victory of love is placed by Chrétien between the question of yielding and the inevitable answer, which Ovid gives immediately and which Chrétien and his two lovers delay.

Love's arrows that kindle a fire in the heart have wounded Soredamor. She endures all the symptoms. She sighs, trembles, grows pale and at night she lies awake, twisting and turning in her bed. She indulges in long monologues in which she wavers between hope and fear. She weeps and groans. Alexander has a like experience.

All this suffering began on the deck of the ship and it was caused by the sight of the loved one.

Chrétien was much interested in the story of the strange love of Narcissus, that beautiful youth loved by Echo and all the nymphs of the fields and the woods and the streams. Disdainful of the love of all these eager females, he falls a prey to his own image mirrored in a clear pond deep in the woods. He lies on the grassy edge and gazes longingly at his image, suffering from love that cannot be returned. If he would turn his eyes away the object of his passion would disappear; but his eyes, which deceive him and which he cannot control cause his suffering and treacherously kill him.

Chrétien alludes to this Ovidian story three times in this romance. Soredamor is determined to control her eyes. She knows that she loves what she sees. She has only to turn her eyes away. Her eyes betray her, she declares; but she will not yield to such treachery. It is only a matter of will power. Alexander accuses his heart and his eyes of treachery and declares that they are killing him.

Later in the story Chrétien draws a portrait of Cligès and compares him to Narcissus.

Like Pyramus and Thisbe, Alexander and Soredamor dare not reveal their love; and keeping it hidden, the fire in their suffering hearts burns more ardently because they keep it hidden and nurse the fire by secret glances.

Another most important source of inspiration is the description of Medea's love for Jason with whom a comparison with Alexander is so natural.

Jason's adventures place him among the greatest heroes in all literature. His voyage in his loved ship Argo to Colchis has always been symbolic of a long and dangerous journey over the water. The Golden Fleece he sought is symbolical of any great adventure in a distant land with a reward of glory. Along with the Golden Fleece he won the love of Medea. Medea, her powers of enchantment and her knowledge of healing and herbs, fascinated Chrétien and served him frequently in his romances.

In her meditation, Soredamor resembles Medea. Her thoughts are similar in style, meaning, and actual wording in eleven identical elements. There is the same wavering from assurance to doubt, from fear to confidence; and emotional fervor tends toward a loss of reason and will power almost to the extreme of insanity.

When Medea sees the god-like beauty of Jason, love enters her heart and so upsets her reason that she declares herself mad. She exclaims over the beauty and the nobility of the hero. At first she is determined not to be influenced by the appeal and force of his male attractiveness. She realizes that all her thoughts are centered on the handsome stranger. All the same thoughts fill the mind of Soredamor. Both heroines wish to gaze unceasingly on the features that have infatuated them. Each one questions her love; and each in feverish meditation arrives at the same answer. An absorbing love fills their hearts and controls them. Each one knows that emotion rules over reason and judgment. Each is a helpless slave in the power of love. Each resists in vain; and each one yields entirely to her passion.

Much is made of the idea of learning about love and the comparison of lovers to oxen that after training and punishment with the goad finally learn to bear the yoke.

In the midst of his suffering Alexander speaks of the deep roots of love that have penetrated deep into his heart so that they may not be torn away, as is said in Ovid's *Cure for Love*. He alludes slyly to the possibility of a cure if he could have consulted a doctor.

Of course the only doctor would be Soredamor whom he dared not consult because young lovers are timid. And the cure would be the love of the maiden.

He dreams in wakeful bliss and mingled pain of his love and the cherished wound of Cupid's arrow in the maiden's glance and the image of the girl becomes the arrow of love. She reappears in a clear vision and his memory makes a portrait of the arrow that is Soredamor herself:

> The feathers are colored like gold,
> And though they were really gold
> No brighter could they shine.
> Less clear the gold would gleam
> Than the glory in the arrow's sheen.
> Those feathers are the tresses fair
> That I saw on board the ship.
> It's the arrow that caused my love.
> God! what a treasure to possess!
> Could any one who had such luck,
> In all his days on earth,
> Desire any other wealth.
> For all the gold in Antioch
> I'd never give the feathers
> Nor the notch of this loved shaft.
> And if such value I proclaim
> For just the feathers and the notch
> How would I prize the rest,
> So fair and full of charm
> So precious and so dear to me
> That longingly and ardently I wish
> To gaze again upon her brow
> That was created pure and clear.
> No mirror nor jewel could compare.
> A light shines in her eyes
> That stars could never give.
> None could worthily describe

Her perfect nose and face
Where roses cover lilies,
To mingle white and red,
And give more luminous effect,
Nor tell the beauty of her mouth.
So cleverly her Creator worked
That her lips seem made to laugh.
In even rows her teeth are set.
— — — —
Her throat in purity excels
The brightest crystal ever known.
— — — —
The breast is whiter than snow
Where it appears above her dress.

At this point the arrow disappears in the quiver where it is enclosed and covered. In reduplication and metaphorically, he tells how he could be cured of all his suffering and pain. The loved woman is the doctor and her love the cure. So if he could see the rest of the arrow his agony would be assuaged.

After a lengthy visit in Brittany news comes to King Arthur that Count Angrès has turned traitor. He has assembled a great army and established his headquarters in Windsor Castle; and he intends to usurp the ruling power in England. In wrath Arthur assembles a mighty army and with the boats that are to carry this tremendous force across the channel they are so numerous that the sea beneath them is covered and the water cannot be seen. Thus the sea is hidden by Aeneas' ships when he leaves Dido and Carthage following the command of fate and the gods.

The main elements of the struggle to capture Windsor Castle and defeat Count Angrès come from two famous passages full of tragedy, bloodshed and horror in Virgil's *Aeneid*.

Before the battle really begins Alexander and a number of his Greek companions encounter some of Angrès men and take four of them prisoners. These captives are drawn by horses around the castle just as Hector was drawn around Priam's castle in the sight of the Trojans.

Angrès and his army are besieged in Windsor Castle and the situation becomes desperate for the starving besieged. They take counsel and form a plan in accordance with which they make a bold sortie in the night from an unused and unsuspected postern gate along a secret path in the hope of slaughtering enough of the enemy in a surprise attack in the dark so that victory may be won. The success of this venture was prevented by the betrayal of sudden light in the darkness as the moon came from behind black clouds and glittered on the armor of the attackers. If the victory had been won by Angrès' men, they thought the battle would be remembered throughout the history of the world. Eight points of similarity clearly reveal the source of inspiration for this attack and failure.

Aeneas had left his camp, in the ninth book of the *Aeneid*, to seek reenforcements for the Trojans, whom he has left under the command of Ascanius. Turnus takes advantage of this absence of Aeneas to attack and besiege the camp with superior forces. The situation becomes grave. A council of war is called and a desperate plan is formed. Two extremely valiant young soldiers, Nisus and Euryalus undertake to penetrate the army of the besiegers, to slaughter many in the night and to escape in the confusion. Their dangerous venture would have succeeded if the moonlight had not betrayed them and unexpectedly, on this dark night, which seemed to favor their attempt. Suddenly the moon came from behind the clouds and revealed their presence by glistening on their arms. Virgil declares that the brave deeds of Nisus and Euryalus will be remembered eternally.

The attack of Angrès' men was a complete failure. There was no escape for most of the traitors. They were entirely hemmed in by their enemy and the sea—a slight exaggeration since the sea was some distance away but a reminiscence of a Virgilian passage, in the tenth book of the *Aeneid* where the Arcadians, under the leadership of Pallas, found themselves completely surrounded by the sea and the enemy when they were put to rout by Turnus.

Angrès himself with some of his followers returned to the impregnable castle by a secret path. They are espied by Alexander, however. Some of the enemy are killed and their shields and lances are taken to serve as a disguise. By this means they are admitted to the castle where only a few of Angrès' men are now armed. The central tower is taken and Count Angrès is captured. A surrender of the whole castle follows; and Alexander has won a cup, which King Arthur, in imitation of similar awards frequently made by Aeneas, had promised to anyone who could take Windsor Castle.

This strategy recalls the adventures of Aeneas, when aroused from sleep on that terrible night when Troy was burned and sacked by the Greeks. Aeneas was able to assemble a few followers. They were able to defeat a group of the Greek soldiers and defeat them. The Trojans then took the helmets, the swords and the shields of their fallen enemies. Thus disguised they were able to kill many of their foes and to mount by a secret path to Priam's citadel and enter by an unknown postern gate.

This postern gate that came to Chrétien from Virgil's *Aeneid* found its way into the *Roman de Thebes*, which has been considered by scholars, erroneously, the first of the French twelfth-century romances. The passage, in *Thebes* is copied directly from Chrétien's *Cligès* and, in itself, disproves the generally held chronology of the early romances as it appears in most histories of literature.

This chronology is extremely important because the contention in this book is that Chrétien de Troyes is the inventor and first author of romances in France.

In this connection it is necessary to know and to keep constantly in mind that scholars have definitely proven that either Chrétien copied passages from *Thèbes* and other romances or those romances copied Chrétien. There are so many elements of similarity in rimes, ideas, and actual wording that copying cannot be denied. But we have shown that this postern gate comes to Chrétien directly from Virgil. Chrétien therefore did not copy *Thèbes*. Consequently

Thèbes must have copied *Cligès* and was written after several of Chrétien's works.

To make the whole question of chronological order clear, the *Roman de Thèbes* is a translation with adaptations from Statius' *Thèbaid*. In the *Thèbaid* there is no secret postern gate. Fifty horsemen leave one of the main gates of the mythical city of Thèbes in broad daylight. They pursue a single man. Therefore no postern, no geographical direction, and no secrecy. The author of the *Roman de Thèbes* copied these elements from *Cligès*.

Soredamor thinks twice of taking the initiative and telling her love to Alexander—this in imitation of Ovidian characters who actually do offer themselves to the men they love; specifically Echo, who vainly strives to win the love of Narcissus, Scylla, Byblis, Myrrha, Venus in love with Adonis, and Circe pleading for the love of Cyniras and again appealing to Picus. Soredamor resists the temptation the first time for fear of losing Alexander's respect.

The second time Alexander has come, as he frequently does, to the Queen's tent, where he can always find the object of his passion; and Soredamor, deeply in love but bashful and timid, hopes to hear Alexander confess his love for her. She is tempted to speak herself as he sits beside her. She hesitates; and she is afraid to speak his name for fear that she might stop in the middle because her emotion and shame might make her speechless. Thus Byblis in the ninth book of the *Metamorphoses* hesitates to speak Caunus' name, and to tell him her love for fear that shame would check her tongue. She asks a servant to take a letter to him. After the word "my" she stops and only after a long pause can she add "brother."

The story of Myrrha is another source for this little trait. In the tenth book of the *Metamorphoses*, Myrrha loves her father, Cyniras. Her nurse, who is in part the model for Thessala, Fenice's nurse in the second part of this romance, heard Myrrha's voice in the middle of the night. What she heard was indistinct but the nurse was alarmed by the tone of Myrrha's voice and words that sounded like "my death." The loyal and affectionate nurse arises from her bed and enters Myrrha's room where she finds the girl about to hang herself. The nurse saves Myrrha from her contemplated death, tries to comfort her, and insists on learning the cause of despair, promising help, no matter what the trouble may be. The nurse has magical powers and knowledge of healing. She pleads with Myrrha until the girl finally tries to speak and tell of her incestuous love for her father; but her voice fails her and she is choked by her sobbing. The nurse also hesitates as she promises Myrrha the "love of your . . ." She hesitates to say the word "father."

After the capture of Windsor Castle there was a false report that Alexander had been killed. Following the Ovidian style in treating of love, Soredamor fainted on hearing this news. Her love was not revealed at this time because there was so much grief among all members of the court that Soredamor's swooning did not seem unusual.

Soon after this, however, the Queen guesses Soredamor's love and serves in a mild way as a sort of go-between; thus giving a prefiguration of important personages such as Thessala, Fenice's nurse, in the second part of *Cligès* and Lunete the lady's maid of Laudine in *Yvain,* confidantes who help further a love affair, as recommended by Ovid, and exemplified by the famous Ovidian go-betweens Dipsas, Cypassis and Nape of the *Amores.*

Alexander and Soredamor were married. A son named Cligès was born. Now the Emperor of Greece and Constantinople died and messengers were sent to inform Alexander of his father's death. Remembering an incident from the *Aeneid,* when to trick the Trojans and persuade them to take the huge horse that the Greeks had left into the city, an individual arrived claiming that the Greeks had intended to sacrifice him to the gods in order to propitiate them and obtain fair weather and a safe return to Greece. He had escaped, he said, and the Greeks had sailed away.

He explained that the mountain-high horse had been constructed in honor of the goddess Pallas and had been made tremendous in size so that the Trojans might never be able to get it into their city.

So, with considerable variation, a single individual returns from the ship in which the messengers had been sent to tell Alexander of his father's death and summon him back to Greece. So, lying to deceive the Greeks, this man, favoring Alis rather than Alexander and deceiving the Greeks with a lie, states that the ship on which he had sailed had reached England and, returning with Alexander, had been wrecked and all had been drowned except himself. Believing his story, Alis was crowned Emperor of Greece.

Naturally Alexander, the rightful heir to the throne, would not accept this situation. He returned at once to his native land. A considerable portion of the romance from this point on is influenced by the *Thebaid* of the Latin poet Statius with modifications.

Chrétien does not conceal the source of his inspiration. In frank and open revelation he compares Alexander and Alis to Eteocles and Polynices, whose fierce struggle over the throne of Thebes caused cruel and tragic suffering. It is unthinkable that Chrétien would allow his characters to resemble the cruel and ruthless brothers of the *Thebaid*. His constant purpose of creating personages of high nobility is applied in the perfection of Alexander's personality. He will not even accept the tremendous and invincible army that King Arthur offered him so that he might easily regain the ruling power in Greece by force of arms. With only a small group of loyal Greeks, who went with him to England, he returns to Athens, anchors his ship and sends a messenger, who resembles Tydeus of the *Thebaid*, to Alis demanding the surrender of the throne. Both messengers speak with similar courage and arrogance.

In order to avoid the horror and tragedy of the struggle between Etiocles and Polynices in the *Thebaid*, Alis, with the consent and advice of his barons, agreed to turn over all the land and the government if he were allowed to retain the rather empty title of Emperor. Thus it was arranged.

Alexander soon died; and the words of Horace are repeated; namely, that "Pale Death knocks impartially at the cottage of the poor and the palace of the rich."

Alis had promised never to marry, so that he would have no heir and the throne would go to Cligès. This is the situation in *Tristan and Isolt*. Marc, too, had promised never to marry, so that Tristan would always be the heir to the throne. Both Marc and Alis kept their promises for a while; each of them was urged to marry by their barons. Alis finally decided to marry the daughter of the Emperor of Germany.

Now the source for much of the next large section of *Cligès* is Virgil's *Aeneid*. Alis is obliged to fight against the Duke of Saxony just as Aeneas had to fight against Turnus, to whom Lavinia had been promised by the Queen of Latium. The Duke of Saxony would not give up his promised bride without a fight. Like Latinus, the Emperor of Germany preferred to marry his daughter to the more illustrious suitor. Mingling a trait from Statius' *Thebaid,* the Duke sent a messenger. This messenger, who, by a slight variation, is the Duke's nephew, reminds us of Tydeus first because he delivers his message, contrary to the manner of Tydeus, without pride or insult; and second because, like Tydeus, the Duke's nephew leaves defiantly after a scornful reception. Like Tydeus, this messenger does not escape without a fight; but to continue the seasaw of similarities and the differences, that point the way no less significantly, there is no treacherous attack in *Cligès*. Cligès challenges him in knightly manner. Contrary to the fate of Tydeus the Duke's nephew is defeated in battle. Unlike Tydeus he was not alone; but, rather, was accompanied by a retinue of three hundred who fought with him against an equal number of Greeks.

In the battle between the two armies, in a trait resembling the one from the *Aeneid* already mentioned in the discussion of the first part of this romance, Cligès' men seize insignia of the enemy—a shield and sword—in order to deceive the enemy and take them by surprise. This trait is used again with the variation that Cligès is able to approach more closely to the Saxon soldiers who have abducted Fenice, the heroine of the romance, daughter of the Emperor of Germany and the promised bride of Alis, by riding on the Duke of Saxony's white horse, which he has captured. The abduction had been accomplished by approaching the abandoned camp of the Greeks during the battle just as Aeneas attacked Latinus' city under a similar circumstance. The Saxons reach the camp unobserved by using an old secluded path which is, of course, a replica of the secret path up to Windsor Castle, described earlier and the secret way that Aeneas took up to Priam's citadel.

In Cligès' valiant rescue of Fenice he defeated twelve opponents and allowed one of them to escape in order that he might carry disappointing news to the Duke just as Tydeus defeated a great number of opponents, leaving a single one alive to return to Thebes with news of the startling defeat of those who expected to kill him.

The war was finally decided by single combat between Cligès and the Duke just as the fate of Lavinia and the war between Turnus and Aeneas was settled. The undertaking of this combat by the youthful Cligès recalls the fight of Tristan against the Morholt with similar protests on account of the youthfulness and inexperience of each successful hero. The fight itself bares a noticeable similarity to the battle of the Cestes between Entellus and Dares in the fifth book of the *Aeneid*. Each victor falls and is supposed, by his grieving friends, to have been defeated, only to rise and rush more furiously into the fray. Each combat is stopped before the end. The reason is not the same. Aeneas stops the battle of the Cestes. In *Cligès* the Duke realizes that he will be inevitably defeated and in a prudent and cautious manner gives up the battle and Fenice. The Virgilian ending does occur later in this same romance when King Arthur stops an equal contest between Cligès and the never-yet-defeated Gawain. The same situation is repeated in *Lancelot*, when King Bademagu stops a fight between his son and Lancelot to save his son from defeat.

As he fights furiously in the battle Cligès is compared to a top driven by a whip lash. This simile comes straight out of the *Aeneid* where Amata, Lavinia's mother, in the seventh book, infuriated by

Latinus' determination to give Lavinia in marriage to Aeneas, rushes furiously through the town "like the top that spins about vast porticos driven by the whip that children wield."

Following the general pattern of *Tristan and Isolt* Cligès and Fenice fall in love. Cupid's arrows fly from the eyes of this charming pair. The radiance of their beauty fills the palace of the German emperor. Their love is secretly and timidly given and the god of love holds them in his power. The dangerous situation of an empress madly in love and adulterously in love was tremendously thrilling in the twelfth century and the theme has been reworked many times in the world's literature. Chrétien puts a twist into the Tristan theme that he has woven into the conjuncture of the *Cligès*. Fenice declares that she will not give her body to two men as Isolt did. Neither her heart nor her body will be shared. In order to work out this problem Chrétien adds to his romance the theme of the Oriental story of Solomon's Wife, whereby Fenice is to appear to die, to be buried and ressurected secretly by Cligès, using a devise that has been made familiar to modern readers by Shakespeare in his *Romeo and Juliet*.

In order to simulate death Chrétien provides Fenice with a nurse with the name of Thessala, which is derived from the name of Medea's native country. Thessala has all the knowledge of herbs that Medea possessed. This personage is compounded of Medea plus the nurse of Myrrha; and the story of Myrrha is adapted to bridge the gap between the Tristan theme and that of Solomon's wife. The resemblance in the illegal and disloyal love affair, the need of committing a crime, palliated in *Cligès* by casuistry, in the relation between the lady and her nurse, the magical and medical knowledge of each nurse, the arguments used to learn about the love affair and the willingness of the nurse to help even to further a crime is close.

The idea of a potion came to Chrétien from Ovid who says in the second book of the *Art of Love* that the art of the Thessalian sorceresses and the herbs of Medea have the power to impart the semblance of love only, while disturbing the reason, and cannot create real love. Chrétien applies this suggestion literally. The potion that Thessala brews and serves to Alis makes him believe that he enjoys full marital rights with Fenice while asleep and prevents him from having any amorous desire while awake. A most amusing disturbance of the reason and the will.

Alis, on his wedding night, had voluptuous dreams of love resembling those of Byblis in the ninth book of the *Metamorphoses,* when in her sleep she dreamed of the fulfillment of her carnal love for her brother.

For the burial and exhumation of Fenice whose name derived from that of the phoenix which is reborn from its ashes, is thus suggested, Chrétien needed an artificer capable of constructing a suitable tomb and after her rescue from the tomb a house of proper construction so that Fenice could live there comfortably and secretly. The idea may have come to Chrétien from the stories of Virgil as a necromancer.

Symptoms of Ovidian love are repeated in the second part of the romance.

This romance has many sources of inspiration: Geoffrey of Monmouth's *Historia, Tristan and Isolt,* the *Thebaid* of Statius, Virgil's *Aeneid* for warfare and military strategy, Virgil the Magician and Ovid for the style and manner in which love is described.

CHAPTER VII

Lancelot

All of Chrétien's romances are medleys in the better sense of the word. They are not confused jumbles, but *Erec, Cligès* and *Yvain* are certainly well ordered compositions, constructed with as much art and precision as a master joiner puts into his careful craftsmanship. Many analyses by scholars have shown, in detailed studies, that the structure of Chrétien's romances is coherent and logical, carefully planned and artistic in arrangement and effect.

Lancelot is less carefully written. It may have suffered in transmission. Chrétien may have worked hurriedly and with some dissatisfaction. He did not finish the romance. The conclusion was written by another author.

This romance is the first to mention Lancelot, Queen Guenivere's lover, who later became the most famous of all the Arthurian heroes in the prose romances. The faithlessness of Guenivere, Arthur's queen, was already displayed in Geoffrey of Monmouth's *Historia Regum Britanniae* where her affair with Mordred, the traitor, is related.

Lancelot might be called a literary cocktail, but one with many ingredients so thoroughly mixed that only the intriguing and illusive flavor of some of them is discernible.

Fundamentally it is the story of an abduction and rescue. The classical story of Helen of Troy was, no doubt, in Chrétien's mind; for *Lancelot,* as well as the classical story, deals in an abduction of a lady who is carried to a distant land and rescued with difficulty and fighting. This long and arduous journey recalls the search of Cupid for Psyche as related in Apuleius' *Golden Ass* which was known and imitated elsewhere in Old French literature.

The arrival of Meleagant to taunt King Arthur about subjects of his realm who are held captive and his demand that the Queen go with him unless he can be defeated in combat, and the promise that all of Arthur's people will be released from captivity if Meleagant is beaten in the struggle recalls inescapably the Morholt of the Tristan story and consequently the Minotaur, the tribute exacted by Minos of Crete from the Athenians, and the defeat of this monster by Theseus, resulting in the end of the tribute—a theme used repeatedly by Chrétien especially in the Joie de la Cour episode of *Erec and Enide* and again in *Yvain*.

The fact that the abduction, which follows the combat between Meleagant and Kay, occurs in a wood or clearing and the clear implication of otherworld mystery with Gorre, the land of Meleagant, comparable to the realm of Pluto, since the statement is repeatedly made that neither Guenivere nor any of the other captives may ever return, the sad attitude of resignation of King Arthur to fate, the tombs reserved for knights not yet dead, and the River of the Devil, all this points to the classical stories of the abduction of Proserpine and that of Eurydice, whom Orpheus was nearly successful in rescuing.

The story of Orpheus was used repeatedly in Old French, Middle High German, and English literatures, and through numerous variants, can be traced to the title and contents of the Middle English poem *Sir Orfeo* so that the relation between the classical stories of Orpheus and of Proserpine with their otherworld suggestions and a whole series of abduction and rescue stories stemming from and imitating Chrétien's *Lancelot*.

Such faint Celtic influences as may have existed are so elusive, so difficult to establish or explain as to be negligible. Chrétien's romances are eminently French in style and content. Popular story material everywhere existant and classical material and artistic inspiration are mingled with original inventions of Chrétien himself and realistic observations of the life around him, to the exclusion of other influences in any important amount or in any unadulterated and pure form unmixed with material at hand and in a language known to Chrétien.

The initial impulse of the action in this romance is the rash boon granted to the eager but incompetent Kay. The seneschal asks for a boon which King Arthur rashly grants before he knows what he is promising. Such a boon had been granted to Alexander by his father, the Emperor of Greece and Constantinople. King Arthur has powers as vast as those of the gods of classical literature, and like Apollo, whose son Phaeton suffered from a promise rashly given and Jupiter, who kills his loved Semele by the fulfillment of a rash promise which, when known, requires his appearance before Semele in all the effulgence of his full glory—a blazing light unendurable by mortals, so King Arthur allows Kay to go forth with Meleagant to fight with him for the safety of Guenivere and the release of all the captives held in the land of Gorre, or their doom. The outcome could never be in doubt.

In a vain attempt at rescue, the King and the knights of his court set out, but soon only Gawain continues, to be joined, unexpectedly and inexplicably, by Lancelot, his name being withheld, for reasons of suspense, for a long time. Lancelot will eventually achieve the impossible rescue. It would be necessary to repeat the whole story in order to recount all the difficult feats performed by the hero ending in a combat with Meleagant after arriving, nearly dead, in the land of Gorre, horribly mutilated by cuts received in crossing a bridge like a sword over whose sharp cutting edge Lancelot was obliged to crawl.

In this frame of an abduction to a distant land, difficult to reach, difficult to enter and from which it is supposedly impossible to return, with a culminating combat, to rescue a lady, is set the underlying conception and all-important burden of the romance. This conception is based on the Ovidian type of love as developed by Chrétien. Here the emphasis is not on the beginning of love, but on love service which requires courage, endurance, patience, and humility carried to the extreme of enslavement to the loved lady's every whim and command. An arrogant lady has taken over the very functions of Love, who tortures and humiliates his victims.

Lancelot's horse is killed and he is obliged to continue for a while on foot; but in the company of Gawain mounted on a horse. Soon they encounter a dwarf driving a cart. When they ask him whether he has any information about the Queen, he tells Lancelot that if he will get up into the cart and ride with him he will soon have news of the Queen. Lancelot hesitates for a step; but then, compelled by love, he gets into the cart. This was a most humiliating act, because, we are told, knights never rode in carts which were used only to convey criminals to jail or to a place of punishment or execution. Lancelot suffers grievously and is the butt of universal mockery when he arrives in a town where he is to spend the night.

This is the first of a series of humiliations and trials to which Lancelot is subjected in his love service. This is not the Provençal type of love as many scholars have thought. The Provençal lover complains of his loved lady's cruelty but her cruelty consists only in not returning his love. She does not torment her lover. This torture and humiliation is Ovidian.

In the morning he looks out of a high window and sees the Queen riding away. He leans out of the window and would have fallen and killed himself if he were not restrained by Gawain. This is one of several incidents in which complete absorption by love endangers the lover. The idea comes from Ovid, who often uses this trait; and this particular incident has a direct source in the fifth book of the *Metamorphoses* where after enticing the Mnemonides into his palace with amorous intent and they in terror race to the top of a high tower from which they throw themselves, but wings are given to them, Pyreneus carried heedlessly on by his mad passion leaps after them and is dashed to pieces on the ground below.

Among numerous passages in the *Metamorphoses* that show this same heedlessness that leads to danger, when love completely absorbs the attention of the lover, a familiar one is that of Scylla who loved Minos, the enemy of her country. She betrayed her father and his city to the handsome hero who spurned her, but her love was so all-absorbing that driven by its mad fury she leaped into the water and tried to swim after the departing ship of the man who, though he profited from her help, cursed her and loathed her as a traitor.

Again Lancelot sank so deep into thoughts of his love that he rode into a ford unheeding of the warning of one who guarded it and forbade him to cross and never came to his senses until he felt the cold water of the stream into which his adversary had dumped him.

The story is lengthened by tests of the hero's courage and the faithfulness of his love for Guenivere, the suffering and pain of his love and still delight in all the agony of his passion. Near a spring he found a comb forgotten by the Queen with a few hairs from her dear head clinging to its teeth. And there he stood in wrapped admiration worshipping this memento so absorbed in love that consciousness of anything else ceases, physical existence became so unsubstantial and shadowy that a sort of coma ensued and he nearly fell from his horse.

In the third book of the *Amores* and the second selection the poet, Ovid, imagines himself sitting beside a beautiful lady and watching a chariot race. Gallantly he praises her loveliness. He waxes eloquent and in exalted tones declares that her love would so strengthen his courage and invigorate his mental and physical stamina that he would gladly brave all the dangers of the race and drive a chariot himself in mad career. Instinctively and inspired by strength-giving love he would have all the skill of the charioteer who risks his life amidst the whirling dust and the threatening wheels of rash and merciless opponents. And yet, if he should happen to glance at the loved lady, he would, drop the reins, overcome by the absorbing trance of his love, and allow the horses to slacken their speed. He alludes to Pelops, whom Neptune had taught to drive horses and who provided Pelops with winged horses to match those of the King of Pisa that could run with the speed of a cyclone. Pelops loved Hippodamia, the daughter of the King. To win this beautiful lady of his dreams Pelops must win a race against her father who would kill him with a spear, if he could catch him. Thirteen aspirants had already been killed in this competition and since it had been prophesied that the King of Pisa would be killed by his son-in-law, he did not intend to lose the race. Ovid says that while contemplating the beauty of Hippodamia, who was watching the race, Pelops was nearly defeated; but it was the love of Hippodamia that brought him victory. Ovid seems to cheat a little here because the story runs that Hippodamia bribed Myrtilus, her father's charioteer to remove a bolt from the King's chariot and replace it with wax.

This poem is the source of an incident in the combat between Lancelot and Meleagant to determine the fate of Queen Guenivere and the captives from King Arthur's realm. Lancelot sees Guenivere sitting high up at one of the windows of the castle before which the combat takes place. He cannot turn his eyes away and fights awkwardly because his opponent is behind him. His mind and will are so completely dulled by the mental absorption of love that he is about to lose the fight through the stupor that dominates him, until a shout arouses him and the warning to get Meleagant between himself and the Queen penetrates his bemused consciousness in time for him to follow this timely advice and then the sight of his loved lady increases his valor and his strength.

Following again the model of Aeneas who stops the duel of the Cestes, Bademagu the father of Meleagant and King of Gorre stops this combat to save his son's life. Chrétien uses a unique method in varying this source. He has the King ask Guenivere to stop that fight. Guenivere merely says in a quiet manner that she is willing; and Lancelot, the willing slave of love's slightest wish immediately stops fighting and docilely receives the blows that Meleagant now rains on him until, at the King's orders, he is restrained.

The Queen was released on the condition that Lancelot would meet Meleagant again in combat one year after Meleagant should summon him at King Arthur's court.

Lancelot is now invited to visit the Queen for whom he has endured untold suffering, repeated dangers on a long journey to find her, engaged in numerous combats along the way and finally penetrated into this inaccessible land to win her release from life-long imprisonment. And yet, as he enters the room where she is sitting, she arises and departs, closing the door behind her, leaving her lover heartbroken. This is based on the recommendation of Ovid that love should be enhanced and quickened by such cruel action on the part of the loved lady. A door is thus closed or *not closed* by a loved lady more than once in Chrétien's works.

There was another difficult entrance to this land of Gorre, over a bridge under water. Gawain and Lancelot who had traveled together and shared the dangers of this long journey had separated, each one to try a different entrance to the land where Guenivere was held captive. Now Lancelot hastened toward the bridge under water; but being unarmed, Lancelot is taken prisoner by some overzealous subjects of Bademagu. A false report is borne by Rumor to Bademagu's court. Incidentally the mention of Rumor that flies so fast is borrowed from the *Aeneid* which spread the report of the love of Aeneas and Dido in the fourth book. The report reached Guenivere that Lancelot had been killed. Now using once more the Pyramus and Thisbe motive but with the final denouement of death omitted, Guenivere tried to strangle herself. Lancelot now hears a second false report that Guenivere is dead. He then tries to kill himself, but is prevented by the men who, by order of the King, now escort him safely back to the court.

Now after all this near tragedy Guenivere receives her lover kindly. He asks her why she had treated him so cruelly before, and she replies that it is because he hesitated momentarily to mount into the dwarf's cart. The arrogant lady has outdone Cupid himself in cruelty. Such behavior had a vogue in literary love treatment of several centuries, appearing abundantly in seventeenth-century French novels.

However ruthless the god of love may be, though his function may be to kindle fires of love, to torture endlessly through all time, there is a time when the individual may have the cure and the joy of love. All the suffering inflicted by the adored object of the courageous lover's affection is after all, a sort of test of the male's sincerity, of the true depth of his love. When the service has been completely assuring and the patience of the lover proves the strength and endurance of his love, then the lady may safely relent and bestow her trust and her love.

Guenivere was deeply moved by the double tragedy that was barely escaped. She feels a deep tenderness in her heart and she consents to meet her lover in the secret shadows of the night, for this type of love must be secret. Lancelot will come to the window of the room where she spends the night. The ardor of Lancelot's love has been nurtured by many days of longing, fear of losing the woman he loves so dearly, whom he might never have found, whom he might never have seen after she had been taken to a land that seems like the realm of death, who had repulsed him so cruelly, and whose reported death by suicide had caused him such despair that he had tried to end his own life.

Now his passion has reached a white heat. He can scarcely wait for the sweet moments of secret communion of love. The day seems long, interminable. The poet says that "the dark, obscure night struggled so long to conquer the day that finally it enveloped it and placed it beneath its cloak." This pretty figure has had great popularity in French literature and has been repeatedly used by French authors through the centuries. It would be most gratifying if we could proclaim Chrétien the first to have used it; but the credit must go to Ovid who used it in the fifteenth book of the *Metamorphoses* to indicate the passage of time during a long debate in the Greek senate:

> While they were wavering in their debate, twilight
> routed the last rays of day,
> And the night threw its cloak of darkness over the
> earth.

Finally the moment of ecstasy arrives and Lancelot stands at Guenivere's window, and the lovely woman comes in light attire. She has risen from her bed. They can clasp each other's hand but there are bars on the window that hold them apart; and they long for close embraces. Now Lancelot assures her that he can remove the bars and enter the chamber if she will only give her consent. Her refusal would be stronger than any barrier ever constructed. She gives her consent and Lancelot pulls out the bars and enters the room. He is only following the instructions of Ovid, the teacher of love. In the third book of the *Art of Love* Ovid suggests to the woman in love that she should frequently close her door against her lover. She should make the lover's approach difficult and to spice the meetings with him with the fear of discovery and fatal consequences. "Let him enter stealthily through a window."

The next morning stains of blood were found on the sheets of Guenivere's bed. This recalls well-known tell-tale stains of blood in an episode of *Tristan and Isolt*. The severely wounded seneschal, Kay, had been sleeping in the same room with Guenivere; and now Meleagant accused Kay of having lain with Guenivere during the night. In order to defend the Queen's reputation by ordeal of battle Lancelot fights again with Meleagant and the combat is stopped by Bademagu to save his son from defeat, again in imitation of Aeneas.

Lancelot starts out again in search of Gawain who finally reached the bridge under water; but fell off and was saved from drowning by friends who had accompanied Lancelot. Lancelot himself was betrayed by a dwarf who treacherously leads the trustful hero into a group who take him prisoner.

Concealing her grief the best she can, the Queen returned to her own country, having received a letter containing the false information that Lancelot had returned there safely.

In his prison, the handsome knight inspires a deep passion in the heart of his jailer's wife. Although Lancelot, inalterably faithful to Guenivere, does not return this affection, he does take advantage of it to obtain his release for the days of a tournament, held by King Arthur, news of which had come to him. At the tournament Lancelot was recognized only by a herald, who proclaimed that a great knight had arrived and that this knight would unhorse many opponents, and by the Queen herself.

In order to further test his great love for her and to continue this Ovidian type of love, which is a large part of the System of Courtly Love that became so famous and spread its influence through Provençal poetry into the *dolce stil nuovo* of Italy, the French novels of the seventeenth century, and the love discussions in the well-known *salons,* Guenivere sent a message to Lancelot, who was fighting valiantly and causing great havoc among the knights engaged in the tournament, to do his worst. Carrying his love service to the greatest depths of humiliation, Lancelot, who was in honor bound to return to his prison and might thereafter never expect to have another chance to win glory in combat, obeyed; and he became the butt of jeers on every side as he allowed himself to be driven about in what appeared to be the most consummate cowardice.

In this three-day tournament, which was a popular folk-tale, Lancelot received the same order from the Queen and disgraced himself again. On the third day, however, the order came from the Queen, whose heart was filled to bursting by Lancelot's proof of the devoted worship of Lancelot's heart for her beauty and her love, to do his best; and, as was inevitable, Lancelot defeated every opponent and won the tournament.

On returning to his prison, Lancelot was placed in a lonely tower from which it seemed impossible that he could ever escape again.

The rest of the story appears to have been written by another hand and therefore has no interest for us.

CHAPTER VIII

Yvain

The central core of *Yvain* is the winning of a lady's love at the end of an almost impossible feat of valor in a distant land, a conflict between the claims of honor and valor on the part of the man and those of love, the loss of the lady and the rewinning of her love. There is a quarrel between man and wife just as in *Erec and Enide* with the difference that *Yvain* is in Chrétien's second manner after he has adopted the Ovidian type of love.

In *Erec and Enide,* Erec held the sovereignty of husband over wife as was natural in the real life of that time and for many centuries afterward. Enide was a meek and obedient wife loyal and deeply in love, full of grief over her part in the quarrel. In *Yvain* we have the arrogant type who demands abject obedience from the male lover.

In *Erec and Enide* the wrath of the husband is vented upon the wife and she is subjected to severe punishment. Her suffering is slight, however, in comparison with that of Yvain, whom the fair Laudine, his wife, banishes forever from her realm and her presence. The worst effects of love throw Yvain, negligent of the demands of love, into despair that brings on insanity and attempted suicide.

No literary study could be more exhilarating than to watch Chrétien de Troyes collect the various parts that build up this romance and to see how neatly he puts them together, after shaping them to his needs. Though he borrows a very large proportion of his materials from classical Latin sources and old familiar folk-tales he is very clever and sometimes very humorous in twisting and turning his source material about and so transforming it that its origin often escapes the casual reader.

No one would miss the use of the story of Gyges' ring or that of Androcles and the lion; but scholars have failed to find the very central theme although it is the first of which anyone should think. One is reminded of the letter, hidden in the most obvious place, in one of Edgar Allan Poe's stories or of the man who wandered about the world looking for a four-leaf clover while one was growing beside his doorstep.

For the theme of a man's honor and glory pitted against love one story stands out preeminent then, now, and always, the story of Aeneas and Dido. Chrétien used this episode from the *Aeneid* as the basic theme of *Erec and Enide*. Every careful reader has seen a similarity between *Erec and Enide* and *Yvain*. Horace, Chrétien's artistic mentor, advises the use of a well-known theme handled with consummate art. Virgil dominated the study of grammar and rhetoric in the schools of all romance nations from Roman times down to the twelfth century, when Ovid became more important for the study of literary style. The Dido story has always been the most interesting part of the *Aeneid*. Every reason points to the fourth book of the *Aeneid* as the most likely source; and it is, in fact, the source of the kernel of *Yvain*.

Chrétien read in Ovid's *Art of Love,* the third book, that "Often a woman may find a second husband at the funeral of the first; let your tears stream and your hair fall in disorder: that is becoming to a woman." The passage continues about as follows: "But shun those men who display their comeliness . . . What they say they have said to many others . . . The most magnificent of all these is only a thief. Some men go about wooing under false appearance of love and, by such approaches, seek shameful gains . . . There are, too, certain names of unquestionable ill fame; many alas, bear the reproach of a deserted mistress. Learn from the complaints of another to fear for yourselves; nor let your door be open to a false lover . . . Believe not Theseus' oaths: the gods he will call to witness, he has called upon before, and thou too Demophoon . . ."

This is exactly the situation in *Yvain*. Even the wording of Chrétien's text follows Ovid's closely. Yvain sees Laudine at her husband's funeral. Her hair is dishevelled and she is weeping. In the midst of her mourning she appears so beautiful to Yvain that he falls in love at once. Love wounds him in the heart through the eyes and Yvain becomes the prey of Love—all in the Ovidian manner. He wonders how beautiful this lady might be in a happy mood, and not wailing and tearing her hair. Thus Apollo asks in the first book of the *Metamorphoses* how beautiful Daphne would be if her hair were artfully arranged instead of falling in disorder about her shoulders as he pursues her, in a passage that we shall later compare with one in this same romance.

Now Yvain later appears faithless to Laudine and she uses the very words of Ovid to declare him a traitor, liar, deceiver, a thief. And Chrétien's words are: "Some name men thieves, who go about wooing under false pretenses, stealing hearts for which they do not care." Laudine has sent a messenger to Yvain, whom she considers unfaithful to her because he has broken a promise and has not returned at the appointed time. This messenger takes up a new source that is indicated at the end of the first when Demophoon is mentioned as a faithless lover. This source is the letter from Phyllis to Demophoon second of the epistles of the *Heroides*. Phyllis writes: "Your Phyllis . . . complains that your absence has passed the term promised to my love . . . Counting the moments as lovers count, I do not complain before the day of your promise." These are the very words that Laudine's messenger uses. Laudine has counted the days until the date of Yvain's promised return. The term has ended and Laudine does not complain until Yvain's forgetfulness has delayed his return until after the appointed time. She does not complain too soon.

Between the funeral, when Laudine weeps so despairingly, and the supposed betrayal on the part of a supposedly insincere thief and deceiver, as Laudine falsely declares Yvain to be—and the mistake on the part of Laudine does not matter, she is the arrogant lady who demands abject obedience and can brook no slightest sin of neglect or failure of the male to worship, adore and serve her; this is a serious quarrel, the solution of which is more difficult than that in *Erec and Enide*—there has to be inserted the winning of this lady's love. In order for Yvain to win her love she must be consoled. The theme of the easily consoled widow puzzled scholars for many years.

Foerster, the great German scholar, who edited Chrétien's works and, a foreigner, ardently defended Chrétien's originality against native French scholars less loyal and deplorably less correct in their judgment, chose as a source for this very kernel of Chrétien's best romance the story of the Widow of Ephesus, a pitiable choice that counts as a black mark against Foerster, but not one that condemns him too much, because he was far ahead of all the other scholars of his day and his suggestion was the best with the exception of the correct answer.

The Widow of Ephesus mourned her dead husband as bitterly as Laudine and, like her, desired to follow her husband to the grave. In this story by Petronius, the widow is represented as a model of chastity so renowned that many people came to see her as though to observe a miracle. She accompanied his body to the tomb with hair dishevelled like Laudine and like Laudine she lacerated herself with her nails. Then she established her abode in the sepulchre and wept day and night over the dead body of her husband. She starved herself for days with intent to die.

A soldier who was guarding the corpses of some crucified robbers, nearby, saw a light coming from the tomb and went over to investigate. He found a beautiful woman mourning there in the company of a maid servant. He entered with his meager lunch and persuaded the starving woman to eat with him. She fell in love with him; and when in his absence one of the bodies was stolen from its cross she offered the body of her dead husband to replace the stolen body and to save her lover from disgrace and punishment.

A better source, however, is Dido, who mourned her dead husband Sychaeus and refused to be consoled yet gave her love to Aeneas. The situation, the development of the intrigue and the language used in the *Aeneid* appear in *Yvain* so exactly similar that the proof is simple and sure.

Yvain like Aeneas was a handsome warrior of a famous kingly line whose father, Urien, was well known to Laudine. Both Yvain and Aeneas arrive in a strange and hostile land. Both need protection and concealment until after the first danger is over. A cloud was thrown over Aeneas by Venus, who appeared disguised as a huntress and who he thought might be Diana, Goddess of the moon. Yvain was assisted by Lunete, whose name means "little moon." She furnished concealment by means of a ring. Like Venus she helped win the love of the lady who rules the land. Venus replaces Ascanius, Aeneas' son, with her own son, Cupid, disguised as the Trojan child. Thus Dido holds the God of Love in her lap and naturally succumbs to his power. The same god officiates in Chrétien's romance. Like Laudine, Dido needs a defender for her realm. An attack threatens each woman. Both women are in mourning for their previous husbands. With words almost identical they declare their undying love and loyalty to their dead husbands preferring to join their loved ones in the grave rather than marry again.

Lunete duplicates Dido's sister Anna and each one uses the same arguments to persuade their mistresses to marry the handsome stranger: the lady must not waste her life in unending tears and each one needs a defender for the realm.

When Lunete observes the fearless and noble appearance of Yvain she echoes lines from the *Aeneid* in which Dido exclaims over the nobility and bravery of Aeneas, that "fear always reveals a base soul."

Both Aeneas and Yvain are completely absorbed by their love. Uxoriousness has taken possession of Aeneas. Yvain is in danger of the same sloth created by an absorbing passion. Soon both heroes are awakened to the manly activities ordained by their life and their fate. Gauvain takes the role of Mercury. Leaving their loved women, both heroes go forth to deeds of valor and glory. Each break causes deep suffering. Each lady refuses to forgive. This attitude of Dido must be sought in the sixth book of the *Aeneid* where Aeneas met Dido in the other world. There she eyed him "with scowling looks," and "turning from him, kept her eyes fixed on the ground. She would not speak to him. Her face was hard and her expression cold as stone as she hurried angrily away."

The changeableness of woman is also an important theme. All through the middle ages this was a favorite theme. The most famous expression of this idea at that time as well as today is the Virgilian "varium et mutabile semper femina." Laudine is a personification of Virgil's expression. She is extremely changeable. That is the chief characteristic of her nature and her whole personality. Chrétien does give us a remarkably clever description of the change she undergoes in her consolation and remarriage. At first she appears stricken with grief. She beats her breast, tears her hair and her clothing. Her love for her dead husband is so great that she wishes only to follow him in death. The idea of a second marriage is abhorent. She gradually listens to Lunete's arguments but dismisses her angrily, refusing to listen, but privately she soon realizes that her servant's advice is good. She recognizes her own mistaken idea when alone. She is ready to listen again. She even asks for advice. She promises not to become angry; but she breaks her promise and scolds Lunete severely. All night she worries; and gradually changes her mind. She appreciates the loyal friendship and kindness of her servant. She repents of her harsh treatment of Lunete. Now she casts off her grief and her loyalty to her former husband. Once having decided to marry Yvain she cannot wait. She pretends to love Yvain dearly; she consents to his departure to win fame and glory in tournaments, but makes him promise to return on a given date. When he overstays the term, forgetful because of his absorption in manly pursuits, she becomes arrogant and refuses to ever allow him to return. Her cruelty drives Yvain to madness; but later she again consents to receive him back as her husband.

Chrétien seems to point directly to the source of inspiration for the nature of his heroine. He says of Laudine: "The heart and mood that she now has she will perhaps change later. Rather, I should say, she will change it without any 'perhaps.' " Later Chrétien remarks: "Now, the lady has changed." Chrétien expresses the same

idea in the line: "For woman has a thousand hearts (or moods)."
This line, however, comes directly out of Ovid's *Art of Love,* the
first book:

> Sed sunt diversa puellis
> Pecora, mille excipe mille modis.

The central theme then is the safe introduction of Yvain into
the city and into the presence of Laudine who rules the land. A
short period of uxoriousness but here particularly the threat of
uxoriousness quickly dispelled by Gauvain, who replaces Mercury
and persuades Yvain to seek renown in tournaments, the separation
and quarrel which appears to end the love of the hero and heroine
and the male regarded as a faithless deceiver. Ovid groups Aeneas
with Theseus and Demophoon, all as faithless lovers in the third
book of the *Art of Love.*

In order to reach this central theme based on the Dido story
of the *Aeneid,* Chrétien first connects his hero with King Arthur's
court. Yvain's cousin, Calogrenant, relates the story of his defeat
in a distant land by a knight. The disgrace annoys Yvain; and
he is determined to attempt the same adventure. King Arthur
was much interested and planned to go there with many knights
but Yvain hastens to anticipate the King.

Following the directions as Calogrenant gave them Yvain
came to a dense forest difficult to penetrate. Reaching a sort of
clearing he came upon a ludicrous person, intended, no doubt to
be comic. He is a huge fellow of tremendous strength and gigantic
proportions and of such an odd appearance that Yvain is astonished.
This monster is guarding a number of wild bulls who fear him
and obey him. His great strength suggests Hercules. Some scholars
have thought he was a shape-shifting host identical with the one
who entertained Yvain and told him about the adventure. This
individual also directs Yvain on his way to a fountain deep in the
tangled forest. He could, in such an event, be an original combina-
tion of Minos of Crete and Hercules. Such speculation is rather
futile.

This portion of *Yvain* was apparently developed on suggestions from Ovid. The third book of Ovid's *Fasti* describes a stream that springs from the rocks in a dense and almost impenetrable forest. A nymph named Egeria possesses this secluded fountain, and the fountain is guarded by Numa, who is the King of the land and the husband of Egeria. He is king because he has proven himself the bravest of the brave. His reign will last only until he is defeated in battle; "his successor will put him to death one day." So here is the suggestion and rough pattern for the dense forest, the spring, the death of Laudine's husband and the new husband she wins at the funeral of the first one.

Numa prays to Jupiter to teach him how to stop the violent rain and winds that shake his realm.

Laudine possesses a rain spring in a dense forest. Her husband must guard the spring and he must be the bravest of the brave to protect it and the realm. If Numa wished to have the power of Jupiter over the rain, Laudine's husband must try to control the rain which shakes Laudine's realm destructively. When Yvain reaches the fountain and produces rain by pouring water from the rain fountain on a stone, Laudine's husband comes riding up with such a horrible noise and clatter that any one who has read the *Aeneid* cannot fail to remember Salmoneus of the sixth book, who, in an attempt to simulate Jupiter, the creator of rain, thunder, and lightning drove his horses over a brazen bridge with a terrific clattering of their hooves.

The actual scene of this fountain in the grove is patterned after the fountain in Ovid's story of Pyramus and Thisbe. Each fountain has ice-cold water, that bubbles as though boiling, each is shaded by a large and handsome tree. Near each fountain is a small building. Later in the story the use of the Pyramus and Thisbe story amusingly distorted, in an occurrence located at this spring will clinch our argument.

The rain ceased suddenly, quelled by God just as Neptune silenced the winds that were wrecking Aeneas' ships before Carthage. The winds didn't dare to blow against God's will. So in the *Aeneid*

Neptune asks the winds if they dare to blow without his command; and at once they stop.

Yvain encounters the powerful Esclados, the defender of the fountain and defeats him. Esclados turns his horse about and flees to his castle. For the figurative description of this flight Chrétien finds a model in Ovid's *Metamorphoses,* the first book, where the Latin poet describes the swift flight of Daphne pursued by Apollo:

"The first object of Apollo's affection was Daphne, daughter of the river Peneus. This passion was not the result of blind chance but the vengeance of Cupid's bitter wrath. Apollo, victor in the Pythian games and crowned with oak and glorying in his success, had seen Cupid straining to bend his bow: 'Weak child,' he said to him, 'what are you doing with such heavy arms? This quiver is suitable only for the shoulder of the god who can lay low, with sure aim, ferocious beasts . . . Be satisfied to light whatever flames of love you may, but take care not to aspire to triumphs like mine.' The son of Venus replied: 'Apollo, nothing escapes your arrows, but you will not escape mine . . .' He shot two arrows from his bow: one that inspires, one that repels love. With the latter he wounded the daughter of Peneus, with the other he wounded Apollo, piercing him to the very marrow of his bones. Apollo falls in love at once, and Daphne hates even the name of her lover . . . Phoebus saw Daphne and wished to embrace her and wed her . . . He sees the hair of the nymph floating over her shoulders and he says: 'What would it be like if it were artfully arranged!' He sees her eyes shine like stars; he sees her rosy lips; he admires her fingers and her hands, and her arms more than half bare; and what the veil conceals from his eyes his imagination embellishes still more. Daphne flees swifter than the wind, and vainly he tries to delay her with speech."

Declaring his love, and proclaiming himself a god he calls upon her to wait. He speaks of the arrow that has pierced his heart, more deadly than his own that never miss their mark. "I am the inventor of medicine," he says: "the whole world honors me as the god of healing, and the virtue of plants is known to me; but is there one that cures one of love? My art, useful to all men, is powerless, alas, for myself." She runs and he follows.

"When a greyhound discovers a rabbit in the plain, they race with equal speed, one to overtake his prey, the other for his safety: the dog continually hopes and believes he has caught the rabbit and bites, with mouth stretched forward, at the footprints of the other, who, in doubt whether he is caught, avoids the open jaws and escapes the mouth that almost touches him. Apollo and Daphne are the same: hope makes him, and fear makes her swift. But aided by the wings of love the pursuer is fleeter. He follows relentlessly and leaning over the fleeing maiden he is so near that she feels his breath on her streaming hair."

This passage was well known to Chrétien. The love doctrine indicating the impossibility of curing love, the portrait of the lovely girl, and the simile all inspired Chrétien at one time or another. The figure of speech that Chrétien used in Yvain is very close to Ovid's:

"As a gerfalcon swoops upon a crane when he sees him rising from afar, and then draws so near that he is about to seize him, yet misses him, so flees the knight, with Yvain pressing him so close that he can almost throw his arm around him, yet cannot come quite up with him, though he is so close he can hear him groan . . . "

In another place Ovid uses almost the same birds as those in Chrétien's figure. Describing the flight of Hesperia before Aesacus, he compares them to a duck pursued by a hawk.

Like Laudine, both Daphne and Hesperia are described with streaming hair.

Daphne escapes Apollo, but only in death, turned into a flower. Esclados escapes Yvain, but he is mortally wounded. He gains his castle over a drawbridge. Yvain follows but he is caught inside the castle and now he is in danger like Aeneas at Carthage. Aeneas moves through crowds of Carthaginians in a cloud that conceals him. In a humorous passage Yvain escapes a crowd of Laudine's men who are sure he is in the castle by means of the ring that Lunete has given him. These men beat all around and search in vain as though they were blind.

Here Chrétien has recourse to the story of Gyges' ring, which was used for concealment in a love affair.

Candaules, the King of Lydia was not only deeply in love with his wife, but he thought her the most beautiful woman in the world. This idea became an obsession and had strange consequences. He praised the beauty of the Queen to Gyges and wanted him to see her naked. The King arranged for Gyges to do so in spite of great reluctance on the part of Gyges. The Queen gave no evidence of the fact that she was aware of what had happened, but she was deeply incensed and insisted that Gyges should kill the King and become her husband or suffer death himself. By the use of a ring of concealment Gyges succeeded in killing the King and took his place.

This bridging theme has the element of the slayer marrying the widow of his victim in common with the first episode and that of concealment of the hero in common with the central kernel of the story.

Proceeding now with the central theme of this romance Yvain has penetrated into the realm of Laudine in safety. The lady has won his love at the funeral of her first husband; but now comes the winning of the lady's love. To assist him, Yvain has, according to the recommendation of Ovid, a serving maid in the intimate confidence of the lady. She is very friendly and favors Yvain's suit ardently. She chooses the most suitable moments to urge the lady to give her love to Yvain and to marry him, pleading with her mistress while she combs her hair and attends her morning and evening.

When finally Yvain is admitted to the presence of Laudine he is already a victim and a prisoner of Love. He pledges his obedience to every wish or whim of the lady; and she is pleased at this humility that is entirely in accordance with her own conception of love and the proper relations and attitudes of male and loved lady.

Now the lady is quickly reconciled and the dead man is entirely forgotten. The man who killed him is married to his wife.

This part of the romance in which the lady finds a second husband at the funeral of the first, the protection of the stranger, the winning of the lady's love, the mourning of the lady for her first husband, her protestations of loyalty to him, her refusal to marry again and then the change in her attitude most skillfully affected and described by Chrétien is so clearly derived from Virgil and Ovid as sources, as we have shown, that no question or doubt could possibly exist in the mind of any one.

Now the first of the three Romances of Antiquity the *Roman de Thèbes* has a number of lines that are almost identical with those in *Yvain*. Jocasta knowingly marries the slayer of her husband. This is not the situation in the *Thebaid*, which the French author is translating. There are sufficient horrors in the Latin poem, which consist of the revelation of the double crime, unknowingly committed, of a mother marrying her son, who is also unknowingly the slayer of her husband. The *Roman de Thèbes* distorts the Latin story inexcusably and inartistically. It is perfectly clear that the sources of *Yvain* were not the sources of *Thèbes*. We therefore have the Latin sources of this episode which we may designate as A. Chrétien used those sources, so *Yvain* would be B in our series and *Thèbes* is close to *Yvain* but remote from Virgil and Ovid and must be designated as C in the series A, B, C, which indicates the chronological order in which the original source and the two French romances appear. Since *Thèbes* is unquestionably the earliest of all the other known romances of the twelfth century, Chrétien stands first as the inventor of the romance and therefore of the novel.

King Arthur arrived at the fountain and with his knights was entertained by Yvain and Laudine. There is a slight love affair between Gauvain and Lunete. Since Lunete's name is associated with the moon, it pleases Chrétien to compare Gauvain to the sun because he is renowned above all knights and enhances all chivalry with his beauty, grace, and courtesy. Chrétien had a model for this comparison in the fourth book of the *Aeneid* where Aeneas is compared to Apollo the god of the sun because he surpasses all others in beauty. Ovid compares Augustus to the sun in the second book of the *Tristia* because his marvelous deeds fill the universe and should fill our thoughts entrancingly just as the brilliance of the sun attracts the eyes of the world.

When King Arthur departed Gauvain persuaded Yvain to go with them to win glory and honor in tournaments, urging him not to become slothful and degenerate. On departing, with his wife's permission, but with a promise to return at the end of a year, Yvain was filled with grief and showed the Ovidian love symptoms of weeping and sighing so bitterly that he could scarcely speak. He declared that he would never stay away a full year. Using words like those of Leander in the seventeenth of Ovid's *Epistles* he said:

> If only I had the wings of a dove
> To fly back to you at will
> Many and many a time I would come.

In spite of his great love for Laudine, Yvain becomes so engrossed in tournaments that he forgets the date of his promised return and overstays the fixed date. Then suddenly, one day, a messenger arrives from Laudine bearing the news that he is never to return and never to know the love of that fair lady again. The shock is terrible and the most severe effect of love lost and denied comes upon him. His mind is in a frightful and dizzy whirl. In terror he departs for the wilderness before madness takes complete control of his mind; and there he lives on water and roots, and is stark mad for many days naked and unkempt. He killed wild beasts for food. A poor hermit gave him water and bread. But he had no memory of his previous life and no knowledge or understanding of what he was doing. A beastlike instinct made him hunt for nourishment.

One day a lady, riding through the woods, saw him lying in his comely and naked manliness and was attracted in spite of his brutish appearance. She also needed a strong warrior to protect herself and her land from a neighbor who sought both her land

and her love and was determined to have both. She had in her possession a powerful salve, which she slyly rubbed all over Yvain's body and slipped away before he awoke from his deep slumber. The medicine cured him of his madness. He defeated the lady's enemy and rescued her person and her land. Her desire for marriage with Yvain was unfulfilled; for now that his sanity was restored memory filled his mind with love of Laudine.

The rest of this romance is filled with deeds of great bravery to make this great hero worthy of a great love, to win the admiration of Laudine to prove himself the bravest of the brave and merit the right to defend the loved lady's fountain and her land.

Chrétien wanted to invent some plausible method of getting Yvain back in the good graces of Laudine. The story must end in a reconciliation. Laudine like Enide must serve both as Dido and Lavinia. A solution of the quarrel and a reuniting of lover and loved lady must replace the second wife. He must get back to the fountain. The fountain suggested the Pyramus and Thisbe story; and that story includes a lion. *Yvain* has a considerable amount of humor and the story of Androcles and his lion would bring a fresh element into the romance and one that would interest his readers, who delighted in romantic situations, the more remote from drab reality the better. So Yvain is to win the affection and gratitude of a lion by freeing him, rather than a charming lady, from a dragon more like a snake but spitting fire from its mouth and getting the better of its struggle with the lion. Yvain kills the snake and wins the undying gratitude of the lion, who hunts for his food, follows him like a friendly dog and helps him in the dangerous combats that fill out the rest of the romance, during which he becomes famous as the Knight of the Lion.

Accompanied by his lion Yvain finds his way back to the fountain, where memory stirs the love malady and its symptoms are grave. He nearly becomes insane again. Grieving and sighing he falls in a swoon. And now a most amusingly distorted adaptation of the Pyramus and Thisbe theme develops. The faithful lion thinks that his master is dead. His sword had slipped from the scabbard and wounded Yvain slightly. Now the lion props the sword against a tree and rushes at the point with the intention of ending his own life. Yvain recovers from his fainting and seeing the devotion of his lion, feels shame because he is still alive after losing the love of Laudine. He is about to take his own life thus succumbing to the ultimate effect of unrequited love, when his hand is arrested by a sound that comes from the small building near the spring. It is the voice of a woman. Approaching the building he talks through a crack in the wall to Lunete, who is imprisoned there. We learn that after Yvain's failure to return at the appointed time Laudine's seneschal had accused Lunete of treachery in harboring Yvain and had recommended punishment by burning unless Lunete could find a champion, before noon on the following day, who would be able to defeat the seneschal and two others in combat. Yvain promised to fight in her defense. Thus we have the man and the girl talking through a crack in a wall, attempted suicide, the lion and the fountain with the same scenery as in the Pyramus and Thisbe story.

As Yvain and Lunete talk, each telling the other of his misfortunes, Yvain uses words from Boetius' *Consolation of Philosophy,* a work that had considerable influence on literature of the Middle Ages, saying that the more comforts a man has enjoyed the harder misfortune is to bear.

The next episode is based on a feat of arms by King Arthur as related by Geoffrey of Monmouth in his *Historia Regum Britanniae.* The story runs about as follows, as translated by Giles in his *Six Old English Chronicles.*

King Arthur, who in Geoffrey's book is the hero, performs the great deeds of valor, whereas in Chrétien's works he never enters any contest at arms but welcomes the great knights of the world at his court. Arthur has received news of a giant of great size who has come from Spain and forcibly taken Helena the niece of Duke Hoel, who is King Arthur's sister's son, away to Mount Saint-Michel. The soldiers of the country could do nothing against him. For, like the huge Polyphemus, he destroys their boats with heavy stones when they try to approach the mountainous island. He captured many of them and ate them alive.

King Arthur decided to exterminate this monster and accompanied by two men, who were to take no part in the combat, he landed on the island at night. He learned from Helena's poor old nurse, who had also been captured, that his nephew's niece had died of fright when criminally approached by the giant. Arthur succeeded in killing the giant, who uttered a frightful roar and fell like an oak torn up from its roots by the wind.

The name, Yvain, occurs in the *Historia* as Eventus and his father Uriien is also mentioned.

In *Yvain,* the giant Harpin also lives on a mountain. He pursues, as in the *Historia* the niece of King Arthur's sister's son, who is Gauvain. When Harpin falls to the ground, defeated by Yvain, he is compared to a tree torn up by its roots.

Yvain had been given a lodging in the castle of Gauvain's nephew. All around this castle the land had been laid waste by Harpin who had threatened to come for the lord's daughter, and if she is not surrendered to him, four of her brothers will be killed before her eyes.

Yvain promised to wait as long as he could, but he has to be at Laudine's court at noon to defend Lunete. The giant delays his approach and father and daughter are filled with dismay. Very great suspense is here achieved. It appears necessary to leave the lord of the castle and his daughter to agonizing distress. At the last moment the giant appears and is defeated; but now Yvain is late for his promised combat to save Lunete from burning. When he arrives the fire is lighted and Lunete, held in bonds, is about to be cast into the flames.

When Yvain with help of his lion wins the fight against three opponents, the same punishment is inflicted upon the losers that had been planned for Lunete. This idea came to Chrétien from the first book of Ovid's *Art of Love,* where the Latin poet says that men are justified in deceiving women because they themselves are deceivers. He then tells two stories of just retribution, in one of which a man is burned to death:

"It is said that Egypt lacked any refreshing rain for the soil, which remained dry during nine years. Thrasius then came before

Busiris and announced that the blood of a foreigner visiting in the country poured on Jupiter's altar would appease him. 'You, then,' replied Busiris, 'will be the first victim offered to Jupiter; a visitor in Egypt, you will give her water.' "

Phalaris had Perillus, the unfortunate inventor of that horrible instrument of torture, burned inside of his brazen bull.

"Phalaris and Busiris were right, for there is no law more just than one that condemns the inventor of a form of torture to die by means of his own invention."

A sad interlude describes the searching glances of Yvain to find the loved lady and gaze longing at her beauty once known in intimate love now denied. In spite of his great prowess and deeds of great heroism, he still remains meek. Obedient lover, he cannot disregard the lady's refusal to ever receive him again in her good graces. Though near her, he dare not reveal his identity. Laudine admires his strength and skill. She talks to him and invites him to stay at her court. She wishes to know his name. He tells her only that he is known as the Knight with the Lion. He tells her that he dare not stay with her until he knows that his loved lady has removed her displeasure from him and her anger. In reply to him she even shows surprise that any woman should bear ill-will to such an attractive, brave, and courteous man. Thus Chrétien creates suspense in the reader who hopes that a reconciliation can be effected.

In sorrow and despair Yvain sets out, sorely wounded, bearing his bleeding lion on his shield.

Lunete accompanies him for some distance and promises to use every effort to win back his wife's love for him; and he places great faith in her and though deep dejection fills his heart, he has a glimmer of hope; for Lunete has now regained Laudine's confidence. He will find some safe retreat until his wounds are healed and his dear lion is cured. Then he will continue to strive for glory in knightly combat to make the Knight of the Lion worthy of the love that is his final goal—the only happiness that he will ever value in life.

Then comes an episode that is split in two, as Chrétien often does to admit another inserted within the first.

A nobleman has died leaving two daughters. The elder is determined to keep for herself all the property left by the father, leaving the younger sister destitute. The younger sister plans and threatens to seek a champion at the court of King Arthur where many knights of great renown were always to be found. The elder sister preceded her, however, and obtained the services of Gauvain, but only on condition that she should not reveal the name of her champion. When the younger sister was unable to obtain Gauvain as her defender she hoped to find the Knight of the Lion; and the King decreed that she should be allowed forty days before the ordeal by battle that would decide her fate.

Now Chrétien described the wanderings of this lady, unescorted, over the dangerous highways through dark forests, alone in wind and rain. This must have been very interesting reading for ladies safe within their strong castle walls, too timid themselves to venture outside unattended. The lady fell sick but another lady who was her friend continued the search until she finally encountered Yvain now restored to health. He agreed to defend her friend in battle with her sister's champion. They traveled on together until they came to a town called Pesme Avanture.

Here we have another much varied replica of the story of Theseus and the Minotaur. A large group of pitiful women are held in captivity, who work in a sort of silk factory, so hard that they are in a weak condition made worse by insufficient food. Here is an extremely early protest against exploitation of unfortunate people mingled with a weird adaptation of a classical source. These unlucky women are an accumulation of an annual tribute paid by the king of their country. This tribute will continue until two hideous monsters, born from the union of a woman and the devil, have been destroyed or defeated in battle.

Yvain undertakes the combat and wins with the aid of his lion, thus freeing the maidens and bringing unhoped for joy to a large number of people.

A testing of Yvain's love and loyalty to Laudine is made once more when the daughter of the lord who possesses this castle is offered in marriage. This young lady is represented as so beautiful that Love himself, if he looked upon her, would wish to become human. He would wound himself with his own arrows and render love service to this lovely maiden.

Yvain now returns to King Arthur's court to fight with Gauvain in an ordeal by battle that is to settle the quarrel between the two sisters over their inheritance. The battle is fought by knights of equal skill and strength so, as is always the result, neither Gauvain nor the hero of this romance is defeated. The two great friends who are engaged in this mortal combat finally recognize each other and each one refuses to continue and gladly accords the victory to the other.

In the end Lunete persuades her mistress to take Yvain back. A defender is still needed for the fountain and the land. Yvain has become desperate. He returns to the fountain and creates unceasing storms of wind and rain. Lunete extracts from Laudine a promise to do all she can to restore the Knight of the Lion to the good graces of the lady he loves and who has been so cruel to him. The reader is left to wonder whether the lady has not relented and is filled with admiration for Yvain's great accomplishments. The trick that Lunete plays is mingled with bravery in battle, intended to win the love of a fair lady, and the motive of the bravest still needed to defend the realm.

This romance or short novel is one of the most remarkable stories ever written. The clever dovetailing of the episodes, which are woven and fused together with an unbroken coherence notwithstanding their widely varying sources, the ornamentation with adornments from extremely diversified sources and of varied fashion but always appropriate, the realistic details descriptive of life as the author observed it, the highly developed and entirely new style, the psychological and expertly developed portrayal of the varying moods of a volatile feminine personality, and the intriguing fabrication of an amazingly new relationship and extraordinary attitudes of lover and loved lady, astounding to readers whose whole conception of the social and amorous contacts of lover and loved lady was almost as near an opposite pole as possible, all this constituted an original work of art whose equal in the realm of fiction cannot be discovered in many centuries after this marvelous achievement.

In natural details there are descriptions of wild lands, dense forests and thick tangled undergrowth, storms of wind and rain, leaves falling from trees, birds singing in the sunlight. Life in castles is displayed in garments, food, the maid attending her mistress, courteous entertainment, bathing, changing of clothing, attention for horses, serving of meals, attempts to conceal grief from guests. There is interest among groups of observers and strangers and comments on their appearance as well as speculation on probable success or failure in dangerous adventures that await the hero.

The predatory baron who burns and lays waste the land and property of his neighbor is shown in Count Allier, who wishes to marry the Lady of Noroison—she who spread the healing salve over Yvain's body to cure him of his madness and win a stalwart champion in her dire need. The giant Harpin of the Mountain gives an extreme exaggeration of similar ruthlessness and cruelty by those who will compel women to yield to their brutal lust, in a contrast between a new idealized adoration of manly virtue for feminine beauty and the reality of life as it then existed. This tremendous discrepancy between what was common, real and normal in the actual life of people and this idealized invention of new relations and attitudes between the sexes had a remarkable vogue in literature down through the centuries and in polite society too, revealed by descriptions of discussions of groups at the courts of royal and noble ladies and the *salons* of later centuries. The *De Amore* of Andreas Capellanus is invaluable in its report of the discussions and judgments of groups and noble ladies in the twelfth century.

We have trials by battle, with the belief that God will give the victory to the defender of justice and the right, burning at the stake, jealousy and intrigue.

In this story, where love has exalted the woman to a position of dominance, our interest is centered in the hero, into whose experiences the adventures of many mythological or legendary figures have been packed to maintain, in their highly rationalized and originally adapted versions, never flagging interest in a highly idealized character, in the vicissitudes of his love affair, in the danger-filled experiences of his knight errantry, and in the grief, worry, and dangers of those whom he assists and defends.

The story contains a large fund of humor. Strange and monstrous figures appear. The seneschal Kay furnishes many amusing touches, where he insults various people, accusing Yvain of boasting after drinking when he expresses a desire to avenge the humiliation of his cousin Calogrenant in an adventure apparently beyond human strength and courage. He also accuses Yvain of cowardice when he does not accompany King Arthur and his knights on the very adventure of which he had been boasting, according to Kay. Very soon Kay is to be undeceived and humiliated by ignominious defeat in a combat with Yvain who has arrived at the danger point ahead of him and now defends the fountain. Kay's attempts at knightly contests are ludicrous on account of his ineptness. The groping of a crowd searching like blind people while Yvain is in concealment in Laudine's castle is amusing. The dropping of the knife-like portcullis which cuts Yvain's horse in two so that half of it is inside and half outside, while the rider is invisible and his absence unexplainable is so funny that Baron Munchhausen has inserted part of the incident in one of his hilarious anecdotes. There is a satirical element running beneath the highly polished surface, highlighted by Lunete's remark: "It is evident, My Lady, that you are a woman, for a woman will grow angry when she hears anyone giving her good advice."

The originality of this finely constructed work of art is evident. No single source combines even a small percentage of this story.

An introductory relation of Calogrenant's unfortunate adventure connects the tale with King Arthur's court and outlines the first theme of a man who marries the widow after killing her husband. This theme takes us to the hostile land where the concealment theme links the first theme to the central episode which consists of winning the love of the widow, who is simultaneously consoled. The awakening of the hero from a very short period of sloth is followed quickly by the quarrel between husband and wife resulting in madness caused by the loss of the lady's love. The rest of the story consists of episodes that show the valor of the hero and make him worthy of forgiveness and a reconciliation with his wife. This series is broken by a tragic crisis, when Yvain visits the court of his lady love, sees and talks with her incognito; but this close proximity does not close the breach in their divorced affections. As a final result reconciliation between husband and wife is a necessary conclusion of the normal romance by Chrétien. Apparently there was no way of ending the *Lancelot* in the manner typical of Chrétien's method, at least not to the satisfaction of Marie de Champagne, or in any way that would permit a continuation of Arthurian romances in the established pattern of Chrétien's other romances.

CHAPTER IX

Perceval

Chrétien's last romance was written for Philip of Flanders, whom he praises as a man of great kindness and generosity. Chrétien, no doubt, felt secure. His reputation in his own day and for the duration of the Christian world was established. He seems to have felt no longer a need to strive for the immediate success of each work. A result of complete self-assurance and satisfaction with his achievements appears to be the reason for the inauguration, with the *Perceval,* of longer works, which soon became quite the fashion.

Another innovation was the beginning of the Grail stories, of which *Perceval* was the first. *Perceval* was not finished. Chrétien died while working on it. We, therefore, do not know what significance he meant to give to the Grail nor what the final and complete plan of the work could have been. The love element, in the portion that he wrote, is meager; but it is the same type of love treatment that appears in all his works after the translation of Ovid's *Art of Love.*

The romance is based on the assumption that blood will tell and heredity will be more important than environment. Perceval is brought up in the country remote from cities and courts. His mother has suffered much from the toll that death has taken from her family in tournaments; and she hopes that her son will never learn anything about knighthood. She has kept him ignorant of armor and of the weapons of warfare. He has learned to throw darts with great accuracy and can kill animals in the hunt by this means. She dresses him in homespun clothing of warm material but of rustic style.

When he first hears the clanking of armor as knights ride by near his home he fears the arrival of the devil. Courageous curiosity leads him to investigate and when he sees the gleaming armor of the knight he thinks that angels and God himself are coming. He is not afraid; and enters into conversation with them. They try in vain to extract information from him; but he is very insistent in questioning them about their armor and their weapons. He learns from them of knighthood and of King Arthur's court; and he is determined to go there, and become a knight.

His mother is deeply distressed. She tries to dissuade him from his purpose, but in vain. He leaves her and she dies of grief. Unheeding, he goes his way. This sin of leaving his mother to die affects his life and the lives of others, who suffer because of his negligence which continues and makes him unable to understand or learn about the virtues and the nature of the Holy Grail which he is privileged to see in its bright effulgence but which, on account of his sinfulness, disappears. He is finally aroused from his heedless life of knightly but ungodly adventures by instruction from a hermit who is related to him. He then consecrates his whole life and energy to the search for the Grail. If he finds it he will ask the questions which will heal the wounded Fisher-King. The events of this story are related to the knightly prowess of Gauvain as well as those of Perceval. He, too, seeks the Grail. In this double romance the training of a knight is indicated and given considerable importance as the simple-minded rustic Perceval gradually learns of chivalry and the use of knightly arms. The two heroes, present a contrast because Gauvain is a knight of perfect courtesy, refined manners, and expert knowledge and skill in the art of war from the very beginning.

It may never be possible to find any single source of importance for this romance. Several episodes from his own earlier romances are reworked in this one.

Perceval comes upon a damsel alone in a tent. The knight who escorts her is absent when Perceval arrives. He enters the tent, and since he is hungry takes generous helpings from the food that he finds there. He kisses the lady and takes a ring from her finger. The knight soon returns, sees the hoof prints that Perceval's nag has left, and finds the lady in tears. She tells about the boy that had kissed her and taken her ring. The knight then accuses her of allowing the boy to take serious liberties and here the language of Ovid appears in almost literal translation.

"Even though she refuse," says Ovid, "take the kisses she will not give. Perhaps she will struggle at first and cry 'You shameless wretch;' yet she will wish to be overcome in the struggle . . . He who takes kisses and does not take the rest, will deserve to lose what was allowed . . . You may use force; women like it."

The knight had the same idea and in consequence inflicted a punishment upon the lady similar to that imposed on Enide by Erec. This episode which, by the way, was split to allow the insertion of a considerable number of events including Perceval's training for knighthood, ended with a reconciliation of knight and lady. Perceval encountered the pair later, the lady, who had not been allowed to change her clothing, was now in tatters. Perceval rights the wrong he had innocently and stupidly done the lady and by defeating the knight proves to him that his lady was not unfaithful to him.

Another episode based on Ovid and showing the Ovidian love treatment concerns Perceval's experiences at the castle of Beaurepaire, the home of the beautiful Blanchefleur. A fierce warrior by the name of Clamedeus desires to take both the land and the person of Blanchefleur. He has already laid waste all the land around the castle; and, after a long struggle, he is sure to defeat the exhausted and starving defenders of Blanchefleur's castle. Thus we have a repetition of an often repeated situation in the romances of the time, both those of Chrétien and of his followers and imitators. Perceval undertakes the defense of castle and lady to become enamored of the lady and she of him. Very cleverly Chrétien has mingled the battle over the castle and the lady herself and her suffering with the battle and the pain of love. In the night fear and love keep Blanchefleur awake and in her terror she comes to Perceval's room. Love, also, is impelling her as well as fear. Perceval comforts her and takes her into his bed. The love symptoms appear. Blanchefleur trembles with fear—and love—sleepless in her bed, tossing and turning, weeping and sighing.

On the next day Perceval defeats Clamedeus and rescues Blanchefleur from his attacks and his cruel impositions. The two young lovers promise each other their undying love; but Perceval delays his marriage until he can return home and learn about the health of his mother, whom he had seen to swoon as he left. His conscience finally troubles him and he wants to know whether she is alive or dead.

His journey is broken by a night spent in the castle of the Grail, owned by the Fisher-King. He saw the bleeding lance that later became so famous in Grail stories and the shining Grail studded with jewels. Perceval wondered about the meaning of these symbols but did not ask the questions that would have been so important and helpful.

On the next day he left the castle and the castle suddenly vanished from his sight.

He met a cousin who chided him for asking no questions about the Grail. She also informed him of the death of his mother.

He soon came near King Arthur's camp. The King had started out with his court to see whether he could find Perceval, of whose exploits he had heard. It was a winter's day and a hawk had wounded a wild goose. Three drops of blood had fallen on the snow and the rosy coloring against the white of the snow recalled the complexion of the lovely Blanchefleur; and all day long Perceval stays to look, completely absorbed in thoughts of love, to look at the blood on the snow. Two knights come out from King Arthur's camp and disturb Perceval's meditation only to be severely punished. Finally Gauvain comes and through his courtesy prevails upon Perceval to accept hospitality in the King's camp.

Gauvain's attempt was made easy because the drops of blood had now disappeared in the melting snow.

For five years Perceval sought the Grail, meanwhile engrossed in furious combats at arms. This period is represented as one of sinful neglect of all religious thoughts or duties. Finally he meets a hermit, who is his uncle. The hermit confesses and absolves him, also gives him information about the Fisher-King.

The rest of the romance deals with the numerous adventures of Gauvain.

This romance has very great historical importance because it is the first of the famous stories of the Holy Grail that have never ceased to be of interest. The Grail has appeared in many stories and poems throughout the centuries and down even to modern times, and in the grand opera *Parsifal* by Wagner.

The structure of this romance is similar to the others. No single source could be found. Mingled with the reworking of numerous themes that appear in his earlier works is a great deal of original composition. Folk tales such as that of the Great Fool, removing of a spell by asking questions, and a disappearing castle have served. The Augustinian doctrine of punishment induced by the sin itself is elaborated by Perceval's long and arduous experiences that along with all the fame and glory of his prowess bring suffering and shame upon the hero.

The story is skillfully constructed with artful repetitions, episodes coherently linked, often interrupted by comments of observers who heighten the suspense by remarks, encouragement, sympathy, warnings of dangers, bemoaning of the sad fate of one who approaches imminent death. Episodes are split to allow others to be fitted in; but the interrupted themes, or motives, are caught up again to carry the story on with a style that flows on like a current that bears the story swiftly through a great deal of scenery revealed realistically by the keen observation of a great artist.

CHAPTER X

Romances of Antiquity

Chrétien de Troyes was an innovator in the use of Classical Latin material in the vernacular. Many scholars knew the Latin authors well. The praise of the great masters of antiquity rang down through the ages in the well-known saying of Bernard de Chartres, that great teacher whose name still lives today. He taught in Latin—in fact Latin was the language of the classroom in Romance countries down to the sixteenth century—and his famous remark that Fontenelle still repeated in the eighteenth century was made in Latin. He said that if we can see farther than the Ancients, it is not on account of our own vision but rather because we, pygmies that we are, are seated on the shoulders of those giants of antiquity. Thus progress is possible since today we profit from the art and learning of teachers who lived many years ago.

The works of those who wrote in Latin in the twelfth century are full of quotations from classical Latin authors. Authors who wrote in the vernacular knew Latin. For example Jean de Meung, who wrote the second part of the *Roman de la Rose* in the thirteenth century, cites many a Classical Latin author in an astounding display of erudition. Classical Latin authors are cited by many French and Provençal authors of the twelfth century. It would be folly to suggest that the authors who wrote in the vernacular in the twelfth and thirteenth centuries did not have a personal acquaintance with the literary masters of antiquity. However, many of their references to Classical sources are sufficiently inaccurate to arouse a doubt of their first-hand acquaintance with the sources that they cite. Where Ovid is concerned the question naturally arises as to whether in a great many instances the French or

Provençal author had need to turn to the works of that Latin author. Chrétien de Troyes had translated Ovid's *Art of Love*. We do not have that work but we do have his translation of Ovid's story of Philomela. When we note how extensively Chrétien amplified that story, we can imagine that Chrétien expanded the *Art of Love*. It is probable that many of the stories of personages mentioned in the *Art of Love,* which appear in other parts of Ovid's works such as the *Metamorphoses* and the *Epistles,* stories that furnished material for Chrétien's other works, to which attention has been drawn in our study of the various romances, were inserted in Chrétien's translation. Translations of Latin works made in the twelfth century were commonly elaborated and extensively modified.

This fashion of attempting to modify the Latin works and adapt them to the taste of contemporary readers was started by Chrétien in his *Art of Love* in *Philomena* and perhaps in *The Shoulder Bite*.

The vogue that Chrétien inaugurated became tremendous. First came the *Roman de Thèbes,* a fairly long work of over ten thousand lines. The idea may have come to the unknown author to make this translation on account of the allusion to Etiocles and Polynices in *Cligès* and the evident use of a portion of Statius' work as material for *Cligès*. The *Roman de Thèbes* is the least inter-esting of any of these adaptations of Latin works. It evidently lends itself less to the purpose. However, the most interesting part of the Old French romance is written in almost literal imitation of the very kernel of Chrétien's *Yvain*. It is an added theme, non-existent in Statius' poem. This added theme is not in keeping with the story as Statius wrote it. The *Thebaid* was planned to have a son unknowingly kill his father and marry his mother to learn of these horrors later. Oedipus who had been exposed and left to die by his father, who had also been informed, by an oracle, of these crimes, had been rescued by a herdsman of Polybus king of Corinth and brought up by Polybus whom he considered his real father. Oedipus, informed by the oracle of Delphi that he would kill his father and commit incest with his mother, left Corinth and went to Thebes to escape his father. There he killed his real father. Then he destroyed the cruel Sphinx and, in gratitude, was accorded Jocasta as his wife by the Thebans. When later he learned of his crimes, he blinded himself and Jocasta hanged herself. The dramatic effect is produced by the revelation of these crimes long after they were committed. To introduce a third crime and to have this one committed knowingly is quite absurd and demands an explanation. The only possible explanation is obvious. Chrétien's tremendous success led the uninspired author of the *Roman de Thèbes* to borrow several of the most interesting lines in all of the *Yvain*. Chrétien had other influences on this romance. The author of *Thèbes*, anxious to adorn his romance with borrowed finery, since he could furnish so little himself, took lines from Chrétien's *Cligès*, which also produced an absurdity. The fifty horsemen who left one of the main gates of Thebes in broad daylight are said to leave secretly by a postern gate; said postern gate having entered *Cligès* from the great epic of Virgil. The portraits of Antigone and Ysmeine are copied from *Erec and Enide* and also the strange coloring of Antigone's horse as well as the sparrowhawk that Ysmeine carries on her wrist, which with the rime and the plover which she feeds the bird of prey all come from *Erec and Enide,* in which story Enide carries the sparrowhawk that Erec had won for her as the prize of beauty. Even the clothing of Ysmeine and Antigone, though rich, reveals the beauty of their figures as fully as the tattered garments of Enide. The conference of the lords of the realm with Etiocles shows influence from *Cligès* in three respects. Etiocles' followers in the *Thebaid* were always loyally behind him and so completely in sympathy with him that they urged him to begin the cruel and devastating war against his brother. Jocasta tries to make peace between her sons and Polynices is almost persuaded to yield to his brother, who has usurped the throne. In *Thèbes,* however, a messenger from Polynices appeals to the barons at Etiocles court to repudiate their king. The barons are favorably inclined toward the ousted brother, and the king decides to yield the land but not the crown. Here are three new elements that lengthen the story and delay it unnecessarily and to no purpose, all borrowed from *Cligès*.

The next translation from the Classical Latin, following the vogue initiated by Chrétien, was an adaptation of Virgil's *Aeneid* with surprisingly extensive variations. This romance could never have been written without Chrétien's earlier works, especially *Cligès,* which the Old French *Eneas* resembles in a striking manner and follows as an evident and obvious model. Chrétien had already combined material from Ovid and from Virgil several times. The use of Classical Latin sources in such amounts as appear in Chrétien's works could not escape the perception of an author who contemplated the translation of the *Aeneid.* To completely revise Virgil's work by the insertion of suggestions from Ovid was not an innovation on the part of the unknown and greatly inferior author of the *Eneas.* His romance has none of the qualities of an inventor or originator. One has only to read the *Eneas* and the evidence of an imitator is convincingly present: exaggeration in the style and the use of love symptoms and effects in inartistic heaps and childish and tedious repetitions, improbable, unbelievable indications, such as fainting at the mere mention of a loved person's name—understandable to readers only after the vogue and fashion of treating love in the manner developed by Chrétien had become familiar—carrying off a heart under one's arm like a package would arouse only hilarious amazement if the readers had not been long accustomed to the metaphorical idea of a heart leaving one person to be carried even to long distances by a departing lover—variations in source material impossible except where the heedless author is influenced by Chrétien, for example when the same people who have been courting Dido for a long time and deplore her extended mourning for Sychaeus long since dead, declare that Dido has quickly forgotten her first husband. Here is an evident borrowing from *Yvain,* where the lady remarries in a few days.

No scholar would have failed to see in *Eneas* the second-rate imitation of Chrétien and eager adoption of his style, if he were not blinded completely by a false notion of chronology. No words can describe the unfortunate waste that results from the utter disregard of the importance of a basic chronology before voluminous studies have exhausted the mental strength of hundreds of brilliant scholars in futile wanderings in the dark and tangled wood of misapprehension.

Without the models that Chrétien's works offer it would never have occurred to the author of the *Eneas* to elaborate the love story of Dido and Aeneas with the metaphorical style that Chrétien had developed in imitation of Ovid. In words that recall those of Chrétien the various symptoms of love appear: insomnia, a burning fire in the heart, turning of reason to folly, fainting, sighing, weeping, love as a cause of death. Like Alis who, in his sleep thinks he holds Fenice in his arms, Dido has a similar dream and believes that she embraces Eneas in her sleep.

The author of *Eneas* imitates the monologues in which Chrétien's lovers commune with themselves with mental question and answer often breaking the line in a conversational style, wavering in doubt and hope that their love will be returned, wondering whether some direct action should be taken toward the loved one, to reveal one's love or plead with the other. This type of monologue was an innovation by Chrétien in imitation of Ovid.

There is a passage in *Eneas* which speaks of Fortune, who turns her wheel and changes a person's fate from bad to good or from happiness to grief. It is copied almost word for word from Chrétien's *Lancelot*.

Chrétien's device of heightening the action and the suspense by remarks that bystanders make as they view the hero and comment on his handsome appearance and strength are also imitated by the author of the *Eneas*.

Many lines are copied literally. For example *Eneas* repeats the line from Cligès: "The day was bad and the night worse." Tantalus is described in similar terms as he tries in vain to reach the apples above him and the water that recedes from his lips as he bends his head downward. The combat between Turnus and Pallas is a good example of copying from Chrétien. In the tenth book of the *Aeneid* Pallas hurls his spear and inflicts a slight scratch on Turnus' body. Then Turnus hurls his spear and with one blow pierces Pallas' shield and mortally wounds him. Both are on foot. In *Eneas,* however, in imitation of Chrétien, in words copied almost literally, these warriors spur toward each other on chargers, strike each other so hard that their shields are broken and each one is unhorsed. Then they draw their swords and deal terrific blows, hack each others shields to pieces and Pallas cuts a portion of Turnus' helmet away stunning him with the blow. All this is similar to Erec's combat with Yder in Chrétien's first romance.

Most amazing and most impossible, were it not for the models offered by Chrétien, is the insertion of a description of an imaginary love experience on the part of Eneas and Lavinia with all the symptoms of the love sickness, the power of Love, the torture and suffering, the yearning for a cure in long love monologues, the wounding of the heart through the eyes with no damage appearing externally, learning of love as in *Cligès,* even the prodding of oxen with the goad more severely before they have learned to bear the yoke with patience, the injustice of Love and the tricks he likes to play on his victims. Like Soredamor, Lavinia rejects love and Love takes vengeance on her. All this with frequent literal borrowings from Chrétien's works and repetitions that become tiresome.

Lavinia sees Eneas from a window in a high tower and gazing lovingly on his figure, watches him and keeps her eyes upon him until he disappears from her view. This passage is imitated from *Lancelot,* where the hero observes Guenivere from a window in a tower and allows his gaze to follow her as long as possible while she rides away. From this tower Lavinia has a letter wrapped around an arrow shot so that it drops near Eneas. He takes the arrow and reads the letter.

In *Cligès,* Alexander compares Soredamor to Cupid's arrow in a striking and pleasing passage that made an unforgettable impression on Chrétien's readers. The author of *Eneas* imitates this passage in a less happy manner. He compares the letter to Cupid's arrow and says that it has wounded him. Then, in a rather ludicrous manner, he argues over the absence of any wound caused by the letter appearing on his body.

Amata, Lavinia's mother talks to her about love somewhat in the manner of Thesala, sees evidence of love sickness in Lavinia's appearance and discovers that it is not Turnus but Eneas that Lavinia loves. In imitation of Soredamor who feared that emotion would interrupt her speech if she tried to speak Alexander's name, Lavinia is unable to say "Eneas" in a natural manner. Sighs interrupt her attempt and divide Eneas' name into three syllables.

Among many more details which show the direct influence of Chrétien's works on *Eneas* there is a passage in which Eneas complains of the slow passage of time while he longs for the time to come when he can marry Lavinia. The complaint is repeated. One day seems like several and the night delays exceedingly in arriving. This is based on a very pretty passage in Chrétien's *Lancelot* that has already been mentioned and its source in the *Metamorphoses* of Ovid indicated.

The *Roman de Troie,* written several years later, has similar borrowings from Chrétien. The love that Chrétien has introduced into Old French literature had become very popular and, naturally, appears in this lengthy romance by Benoît de Sainte-Maure.

CHAPTER XI

Provençal Literature

The relation of Chrétien de Troyes to Provençal literature has not been made clear. Questions of chronology have made it difficult to determine influences from South to North or from North to South. Wrong notions of chronology should never be allowed to persist. One of the most amazing mistakes of scholars in the field of the Arthurian romances and of the development of literature at the middle of the twelfth century is the indifference of scholars to the need of establishing correct dates before undertaking studies whose conclusions are worthless if the chronology is incorrect.

It is clear enough that Chrétien had a very great influence on later Provençal poets; but the question as to the beginning of that influence has never been determined. The System of Courtly love as developed in Provence has predecessors who wrote earlier than Chrétien. Chrétien wrote in a style that has many of the elements of courtly love. For these reasons scholars and literary historians have taken it for granted that Chrétien was strongly influenced by Provençal writers. Thus the current would have flowed in two directions, first from South to North and then from North to South.

This theory is definitely incorrect. Whatever influence moved northward to effect the works of Chrétien must have been very slight.

William the Ninth, of Aquitania, the first of the Provençal troubadours, shows evidence of a slight influence from Ovid. A half a dozen of those of his poems that have come down to us show a faint tinge of the Ovidian type of love. He speaks of the joy of love and the charm of his lady, which can cure a sick man. The lady's anger would kill him. He accepts the bondage of love and declares himself in the control and power of his lady. He would never wish to break the chains of love. The loss of his lady's love would cause his death. His heart aches and he trembles with the chill of love. He promises to keep his love for his lady a secret.

Similar faint traces of the Ovidian love or suggestions from Arabic love poetry also appear in a very few of the poems of Cercamon. These meager indications do not show a vogue for analytical and metaphorical style in the treatment of love.

Macabrun decried false love with a satirical vehemence and extolled fine love, but with little use of metaphors.

Jaufré Rudel, who is famous because he is supposed to have loved a distant princess, whom he had never seen and whom he tried to reach, was not a great poet. In those of his poems that we have today there is very little of the metaphorical style in writing about love. Moreover his dates are uncertain. If, according to the tradition he loved Melisendis, the daughter of Count Raimon I of Tripoli and his poems filled with complaint of the hopelessness of his love were written for her, then they were not written before 1160, which was the year when she was betrothed to Emmanuel of Constantinople. It was on account of the faithlessness of Emmanuel that she became famous; and she was not born until 1142. For these reasons Janfré Rudel could not have influenced Chrétien, who had already translated Ovid's *Art of Love*. As for the others, they wrote before Chrétien composed his *Erec and Enide,* which contains none of the Ovidian type of love treatment. It is therefore evident that it was his study of Ovid and not his knowledge of Provençal poetry that influenced Chrétien in his use of metaphor and the analysis of the effects and the symptoms of love which appear in all the rest of his works.

The real essence of courtly love as it appears in the Provençal poetry, before a metaphorical style formed an essential part of it, as it appears in literature, and before extensive enumeration of the symptoms and effects of love characterize it, was a mystical element that lifted woman to a moral superiority commanding the worship of the male and a feeling on his part of being lifted through the love of a woman to an ethereal plane above the petty and the sordid in mortal life. Now this ethical and mystic conception is never to be found in any of Chrétien's romances. Thus any important influence on Chrétien by any of these early poets is ruled out.

There remains then only the consideration of Bernard de Ventadour whose poetry is the first in Provence to show abundantly the Ovidian type of love; and he is the first Provençal poet to use metaphors abundantly in treating of love. The question is whether he could have influenced Chrétien or was himself influenced by the French poet. They both were in England after Eleanor became Queen. Since Bernard's dates are uncertain and since he is known to have entered a monastery in 1194, he may have lived until 1215—and Chrétien died in 1175 or shortly before or after, it would seem safe to conclude that Bernard was several years younger than Chrétien. The influence where the romances of Chrétien are concerned, must then have been from North to South. The metaphorical treatment of love had not become the fashion before Chrétien translated Ovid's *Art of Love,* around 1150, and thereafter it created a new style that became extremely popular in the North and in the South through its adoption by Bernard de Ventadour, Bertran de Born and innumerable followers. It should be carefully noted that the above statements have nothing to do with the question of the influence of the troubadours on lyric poetry in the North of France.

Bernard has adopted the metaphorical treatment of love that Chrétien created and of which he established a vogue that developed rapidly and strongly in Southern France. The power of love and its full control of the lover is repeatedly expressed in the poems of Bernard de Ventadour. The various symptoms of love, sighing, weeping, sobbing, loss of sleep, pallor, emaciation, great pain but a sweet and delightful torture, appear. Love kindles a fire in the heart of his victims that burns fiercely.

This love is communicated through the eyes. It absorbs the attention of the mind, dulls the senses and even tends toward madness. Many times the poet fears that love will cause his death. The idea of learning of love, of obedience to the teaching of Love, and to his every command appears and is emphasized. Love as warfare ends in the total defeat of the victim and the complete victory of Love. The loved lady is described as cruel and unyielding, but patience and long service in love are extolled.

Although the metaphorical style and the precepts, symptoms, and effects of love show the strong influence of Chrétien on this poet and similarly on two centuries of Provençal poets, Bernard has fine qualities that are his own and which spring from the exalted attitudes toward love as a tremendous force for moral uplift and pure joy that had developed among his predecessors.

The sheer beauty and loveliness of his poetry cannot be rendered:

> Whene'er I see the happy lark
> Spreading its wings against the sun
> Then lost in ecstasy, that fills its heart,
> Forgetful of all else but joy,
> Downward seem to slip and fall,
> My soul with envy seems to burst
> For the bird I love to watch.
> I wonder why at once my heart
> In longing does not melt and break.
>
> Alas, I thought I knew so much
> Of love, and yet so little did I know!
> I cannot tear myself away
> From her who ne'er will give me joy.
> She has taken my heart and my very self.
> She has taken herself and all the world away.
> And since she took herself away from me,
> She left me nothing but longing and pain.

The fourth line of the second stanza is taken word for word from a line in *Cligès* where Alexander says the same of Soredamor.

Flamenca, a tale that shows much originality and surprises the reader, who scarcely would expect its like, so many years ago, away back in the thirteenth century, still owes much to Chrétien's teaching.

Distinctively Provençal elements seem to be the satirical condemnation of jealousy, the exaltation of extra-marital love, and the joy of love in itself without any restrictions or any hint of conventional or moral reservations. In spite, however, of advanced notions of freedom from moral restraint, from the social barriers to adultrous indulgence and free love among the unmarried this love calls for secrecy. The husband also holds sovereignty in real life and is represented, even in the story, as having tyrannical rights and power over his wife.

The love story presents a jealous husband, who suffers grievously, but without pity, a handsome lover and a young wife unequalled in beauty. The portraits of these people, the adornments in the apartments, the rich cloth in their garments, the extreme generosity of the hero and the husband, the gay tournaments, the invincible strength and valor of the hero, his courtesy, the tremendous number of guests summoned from every geographical extent and direction, the decorations in the town, the streets draped with rich tapestries and silken cloths, the style in which the love symptoms and effects are described are all elements for which Chrétien de Troyes gave the models and furnished the inspiration at least indirectly and to a large extent directly; for the author was well acquainted with the great French poet and creator of the novel. He mentions some of Chrétien's stories.

Line 1696 is taken word for word from Chrétien's *Erec and Enide:*

"He takes knights and wins horses" in a tournament. The statement that follows also recalls Chrétien's Erec, when it is said that William either spends them or gives them away at once. Erec gave one horse for a breakfast and seven for a night's lodging.

Also, the entertainment after a meal with indication of the stories of the *jongleurs* and the various instruments they play is directly copied from *Erec and Enide* as well as the decorations in the streets where cloths of silk and colored tapestries are hung.

The husband became jealous of his young wife almost as soon as they were married. Jealousy seems to have the same effect as love, and, although this man, whose name was Lord Archambaut, was a brave knight and a generous and courteous gentleman, he became slothful in a curious way. He gave up all knightly or social interests, applied all his efforts to guarding his wife, and allowed himself to become dirty and unkempt.

William, her lover, also gave up all manly pursuits and applied all his wealth, time, and intelligence to outwit the jealous husband and win the love of a lady so carefully guarded. Flamenca finally aroused both of these men from their sloth and sent them forth to fight and win glory in tournaments. This slothfulness and the awakening from it seem to stem from Chrétien's *Erec and Enide*.

Archambaut kept Flemenca locked in a tower. She left the tower only to go to church on Sundays and on church holidays, and to go to bathe in baths owned by a man named Gui. William, the lover, took an apartment in Gui's house; and it happened to be adjacent to the baths, from which it was separated by a wall of soft stone.

William won the friendship of everyone, even including the priest, by means of presents and hospitable entertainment. He attended church and sang all the responses. He soon offered to send the priest's assistant away to school and pay all his expenses. The offer was accepted and the priest took William as his new assistant. This office gave William an opportunity to present the breviary to Flamenca for her to kiss an open page. As he did so he started his courtship, saying a word or two softly so that only she would hear. The first time he said "Alas." The next time he passed her the breviary she asked softly: "Why?" The conversation went on for months, a word or two by William, the next time an answer or a question from Flamenca, so that the dialogue continued as follows: "I am dying." "Of what?" "Of love." "For

whom?" "For you." "And I?" "Heal me." "How?" "By a means."
"Take it." "I have." "What means." "You'll go . . ." "Where?"
"To the baths." "When?" "Soon, for my joy." "Gladly."

So it was decided that Flamenca should go to the baths on a
certain day. She pretended to be very sick and to need to take the
baths, and her husband consented, ordered Gui to prepare the
baths; and Guillame heard the arrangement.

Meanwhile William had secretly had masons cut a hole in the
wall, so that he could enter the baths, unknown to anyone excepting,
of course, only those who were already in the baths.

Archambaut conducted Flamenca and her two maids to the
baths and locked her in. She was to ring a bell when she was ready
to come out. The door that the masons had made and that led
to William's apartment could not be detected; and Flamenca was
surprised when William appeared. The two young people loved
each other dearly and met frequently in this secret way.

The idea of this secret means by which the lovers could join
each other may well have been suggested by the double construction
of a tomb that could be entered and a house cleverly constructed
for concealment in *Cligès,* where Fenice was buried alive and
then exhumed to live secretly with Cligès.

Here we find in profusion the love symptoms that Chrétien
collected from Ovid's works and spread in gleaming masses in
Cligès to delight a dazzled society, that thrilled with the exquisite
novelty, and set a style of writing in that and other models to be
the absorbing interest of centuries of followers, in literary propaga-
tion, often in exaggeration, but in tender and natural fulfillment
deeply felt and artistically expressed by the Italian poets of the
dolce stil nuovo especially by the charming Guinicelli and the great
Dante, still to be robust in Cervantes' works and Spenser's, roman-
tically continued by the great French dramatist Corneille and
delicately though somewhat sparingly and tastefully admitted to
the tragedies of the greater Racine. Centuries of social groups
spent long and joyful hours in endless discussions of love topics and
intricate theorizing on questions that this great vogue suggested
and inspired and which reached a culmination of historical impor-

tance in the *salons* of seventeenth century France, to be satirized in delightful and exhilarating comedy by Molière especially in his *Précieuses ridicules;* and still present in grand and glowing lyricism in the poetry of the greatest of all French writers, Victor Hugo. In *Hernani* we read for example:

Dona Sol: Tell me whether you are cold.

Hernani: I burn when I am near you.

And in *Toilers of the Sea,* Gilliatt commits suicide in the famous rocky armchair, where he sits at the end of the novel until the tide rises above his head. Despair on account of unrequited love was the cause of his death.

The portraits that Chrétien developed from Ovidian models show one feature after another in a rather comprehensive list. The same procedure appears in *Flamenca* including even the hero's fingers. In like manner rich interiors, jewelry, food, service at the table, and after the meal the description of the *jongleurs* who recite stories and play various instruments is almost word for word from Chrétien's *Erec and Enide,* and fine raiment of silk, satin, exquisite fur, and, bright colors all seem to be a reflection of similar details in Chrétien's romances.

Archambaut shows the love symptoms aggravated by extreme jealousy. He burns with a searing fire, love pours its flames over his heart but nothing like a wound or a burn shows on the outside, on his face or body. Chrétien explains this penetration of Love's arrow through the eye to kindle a fire in the lover's heart, without any evidence of the hurt or the fire appearing on the lover's face, in a long passage in *Cligès* that interested many Medieval authors. The jealous rage of this unhappy man almost reaches the extreme of insanity.

The idea of a cure for love is elaborated. No herb or ointment is of avail. Flamenca is described as a personification of that cure in a manner that recalls Chrétien in this detail and also in the personification of Love's arrow by Soredamor in *Cligès.* William asks Flamenca to heal him; and he, too, is a cure for her.

Enslaved by love, enduring its sweet pain, sighing and weeping William lies awake all night. Like Alis in *Cligès,* he dreams that he holds Flamenca in his arms while asleep.

By day, he shows palor and emaciation, he sobs and faints. Absorbed by thoughts of love he loses the sense of hearing and the power of speech.

When Flamenca falls in love she sighs, weeps, and sobs, crying out with the pain. She is sick and dying of love. She lies awake all night. Speaking to Guillame she gives herself wholly to him but sobs interrupt her and make her pause just as Soredamor feared that she would be compelled to stop if she tried to tell her love to Alexander in *Cligès.*

The comparison of Flamenca to the sun—"for just as the sun is supreme by virtue of its splendor, so did she take rank above all the other ladies by reason of her beauty"—recalls the comparison of Gauvain to the sun in Chrétien's *Yvain.*

The extreme jealousy and the satirical attitude toward jealousy, the exaggeration of extra-marital love, and, especially, the use of church services and the psalter, the device by which the hero became the assistant of the priest in order to outwit the jealous husband and win the love of Flamenca are original or eminently Provençal. All the rest of the romance or novel is modeled on Chrétien's stories. The author shows some erudition, a knowledge of various Latin authors such as Ovid and Boetius and a great familiarity with the literature of Northern France.

Love as treated by the early Provençal poets was quite different from that of Chrétien. In *Erec and Enide* the love is natural, fresh and unadorned. Although Erec was unquestionably deeply impressed by Enide—he saw at once that her beauty was transcendent —his thoughts were more concerned with his own honor. Enide offered a good means of taking vengeance on the arrogant knight whose impudent dwarf had lashed his face. To prove her beauty in the contest he could enter the tournament against Yder. His offer of marriage was the matter-of-fact request for a woman whom the noble father could give away as he might give an animal or a generous gift. To be sure, a maiden was the hero's prize after victory in a dangerous adventure in classical and in Medieval literature. After the combat in which Enide's great beauty was defended and the prize was won, Erec appreciated Enide's loveliness and feasted his eyes upon her beautiful features. Love is now evident between the two. His uxoriousness is not elaborated. When a quarrel develops between husband and wife Erec treats Enide very harshly. He asserts his authority and his sovereignty and Enide meekly and obediently submits to the punishment that her pride and her reproaches have brought upon her. All this is typical of the accepted attitude of man and wife in the twelfth century.

In Provence the early literature of worth was lyric poetry written and often sung by troubadours. These troubadours were numerous in Southern France, so numerous that sometimes they were driven away with sticks by order of an impatient noble, whom they pestered. They needed a patron who would furnish food and lodging in return for the entertainment they hoped to furnish. Often young men of noble lineage wrote and sang. They pleased their audiences more when they were young. In the castle town many people sought the protection of the rich and powerful lord. There were maid-servants, waiting maids, and female relatives but above all the other women in the castle reigned the lady of the manor exalted, remote, adored, worshipped as the source of kindness, virtue, and purity. A harsh word from her fell like a bolt to wound the hearts of youths who hoped for a gentle nod or radiant smile to glorify a joyful day. Whoever could sing a song of lyric beauty to express his adoration of a goddess enthroned in ethereal heights above hoped to win commendation. He sighed for unattainable affection. He professed enslavement in loving adoration. He prayed for a caressing look or touch of hand or lips, begged the privilege of a kiss on snowy neck, preferably below the garments' edge. More courageous poets with the prestige of noble birth or growing fame waxed bolder, sometimes coarse or lascivious; but the fashion was to beg for love and complain of cruelty when one dared. The lady was usually the mystic idealization of goodness and nobility, capable of lifting the male to higher planes of morality and joy. A religious element was present and later mingled with the adoration of the Holy Virgin. The loved lady became the representative of God on earth—such was Beatrice for Dante. She could cure love sickness and finally any ill. A leper was healed if he touched her skirt.

This was the element of exaltation.

There was also the thrilling joy of love, a sort of pagan uplift that could not be curbed by the protesting clergy; freedom from negative morality and the restrictions of the prohibitive teaching of the church and the "thou shalt not" of priests who struggled to stem the wild currents of brutality, obscenity, and self-indulgence.

There was the element of extra-marital love that grew first out of social conditions. Marriage was a contract entered into for practical reasons political or financial. Two adjoining estates were thus united, political power was increased or consolidated, peace was thus established and assured by a union of two neighboring families. The contracting principals rarely had a voice in the arrangement. The woman passed from under the authority of her parents into enslavement to a husband. She became the great lady of the castle. She was adorned with fine raiment. She commanded her servants, pages waited upon her, *jongleurs* and troubadours served her and entertained her; but however high enthroned above the household, she was still the property of her lordly husband. She enjoyed the adoration of males who admired and flattered her. Such humble worship was a satisfying delight in marvelous contrast with the brutal dominance of a husband whose children she bore as a duty and a chore.

Page or troubadour had some moments of social intimacy in service of the lady. They were even allowed to assist in disrobing her, knelt before her to remove her shoes, touched her delicate feet and divinely turned ankles. Love often burned within them and truly filled their hearts with pain, their minds with longing.

The husband sought adventures of love outside the uninteresting marital chamber. Bastards swarmed, polluted the nobility and debased it. Each wayward husband strove to keep his own wife faithful while eagerly maneuvering to steal another's. The game was exciting for the male, dangerous for the woman. Secrecy thus was essential. The deceived husband was a cause of amusement, but the obviously jealous husband was the butt of jeers and scorn.

This was the brutal realistic element. Both the ethereal and the bestial united to form a background out of which the literary love of Southern France developed. This purity, this worship rising above the sordidness and mediocrity of real life and the reality of a pagan *joie de vivre,* a love that sought fulfillment outside of unstimulating, homely familiarity united in poetic souls blessed with artistic genius that produced, by unexplainable magic, the sweet music of Provençal poetry.

Chrétien did not adopt this type of love. He preferred marital fidelity. If he used the Tristan motive in *Cligès* and had his hero love the wife of another, he covered the crime with casuistry and justified it by the broken promise of Alis, Cligès', uncle, and the unlawful usurpation of the throne by a younger brother. In *Lancelot* the theme was chosen, apparently, by his patroness Marie de Champagne and the illegitimacy of Lancelot's love for Guenevere is covered by long and patient love-service in dangerous adventure and battles. King Arthur, the legal husband is scarcely a real figure. The cruel torture to which the enslaved lover is reduced by an arrogant mistress is purely Ovidian. Nothing like it is to be found in the early poetry of the troubadours. The only cruelty of which the Provençal poet complained is the lady's indifference to his passionate love.

Courtly love as developed in Southern France is based to a large extent, at least in its beginnings, on a wide distance that separates the poet, servile lover, from the loved lady, far above him, remote in social eminence; but love has a tremendously leveling force and the loved lady has a power of uplift that raises the lover morally. His fear is due to the lady's elevated caste and dread of the consequences if boldness on his part is discovered by the brutal and merciless husband.

The timidity of the Ovidian lover is caused by Love, the god, who put it in his heart. In the frivolous escapades that Ovid has in mind in his *Art of Love,* the mistress is on no higher social stratum than the lover. When Chrétien took over the Ovidian style and theory, he tossed aside the base and light-hearted frivolity and fitted it to the high ideals and lofty virtue of his heroes.

It was not a social difference that made the hero of Chrétien's romance subservient to the loved lady, her obedient servant and humble slave. It was love itself that set the lady so high and made her so arrogant that she tried the lover, compelled his service, withheld her favors, and assuming the very functions of Cupid, tortured the patient lover.

These two concepts of love were widely separated. Chrétien never absorbed much of the Provençal love treatment. It did not fit his ambitious purpose of setting before his readers nobility of character so ideal that time and civilization may keep it everlastingly as a model and goal, never to be fully attained, but always an inspiration and a glorious splendor radiating the delight and the charm of chivalry in its grandest imagined conception.

Chrétien influenced the literature of the South by pouring into it all the refinement of his metaphorical style and the full measure of the Ovidian analysis of love in all its symptoms and effects.

CHAPTER XII

Imitators of Chrétien

In France many Arthurian romances were written in verse. They have the same structure as Chrétien's romances. A string of episodes is connected by the love story of the hero running through a longer or shorter portion of his life. There may, of course, be more than one hero. These romances are usually written in the same meter and rime scheme as Chrétien's poems. They often have prologues similar to Chrétien's which repeat more or less of the Horatian precepts for good writing with an occasional allusion to Solomon. They deal with knightly adventures and tournaments, treat of love in the Ovidian manner developed and taught by Chrétien. They imitate the monologues that he introduced into French literature. Like Chrétien they give pictures of the life of the time on the road and in the castles, describe shining armor, bright colored cloth and raiment, hospitality, food, service, washing of hands before eating, removing of armor and furnishing of comfortable clothing, and bathing. Chrétien's detailed portraits are repeated in similar terms. The story-telling, singing and playing of various instruments all are described in words that recall Chrétien's poems but miss the elegance of his style.

These poems not only represent the life of the twelfth and thirteenth centuries, they influenced it and raised standards of morality and courtesy.

It is not sure that André de Chapelain consulted Ovid directly. Whether he did or not, the vogue for the Ovidian type of love as described in Chrétien's romances was well established. The probable date of composition of his *De Amore* is around 1180.

The burning torment of love is featured and the element of fear. The desire on the part of the lover to find an intermediary recalls *Cligès* and *Yvain*. The impatience of the lover can only be a suggestion from Chrétien's *Lancelot* and the passage where Lancelot is waiting for day to end and night to come so that he may visit Guenevere. Words are taken directly from Chrétien's romance, when André says that a day or an hour "seems like a year."

The idea that love enobles a man may come from the poetry of the troubadours of Southern France; but the lovers in Chrétien's romances are perfect in every respect. Their valor is expended in part to win the respect and love of their ladies. As for loyalty to one woman, no author displayed such constancy and loyalty to one love as the characters of Chrétien's stories.

The notion that a blind man cannot love is developed naturally from the idea that the eyes are the messengers of love, that the shafts of love pass from eye to eye; and this was learned from Chrétien who took the idea from Ovid's story of Narcissus as was explained in the chapter on *Cligès*.

Also the idea of the injustice of Love, who torments his most loyal followers is to be found in *Cligès*.

The insistence on secrecy and on extramarital love are suggestions that come rather from the South. Love was extramarital in four of Chrétien's works and secrecy was essential. These were his *Tristan and Isolt, Philomena,* the second part of *Cligès,* and *Lancelot.* These elements were not accepted by Chrétien as fundamental or necessary—his natural tendencies seem to be in the opposite direction. They are unimportant in the larger view of literary development, but represent a sort of side current and back water in Southern French literature; and the exaggeration and absurdities of which they were a part ended in the stagnant affectation and finally the sterility of lesser Provençal poets and the early Italian poets, who wrote in the Provençal language, which was ended in a happy rejuvenation with the more enlightened poets of the *dolce stil nuovo* particularly Guinicelli, Cavalcanti, and the great Dante.

Twenty-two cases are set forth and decided by Eleanor, Queen of England, Adèle, Queen of France, Marie, Countess of Champagne, and Ermengarde of Narbonne in accordance with twelve rules as follows:

1. Avarice should be avoided.

2. The lover should keep himself chaste for the loved lady.

3. No attempt should be made to break up a correct love affair of other persons.

4. The love of a person whom one would be ashamed to marry should not be sought.

5. Falsehood should be entirely avoided.

6. Few should know of one's love.

7. One should serve Love and the commands of the loved lady obediently.

8. One should be modest in the enjoyment of love.

9. One should speak no evil.

10. A love affair must not be revealed.

11. Politeness and courtesy are required in all things.

12. In the enjoyment of love the desires of the loved one should not be exceeded.

It is not known whether this treatise is entirely a work of imagination but it is probable that love topics were discussed in social gatherings at the courts of great ladies.

This *Art of Courtly Love* was written for Marie de Champagne.

Not only was Chrétien imitated in France, many of his works were translated into other languages, several in German, a few in Dutch and in Norwegian.

By the end of the thirteenth century the versified romances came to an end but prose romances continued down to the seventeenth century tending in the sixteenth toward the pastoral type. The versified romances were often much longer than Chrétien's and the prose versions very lengthy. These prose romances, especially, combined episodes taken from various romances by Chrétien, added their own variations and jumbled the episodes together in multiplied changes and permutations of their order and significance.

Chrétien is mentioned and praised as an inimitable master frequently and even in the fourteenth century. His reputation was so great that authors in Germany attributed to him works that they translated from the French even when those works were not by Chrétien at all.

Gaston Paris, the greatest of all French scholars who have studied the Arthurian romance, said that most of the authors who followed Chrétien and wrote about Arthur and his knights imitated him even in the smallest details.

Floire et Blancheflor offers all the charm and idealism of Chrétien's poems. Floire is the son of a pagan king who has brought back from France a woman that he has seized there to take back as a gift for the Queen, who wishes to learn French. It happens that this captive is pregnant; and she gives birth to a baby girl on the same day that the son is born to the pagan queen.

The two children are brought up together and, at an early age, are bound together by an ardent love. The pagan king is disturbed by this affection and determines to separate them. The boy is sent away to school with the promise, falsely given and never to be kept, that Blancheflor will soon be sent to study with Floire. Even though their parting is to be short—Blancheflor remains behind to nurse her mother who pretends to be sick—the two children swoon with grief as Floire leaves home.

After several days Floire realizes that Blancheflor is not to join him; and the sorrow this disappointment causes nearly kills him. Deeply disturbed, Floire's parents declare that Blancheflor is dead and have a fine monument erected over her pretended grave. Meanwhile she is sold as a slave, taken to Babylon and there held a prisoner by the Kaliff in his harem.

When Floire learns of the death of Blancheflor he swoons and, recovering, swoons a second and a third time. At the false tomb Floire's emotions break out again with violence. He sobs and utters imprecations against death. He declares that he cannot survive his love for Blancheflor; and he would have killed himself with a dagger if his mother had not snatched it from him.

On account of his unconsolable grief, his parents reveal the truth. Then Floire becomes hopeful and happy. He starts out on a long search, confident that he can find the loved lady.

Searching for the port from which Blancheflor sailed, sitting at a table where he found lodging, sighing and without appetite, he is told of a maiden who sighed the same and ate nothing, his hostess tells of Blancheflor, who sighed the same and refused to eat, and who was taken to Babylon. So Floire now knows where to search for Blancheflor.

Arriving at the port of Babylon he again has news of Blancheflor who sighed and moaned for Floire neglecting her food all in the manner of Floire who resembles her like a twin brother. He reveals his secret and declares that he will die if he cannot find the lady of his love and wakeful dreams.

His host tells him of the dangers attending any attempt to rescue the maiden. He takes over the role that Reason had recently played in a dispute with Love, Reason recommending the abandonment of the dangerous adventure. Love won the argument then as now. Even though Blancheflor is held in a fortified castle guarded without by soldiers and by armed eunuchs within. He learns that the Kaliff marries one wife each year and cuts off her head at the end of the year. He has only one month to rescue Blancheflor before the Kaliff makes his next choice of a wife.

Winning the friendship of the porter by presents, Floire is brought into the palace in a basket of flowers delivered in the rooms of the harem. United to Blancheflor, he lives for several days in heavenly joy in her room until finally they are discovered. The two lovers are in imminent danger of death; but finally their great beauty moves the whole court and the Kaliff himself pardons them and allows them to leave his kingdom together.

A tale of the thirteenth century, *Aucassin et Nicolete* is strongly influenced by *Floire et Blancheflor* and resembles it in many respects, except that the ending is different and the form unique in French literature: passages in verse alternate with prose. This form was used by Boethius in his *Consolation of Philosophy* and it appears in several works written in Latin in the Middle Ages, especially in Italy.

The hero is the son of a great French lord. The heroine is a pagan captive. The hero is most proficient in the use of arms, the true defense of the land. His love for Nicolete and hers for him is indicated according to the style and fashion of Chrétien and his followers. Both hero and heroine are persons of high character and they are thrown into adventures of exciting interest and great danger, in which they both show undaunted courage. Their portraits are presented in the exact style of Chrétien, that of Nicolete being the more complete and most charming. The various symptoms and effects of love appear in conventional form. Absorption in love appears when Aucassin deep in thoughts of Nicolete suddenly finds himself surrounded by enemies in a battle; and he is about to be taken prisoner. He recovers his senses and a realization of his situation just in time to extricate himself with a tremendous display of strength and prowess.

Aucassin's father is opposed to his son's marriage with a slave and a pagan. In order to put an end to this love he has Aucassin thrown into a prison and threatens to have Nicolete killed. The brave girl escapes and passing by the tower where Aucassin is imprisoned, in a subterranean dungeon, she hears his laments through a crack just as Yvain heard Lunete complaining of her sad lot in a building near Laudine's fountain and she talks to him through the crack like Yvain and Lunete in one of many imitations of Ovid's story of Pyramus and Thisbe.

When Nicolete states her determination to escape to a distant land Aucassin threatens to kill himself. She will soon be taken and made the mistress of some captor, and the thought of such an event will make him dash out his brains against a rock. His love is so strong that he refuses to take any interest in his honor, the safety of his country, or his eternal salvation. He declares that he would rather live in Hell with Nicolete than in Heaven without her. Such is the tyrannical and all-powerful force of love.

Nicolete escapes into a nearby forest; and there she makes a bower of branches and flowers, which Aucassin comes upon, as he follows, in an attempt to find her. He recognizes by instinct the work of her hands in this pretty bower and enters. Lying there he gazes upward and through an opening sees a brilliant star that beautifies the night. It reminds him of his love and he says:

> I see you little star
> That the moon draws to itself.
> Nicolete is surely with you,
> My darling blond-haired love.
> I think that God would have her
> A clear light in the evening
> Made by her more beautiful.
> Sweet Sister, how I would like
> To mount straight up to you
> However hard might be my fall,
> And if I could be there with you;
> Quickly I would give you kisses!
> If I were even a prince,
> You'd be all too worthy still,
> Dear Sister, my true Love.

Heedless in mental absorption in thoughts of love, he never feels the scratch of briars; he falls, in distraction, from his horse, wrenches and wounds his shoulder on an unseen stone but cares little for the pain. Nicolete is near. She comes to find him, holds him in loving embrace, and nurses his wound. Now he is happy. The danger of their situation, the difficulty of their escape, the course they may take or how or where they may live is totally indifferent to him now. Love fills his mind and heart.

The two lovers are captured by Sarassins. Nicolete is sold into captivity. Aucassin is returned to his native town of Beaucaire. Thus the lovers are brutally separated.

Nicolete finds her way to Carthage where she learns her identity as a princess of that land.

Aucassin weeps and sighs, longing for Nicolete whom he never hopes to find again. The author chooses to have the heroine seek out her love; and Nicolete comes, disguised as a minstrel, to his court; and the lovers are united again.

Galeron de Bretagne, by the *trouvère* Renaut, has many characteristics that mark it as an imitation of Chrétien's romances. The portraits of Galeron and the heroine Frene are typical. The beauty of both is resplendent. In character, as well, they are superior, charming in manner and noble in their impulses. Galeron is an accomplished knight capable of winning great renown in dangerous adventures and fierce combat. Love holds them in its all-powerful sway. All the symptoms and effects of love appear. They suffer the pangs of love with joy. It fills their thoughts by day; and in the night it holds them sleepless twisting and stretching their limbs that ache, sighing and weeping. They are pale and emaciated, their appetites are poor. Cupid's dart has wounded them and kindled a fire in their hearts that burns them with sweet suffering. In idyllic happiness they wander through charming fields gladdened by the song of birds and decorated with spring flowers, a bubbling brook, charming shade of trees; and fragrant breezes murmur songs of love and joy.

Galeron is the son of the Count of Brittany. Frene was a foundling left under a tree. The two children were brought up together by Galeron's aunt in the Abbey of Beauséjour, in France, of which she is the Abbess.

Galeron is called to his estates in England on the death of his parents. The two lovers are thus separated while Galeron takes his oath of fealty to his suzerain and trains himself to become a knight. Love service demands great deeds at arms to make the lover worthy of his lady's affection and favor. The two lovers suffer all the pain of love with sleepless nights and sad longing.

Galeron is able to visit Frene in the abbey at Beauséant but his frequent coming and going awaken scandal and reproaches because he is expected to marry a lady of high birth. Both lovers suffer from this condemnation and this opposition to their marriage. Their idyllic and innocent pleasure in each other's company is a sort of uxorious dalliance for a youth who should be mindful of virile occupations and knightly glory.

Frene is plagued by scandal and finally dismissed from the abbey. She has, however, seen the cloth of embroidered silk in which she was wrapped when abandoned as a baby and the fine pillow on which she lay. These magnificent objects made Frene believe that she was born of noble parents. She takes up her abode in the city of Rouen in a modest home with a girl of her age and the girl's mother. She is able to earn her living by weaving and embroidering. She lives there for many months admired for her beauty and her virtue, courted and sought after by many men of noble birth. Although her life is monotonous she remains true to Galeron.

Galeron sends messages to many lands seeking to find Frene; but all in vain. Finally he mourns her as dead. Great deeds of chivalry, victory in tournaments build his fame. In the castle of a nobleman named Brundore, he sees the beautiful Fleurie, daughter of his host. She resembles Frene so much that he falls in love with her and his love for the two young ladies seems like one.

The marriage between Galeron and Fleurie is arranged. The news reaches Frene who has held herself aloof all this time perhaps in the hope that Galeron's deep love for her will finally bring him to her. Whatever her pride before, she now yields to despair. She will make a supreme effort. She still has the fine cloth in which she was found as an abandoned baby. Out of this cloth she makes a beautiful dress and goes to the scene of the wedding, appears before Galeron, plays her harp and sings. Everyone present is charmed and Galeron is compelled by his true love for Frene to give up his marriage with Fleurie. Fleurie's mother recognizes her own embroidery on Frene's dress. She recognizes the child that she had abandoned because Fleurie and Frene were twins. Fearing the scandalous suspicions, according to a superstition, that twins are the result of two fathers, she had abandoned one secretly. She now confesses her action and rejoices in the recovery of her child.

Galeron, of course, in his turn must abandon Fleurie and marry Frene.

In *l'Escoufle,* by Renart, Count Richard of Normandy retained in the service of the Emperor of Rome marries the noble Lady of Genes who gives birth to a son named Guillaume on the very day that the daughter of the Empress is born. Her name is Aélis.

The Empress now lives in a castle in Venice. At the age of three the Emperor demands that his child be sent to Rome. The two children of the same age are thus brought together. They are both as beautiful as angels and look like twins. From this point on they are never separated and their friendship as playmates ripens into love. Aélis calls Guillaume "brother" and also "sweetheart" but when she says "sweetheart" her eyes are dimmed by tears and her voice is shaken by sighs and sobs.

The Emperor decides to marry these two children; and, in order to win the consent of his vassals to this mésalliance, he calls them together and uses the trick, made common by Chrétien, of asking for a "don" or free grant of a favor before the favor is made known. Alexandre obtained such a grant from his father in *Cligès* and Kay also from King Arthur in *Lancelot* even obtaining the privilege of defending the Queen against Maleagant with disastrous result.

The vassals grant the Emperor's request; but when they learn what they have granted they demur with loud outbursts until the two charming children are brought in. The Emperor takes advantage of the startling impression they make on the assembly to obtain the oath of all his vassals to allow Guillaume to become Emperor on his death.

Suddenly, however, Guillaume's father dies; and then the vassals and the Empress herself urge the Emperor to give up the idea of this marriage. Being of a weak character, the Emperor yields and orders Guillaume to cease to see Aélis any more.

Thus separated the two lovers pass a sleepless night in tears and sad regrets. Guillaume does not doubt the love of Aélis. He says that as he left her chamber he saw her heart at the windows of her eyes and he knew that she would always be true to him.

Aélis lamenting through the long night declares that she will be his wife or die. And she forms the resolution to go with him to Normandy.

Love gives her courage. In the night she makes a rope of her sheets, intending to escape by the window of her chamber. Now, in imitation of previous romances Reason enters into a debate with Love advising prudence rather than this rash enterprise. Love wins the victory at last, and ashamed of her hesitation, the brave girl slips down into the arms of her waiting lover.

Aélis carries with her, in a wallet, a ring that her mother had given her. After a successful escape on two mules, while they are resting in a beautiful spot and communing in tender loving words and embraces, Aélis gives her ring to Guillaume. Instead of putting it on his finger he puts it in the wallet; and, drowsy, he falls into semi-slumber. Now suddenly a hawk swoops down, takes the wallet in its beak and flies away. Guillaume is filled with shame on account of his carelessness. He cannot bear to lose the ring. So he pursues the bird for a long time until finally he recovers the wallet. Returning to the place where he had left Aélis he finds that she has gone. Each one suffers desperately fearing that the loved one has abandoned him. Aélis goes on toward Normandy; Guillaume toward Rome. For many years they are separated and live in deep sorrow until finally chance brings them back together.

Guillaume de Palerme is somewhat similar to *l'Escoufle*. The hero Guillaume is discovered, in a forest, by the Emperor of Rome while hunting. He attaches this attractive boy, as a page, to his daughter, the beautiful Melior. Guillaume distinguishes himself in battle, defeating the Duke of Saxony. His hopes of marrying Melior are dashed by the proposal of the Emperor of Greece to marry his son with Melior. This proposal is enthusiastically accepted at Rome; and the despair of Melior and Guillaume who have fallen passionately in love, drives them to a courageous flight together.

This romance has an extraordinary abundance of marvelous elements, among them the kind assistance given to Guillaume and later to the two lovers by a were-wolf. Nevertheless, this romance, is in essence typical of the long line of stories of love flowing from

Chrétien's works as sources of inspiration and material. Great adventure, knightly prowess, and the type of love taught by the great master, inventor, and model for centuries of literature characterized by idealism, nobility of character, high adventure, undaunted courage, and love as it has always been described since in lyrics, epics, plays, and novels, though not always in the same concentration of analytical symptoms and effects.

This love is expressed by the coloring of courtly love in its metaphorical style. Great suffering and pain is experienced by Melior and in words that seem to have been taken straight out of Chrétien's *Cligès,* she asks herself, in the typical love monologue, just like Soredamor, what is this sickness that makes her suffer, twist and turn, sigh, turn hot and cold, become pale, and tremble as though feverish. Then, in question and answer, she blames first her eyes, then her heart because the eyes are only servants of the heart and bears its messages. She thinks she should have control of her heart and eyes just as Soredamor said to herself that she had only to turn her eyes away from Alexandre. Finally she must admit that love has her entirely in its control.

A number of short tales in verse sometimes called lays tell stories of love and adventure. They are miniature reflections of Chrétien's style and manner. Some follow his example by using Classical Latin stories such as that of Narcissus, of Pyramus and Thisbe, or of Orpheus.

The lays of Marie de France, written in England, have a freshness and a charm that is given them by a delicacy and rapidity of style and an idyllic treatment of love that is full of youthful sincerity and naive ardor. Some of Marie's lays are based on stories told by Celtic bards. She makes this claim herself. In two of her lays she indicates the subject of stories by a double designation, one Celtic and one English: *bisclavet, garwall* (were-wolf); *laustic,* nightingale.

Though the love of heroes is often for fairies and though it is simple and sincere, it bears the stamp of Chrétien's influence in the symptoms of love and its serious and even tragic effects.

One of these lays tells of a married woman who arises from her bed in the middle of the night to commune with her lover at the window, explaining to her husband that she is listening to the sweet song of the nightingale. The harsh husband gives her a cruel warning by presenting to her one of these little birds that he has caught and brutally killed. She sends it to her lover as a message of parting. Other lays tell of sacrifices for love, betrayals, the suffering of lovers through separation, and their joy in finding each other again.

The *Lai de l'Ombre* brings a courteous knight and a charming lady together at a well where they gaze at their shadows in the water. The gentleman slips a beautiful and costly ring on the lady's finger but she refuses the gift. So he drops it in the well so that her shadow, dear to him, may have it. Such gallantry and tender love melt the lady's heart.

The *Roman de la Rose* of the thirteenth century, written by two poets of very different types and widely differing styles— Guillaume de Lorris first and several years later Jean de Meung —is an elaboration of the doctrine of love as developed and expounded by Chrétien, cast in the form of an allegory and padded with Medieval learning into swollen distention by the later author.

CHAPTER XIII

Influences of the Romances
in Italy and Spain

The infusion of elements that characterize the romances—first of all the love element, but also idealization of the hero, all the courtesy of chivalry, generosity, the magnificent and lavish spectacles of tournaments, that nobility of character that made a promise sacred and finally had its culmination in real life, in the concept of "nobless oblige"—into the epic, in such strength that the epic actually became a romance, reaches its highest point of development and exaltation in Ariosto's *Orlando Furioso,* a poem of the sixteenth century, which is a sequel to Boiardo's *Orlando Innamorato.*

From the romances, too, there is much magic, marvelous palaces richly adorned with many jewels, and impossible deeds of valor.

At the very beginning of his *Orlando Furioso,* Ariosto tells us that he is going to write of loves, ladies, knights, and arms, of courtesies and many a daring deed. This work, then, is a romance grafted on an epic. It is a story of adventure and in spite of the historical background and the problems of Charlemagne, the chief interest is in the actions and the fate of individuals.

The irresistible power of love is an essential theme of the poem. The conventional symptoms of love and its effects, long since established and faithfully copied and transmitted, appear in full force. Angelica, the lady of Catay, at the opening of the action, sways the glowing breasts of both Orlando and Rinaldo. Two knights, who had been friends and comrades in arms are now quarreling over this paragon of beauty. Charlemagne decrees that she shall be awarded as a prize to whichever of the two paladins will slay the larger number of pagans in a day's battle. Charlemagne's plans are disturbed by an unexpected defeat. Angelica escapes and flees, pursued by various knights, whose love is kindled by her extraordinary beauty and a maze of interlocking scenes begins, presenting exquisite pictures that, though appearing in detached focus, are, nevertheless, blended into a coherent and well organized composition.

Although Ariosto's impish sense of humor breaks through the golden surface of beauty, idealism, passionate love, and chivalry in Rabelaisian outbursts, still all the glamor of romance remains to satisfy thousands of ardent admirers, who demanded one hundred and eighty editions, before the end of the sixteenth century, of a great masterpiece that glorified the Italian language then and ever since.

Though Isabella's voice resounded through wood and meadow for many miles, anticipating the lusty bellowing of the giant baby Gargantua, her sorrowful mourning for Zerbino, her dead lover, has always been admired for its pathos, and she would have taken her own life and like many a heroine from Enide on, thrown herself as Thisbe did on her lover's sword. Though Orlando astounded shepherds tearing trees out from their roots and though the reader laughs in amused amazement at his furious rage as, armed with a tree trunk, he struck down farmers, their flocks, and herds, rushed naked through forests where he destroyed wild boars with his naked hands, traversed France and Spain spreading terror and destruction, to swim across the Strait of Gibraltar and storm the shores and fields of Africa, yet his madness is the most overwhelming result of love betrayed and the trip that Astolfo takes to the moon, anticipating Cyrano de Bergerac of the seventeenth century and his imaginary trip to the moon, because Orlando was moonstruck, to recover Orlando's senses and bring them back in a bottle, is burlesque indeed. Another trait of Rabelaisian flavor is the action of Orlando in his defeat of Cymosco and rescue of Berino, when he runs through six opponents and sticks them all as on a spit.

It seems likely that Orlando's madness, which is the center and core of Ariosto's poem was suggested by *Yvain's* madness in Chrétien's romance. Among other traits that remind the reader of

Chrétien are the magic ring that renders Angelica invisible like the one that saved Yvain, in Laudine's castle, from the crowds of her liegemen who probe about in amusing and vain search for the hero. The rescue of Genevra from burning at the stake by Rinaldo, who arrives as her champion for the ordeal of battle, recalls how Yvain fought for Lunete against the treacherous seneschal, who had brought an unjust accusation against her, the same as Polinesso had done to Genevra. Fights with giants remind one of Erec's combat with two giants and Yvain's fight with Harpin of the Mountain. The name of one of those giants, Caligorante, may be derived from a character named Calogrenant in *Yvain*.

The portrait of Alcina in the seventh canto is typical of those that Chrétien placed in vogue. Characteristically feature after feature is listed and described:

> Her shape is of such perfect symmetry,
> As best to feign the industrious painter knows;
> With long and knotted tresses; to the eye
> Not yellow gold with brighter lustre glows.
> Upon her tender cheek the mingled dye
> Is scattered, of the lily and the rose.
> Like ivory smooth, the forehead gay and round
> Fills up the space, and forms a fitting bound.
>
> Two black and slender arches rise above
> Two clear black eyes, say suns of radiant light;
> Which ever softly beam and slowly move;
> Round these appears to sport in frolic flight,
> Hence scattering all his shafts the little Love,
> And seems to plunder hearts in open sight.
> Thence, through mid visage, does the nose descend,
> Where Envy finds not blemish to amend.
>
> As if two vales which softly curl,
> The mouth with vermeil tint is seen to glow;
> Within are strung two rows of orient pearl,

Which her delicious lips shut up or show.
Of force to melt the heart of any churl,
However rude, hence courteous accents flow;
And here that gentle smile receives its birth,
Which opens at will a paradise on earth.

Like milk the bosom, and the neck of snow;
Round is the neck, and full and large the breast;
Where fresh and firm two apples grow,
Which rise and fall, as, to the margin pressed
By pleasant breeze the billows come and go.

There follows, even, the spicy suggestion of hidden beauty that
Chrétien borrowed from Ovid:

Not prying Argus could discern the rest.
Yet might observing eye of things concealed
Conjecture safely, from the charms revealed.
To all her arms a just proportion bear,
And a white hand is oftentimes descried,
Which narrow is and somewhat long; and where
No knot appears, nor vein is signified.
For finish of that stately shape and rare,
A foot, short, and round, beneath is spied.

The portrait of Olympia is similar though in less detail; and
the same suggestion of beauty hidden under the clothing is repeated:

Olympia's beauties are of those most rare,
Nor is the forehead's beauteous curve alone
Excelling, and her eyes and cheeks and hair,
Mouth, nose, and throat, and shoulders; but so down
Descending from the lady's bosom fair,
Parts which are wont to be concealed by gown,
Are such, as haply should be placed before
Whate'er this ample world contains in store.

In whiteness they surpassed unsullied snow,
Smooth ivory to the touch; above were seen
Two rounding breasts, like new pressed milk in show,
Fresh-taken from basket of rushes green;
The space between was like a valley low,
Which oftentimes we see small hills between,
Sweet in its season: and now such as when
Winter with snows has newly filled the glen.

Descriptions of the effects of the love sickness are vivid, for example Jocundo:

He rests not night or day, in sorrow drowned;
His appetite is gone, with his repose,
- - - - -

His eye-balls seem deep-buried in his head,
His nose seems grown—his cheeks are pined so sore--
Nor even remains (his beauty so is fled)
Enough to warrant what he was before.
Such fever burns him of his sorrow bred.

Of Rodomont:

As the sick man who with a fever glows,
And, weak and weary, shifts his place in vain,
Whether he right or left himself bestows,
And hopes in turning some relief to gain,
Finds neither on this side nor that repose,
But everywhere encounters equal pain.

High adventure, indomitable courage, invincible strength in the heroes, and passionate love, and nobility of character and purpose are the dominant characteristics of this poem. They reveal it as a romance inspired by romances and carrying on the tradition invented, molded and transmitted by Chrétien de Troyes.

Chivalry with all its bravery and passionate love is still to be found in Tasso's *Gerusalemme Liberata*.

When Dante first beheld Beatrice, in his ninth year, his heart trembled violently and its trembling was communicated to all his veins. And he wept. Love lorded it over him and held him henceforth in his power, so that he obeyed all of Love's commands. Love weakened him and his love sickness appeared in his countenance.

Weeping and sighs are multiplied. They are caused by Love, who holds the poet in the bonds of his absolute power. They are caused, too, by the denial of Beatrice's salutation. When receiving the salutation of this most charming of all women known or imagined the poet was so filled with the bliss of love that all strength and vitality left his body inanimate in swooning.

With humility and will only to love and serve, like that of Lancelot, he begs his loved lady's pardon for a slight offense; and if she will not pardon, then he will gladly die.

Lovers are the vassals of Love. They must do his will. Often the will of Love brings suffering and grief; and the more loyal the servant of Love the greater his trials and his distress.

The presence of Beatrice near him in a room so fills him with love that he is obliged to support himself against a wall. Love chills him with fear. Trembling he loses control of all his senses. Even sight is driven forth to make way for Love himself, who desires to gaze upon the beauty of the lovely woman, and takes full possession of his eyes.

Transfigured in the *Divine Comedy* and placed there near God, Beatrice becomes, figuratively, Philosophy, full and divine truth.

Dante is clearly in the tradition of Chrétien's creating. His actual knowledge and borrowing from *Cligès* appear in the twenty-fourth sonnet, as Professor Comfort has already shown:

> Oh pilgrims who pass, deep in thought,
> Thinking of things that are far away,
> Do you come from a town as distant
> As your indifferent manner seems to show?

For you weep not as you pass along
Through the middle of a city filled with grief,
Like people who have no knowledge of her woe.
If you would stop a while to hear,
I know in my heart that weeps and sighs
That you would leave the city in tears,
For Beatrice is lost to the sorrowing city;
And the words that are spoken in mourning here
Have the power to wring tears from everyone.

In *Cligès* Fenice is supposed to be dead. The whole city is mourning; and into the midst of the city in grief come three doctors who, for a long time, have lived in a distant town. They do not pass, in apparent indifference, as the pilgrims do in Dante's poem. They ask about the great grief; and they are answered and told what Dante would have the pilgrims learn. The people in the town ask in words like those that Dante uses: "Where have you come from that you do not know what has happened in this City?" All the world would weep if it knew the sad news. Just as Beatrice is represented by Dante as the representative of God on earth, Chrétien has the people say: "God has illumined the world with a great brightness and light." And Death has taken it away.

Flamenca is still a story of chivalry and love. The clever and extravagantly costly love intrigue is only an incident in the lives of knights who fight fiercely and win great glory in tournaments and of ladies who live in luxury and the delight of rich festivities, watching the pageantry and the dangerous combats of the jousting. Nevertheless the love intrigue is the very center and the real interest of the story. All the rest, and even the knightly combats, are accessory, decoration and padding to fill out the poem to the conventional length. The essential part of this romance is a departure from the set form and content of romances of chivalry. It is a transition work opening the way for the still more modern *Fiammetta* of Boccaccio, a novel of manners and also a psychological romance standing by itself in time, unique, and matched only after three centuries by another work that again stands alone with a lapse of several years before a similar work appears in the history of literature. This work is the *Princesse de Clèves* of Madame de LaFayette, the masterpiece of psychological novels until the nineteenth century, and showing much realism when compared with the other novels of the century.

Like *Flamenca, Fiammetta* starts the love story in a church. There Panphilus first saw the lovely Fiammetta and received the fatal shaft from Cupid's bow.

This book is permeated with the perfume and elixir of Ovidian love. This concentrate of Ovid's scattered acid and balm of love, filling fifteen books of the *Metamorphoses,* a long series of love letters, the love lyrics of the *Amores,* the *Art of Love,* and the *Cure of Love,* and not absent from the *Tristia* and the *Fasti,* was distilled by Chrétien de Troyes, made into a systematic prescription and administered to centuries of writers, who drenched their works with the fragrance that was an exhilaration to them and their readers for hundreds of years. He made Ovid the favorite author of the Medieval world and the important text in the schools. If the educated authors of later days turned eagerly to Ovid, the fountainhead of love lyrics and fiction, pouring waters from a pagan world into our Christian era, Chrétien still stands on a high hilltop from which that great stream still gushes with added elements of great nobility and idealism that still elevate the thoughts of men.

The story starts, not with courts where knights await great adventures, meanwhile jousting in huge theaters before admiring women, but with the thoughts of a woman recalling the innocence of her childhood, all too soon clouded by the innumerable male worshippers of her great beauty, who sought to win her love, lovers who burned with an amorous fire, striving to enkindle a like flame in her heart. At first these flames that raged around her did not even scorch her. But looking back in tragic sorrow on the days of her life, she laments over the long and lingering fires that utterly consumed her.

In her youth she had a frightful dream that, if she had heeded it, might have been a warning that would have saved her from the bitter tragedy of later life. She had a dream, which, allegorically, was an oracular description of what her sad fate was to be.

Early one morning she was sleeping in her bed, but she dreamed that she was walking in a beautiful meadow where lovely flowers grew and stately trees with fresh green leaves spread comforting shade. After gathering flowers in the field, tired and heated by the sun she sat down in soft grass under the protection of shade that shielded her from the blazing sun. Soon she fell asleep and suddenly a poisonous snake bit her on the left breast and sent a seering pain through her body; and swelling rose from her flesh in many spots. She took the snake and placed it in her bosom to still with its coolness the burning fever of its bite. Though she tried to hold it the snake left her and left behind its venom and the sores it caused. Now more fiery flames shot through her. She turned and twisted in her pain and thought that she would die. Black night descended upon her and shut out all the light from the heavens and a foggy blackness covered her.

Awaking from this horrible dream, she laughingly cast its frightfulness from her mind and attached no importance to it. She dressed herself in magnificent finery and went to the temple to delight in the pleasant vanity of displaying her beauty to the eyes of many youths whose glances wandered from all others to her divine beauty that transcended the most charming graces of many lovely women. Basking in this adoration, at times she lifted her own eyes for a cursory and furtive glance; and her gaze fell on a gentleman young and handsome who held her attention with a caressing look that seemed to speak and say: "You are, oh Lady my only joy and sole desire." She tried to make her eyes answer: "And you are mine."

She describes Love's arrow as a light that issued from the eyes of the young man, penetrated her eyes and reached her heart. The passage reminds us of Chrétien's *Cligès* where this phenomenon is discussed at some length. Boccaccio uses somewhat different terms and the discussion is very short. The outer defenses of her heart move in defense against this projectile due to fear awakened in the heart itself. This fear and the action of the forces that attempt to ward off the beam produce cold that is communicated to the face, causing pallor. The fear being somewhat allayed, a welcome warmth of passion ended this inward contraction. The blood flowed back again from the heart and in its rush brought a bright flush to her face. The coldness was replaced by a burning heat through all her being. As she contemplated the source of this power she could only emit sorrowful sighs. Henceforth all her thoughts were bent on imagining how she might please this man endowed with such apparent virtues. This man was a trained soldier of Love. He had learned in Love's school. So he knew wiles that intensified his appeal and she was enmeshed in a sudden and unlooked for love from which she was never, in all her life, extricated. This man was the cause of woes that threaten to end only with her death. A free and happy lady was then changed to a miserable and unhappy captive. Just as Alexander and Soredamor stimulate their love by covert glances so Fiammetta's love grows with each sly glance from her new lover and the flames of love are nursed. And in words like those of Gauvain in *Yvain* she compares her love, never known before, to the fire that burns longer in green wood though it is not so soon kindled.

Fiammetta was consumed by an illict love for she was married, and, like the Princesse de Clèves, she had a fine and noble husband who loved her dearly and of whom she was, herself, fond.

She also had a nurse like Thessala in *Cligès*. As in some of Ovid's stories and in the romances this nurse was wise and in the confidence of the heroine. As is always true in these stories, so here Fiammetta has difficulty in revealing her love and, like heroines in the romances, speaks in broken words. This nurse, however, is different from the usual type. She is much more of a character, remarkably developed—an early example of the careful elaboration of a secondary character. She tries to help Fiammetta, by kind, intelligent, and virtuous advice to throw off this shameful love and remain true to a splendid husband—another secondary character, a carefully and cleverly developed one, whose equal will be found first in the Prince de Clèves in the seventeenth century.

In discussing her new love, the power of Love who possesses and rules over her heart, she acts like a lovesick woman of the romances and faints. Such fainting could be only an influence from the romances where the symptoms and effects of love are exaggerated.

Boccaccio puts into the mouth of this new type of nurse, remarkable because of her deviation from the nurses in Ovid and the romances, who, in fact, are really in the nature of a go-between, sensible remarks, which, though imitated from Seneca's *Hippolytus,* are a satire on the society of the time in Italy.

The nurse bursts into a tirade against the amorous company of wilful and wanton women of rich and noble women kindled with burning lust who declare Love to be a god, whereas in truth he is a frantic and furious force from Hell flying swiftly through the world to bring despair and fiendish folly to the rich and idle.

Panphilus imitating William, the hero of *Flamenca* makes every effort to win the friendship of everyone related to or close to Fiammetta.

After the consummation of their love and many days of joy, Panphilus is called home by his aging father. He cannot refuse. The scene in which he tells Fiammetta of his forced departure, his purpose first revealed by tears and moaning in his sleep, is admirably and movingly told.

The rest of this lengthy book is filled with the laments of Fiammetta—for her lover never returns—the attempts of the faithful nurse to comfort her and her husband's efforts to cure her of a disease that torments her and has no remedy.

Torquato Tasso's lyrics celebrating Leonora d'Este are full of courtly love and its metaphors. Love burns in the heart. The lover trembles and sighs. In *Rinaldo,* inspired by Virgil's *Aeneid* and Ariosto's *Orlando Furioso,* unquenchable thirst for glory is mingled with passionate love.

The love element is the more important and more interesting portion of his *Gerusalemme Conquistata.* Tancred, the real hero of the poem, is like its author, who is the spiritual father of Byron, Keats, Rousseau, Senancour, Heine and others whose bleeding and restless hearts bring them pain and suffering mirrored in their works. His heart aflame, he burns with the consuming fire of love. He lives in agonizing fever.

In Spain the *Libro de buen amor* by Juan Ruiz is based both on *Pamphilus de amore* a love story in Latin told in the manner of Ovid and on Ovid either directly or through intermediaries.

He tells us that no medicine will cure the pain of love, that the fire of love burns and that Love creates this fire in the hearts of those most loyal to him. The symptoms of the love disease appear. The victims of love lose their appetite. They become weak and thin, they cannot sleep at night. They rave and become demented. They sigh, weep, tremble, and grow pale.

The lyric poets of Spain have filled their poems with metaphorical descriptions of love and all its symptoms. Love is represented as a cruel person who strikes and wounds his victims sorely. Not satisfied with the conventional bow and arrow, they provide him with swords, lances and every kind of weapon. The love disease cannot be cured by doctor, surgeon, or medicine. Death is frequently the pitiful end of the lover.

A tendency developed to present the other side of the argument, to show how to recover from the dread disease and also to ridicule the whole list of symptoms and deny any outward and compelling force other than the will and natural disposition of the victim. Gaspar Gil Pola summed up the whole debate in the following lines:

> Love is not blind 'tis I
> Who place myself in torment's way.
> Not Love, but I, that in a day
> Hope, fear, laugh, and cry.
> To say Love burns is a lie.
> His fire is only what I say.
> His wings are just my will to play
> With vain hopes that make me sigh.
> Love has no lock, he has no bow.
> To imprison and wound the free and sane

Is only a thought that we maintain;
And poets' claim is just not so,
But a dream quite stupid and vain.
To believe such things is truly insane.

There was a vast number of romances written in Spanish as can easily be seen by reading Cervantes' *Don Quijote*. These romances were written in the form and style created by Chrétien and imitated by hundreds of romances in verse and prose in France that slavishly copied the great master of the twelfth century. The pastoral romances continued this vogue but drew inspiration also from Classical authors.

In the plays of Lope de Vega are still to be found the various symptoms of love that appear in the romances. Lope mentions the romances in *el Desconfiado;* and though he knew Ovid and other Classical authors well, the traditional use of metaphors in writing of love was not without their influence. Love is a disease that cannot be cured. It burns and affects the health in the usual ways.

In the lyric poetry of the sixteenth century in Spain the fire and the flames of love appear in profusion. The suffering of one in love and the impossibility of any relief or cure is no less frequent, nor sleeplessness, tears and groaning with the pain of love.

Cervantes' satire on the romances probably did much more to perpetuate them, their style, and their influence than to put an end to them. They persisted and were fervently read for another century. The pastoral romances which led on to the novels of the seventeenth century were tending, however, at least in part, to supersede the romances.

CHAPTER XIV

Chaucer and Shakespeare

Chaucer wrote a *Court of Love,* translated a good part of the *Roman de la Rose* and shows a use of French sources that saturates much of his work. He studied in France. Later he served in the English army and was taken prisoner in France where he remained for several years.

One of Chaucer's early poems was the Ovidian story of Ceys and Alcyone told in his *Book of the Duchess* with Machaut's *Dit de la Fontaine Amoureuse* as an important source. This story is an evident imitation of French romances.

The story of Troilus and Briseida (Cressida in Chaucer and Shakespeare) was told by Benoit de Sainte Maure in his *Roman de Troie,* a romance modeled and developed on the patterns of Chrétien's stories. With great improvement, Chaucer takes over this story to give it world-wide renown by his amazing gift that places him among the greatest story-tellers of the world.

Benoit's poem had already won great fame. It is preserved in many manuscripts, was translated into German and, in the thirteenth century, imitated in a Latin version by Guido delle Colonna, to be retold by Boccaccio, from whom Chaucer translated it with original additions and the help of Guido della Colonna. Chaucer's version has some resemblance to the French *Roman de Troie,* which he may have known.

Various love complaints are imitated, also, from the French, with perhaps some influence from Ovid's *Heroides.* They have all the familiar symptoms and effects of love.

In the *Parliament of Fowls,* the overwhelming power of Love is expressed and the torture he inflicts on his followers.

A portion of the *Cour d'Amour* was suggested by the *Roman de la Rose*. Rosial, the heroine of the poem is described in terms that seem to show that the model was the portrait of Emilia, the lovely amazon of Boccaccio's *Theseida*. The portrait as painted by Boccaccio is clearly elaborated feature by feature from the portrait of Dame Oyseuse in the *Roman de la Rose;* and this portrait is a replica of those that Chrétien de Troyes put in his romances to furnish models that were passed on from poet to poet and from country to country.

The allegorical style of Guillaume de Lorris and his metaphorical love treatment had a number of disciples including the poets Eustache Deschamps, Machaut, Froissard, Christine de Pisan, Alain Chartier, and finally the delightful Charles d'Orléans all delicately lyric but monotonous, stylized, and tending toward the insipid. Poetry had become highly conventional and uninspired; but these were the writers who carried the torch of Arato in France and they are all direct or indirect imitators of Chrétien. One author, who was listed among the great poetic pillars of French literature in the fourteenth century by Eustache Deschamps was, in his industrious but stupid way, a fervid admirer of Chrétien de Troyes. His name was also Chrétien—Chrétien Legouais. He wrote the *Ovide Moralisé* a work whose title advertises its absurdity. He translated the *Metamorphoses* and drew a moral from each episode. When he came to the story of Philomela he inserted Chrétien's version instead of his own, because of his great admiration for Chrétien de Troyes and thus preserved for future generations the only copy that we have of Chrétien's poem. His praise of Chrétien shows that the great poet of the twelfth century was still the revered master of French poets. The earlier of these minor poets were well known to Chaucer and he borrowed freely from Machaut and somewhat from Chrétien Legouais.

The "Franklin's Tale" in the *Canterbury Tales* is a story of chivalry and love. It displays the typical love that Chrétien developed with its various attitudes and effects. Chaucer has put into the mouth of the Franklin certain of his own commonsense views, particularly regarding some sort of equality between man and wife, eschewing completely any idea of servitude on either side. Nevertheless Chrétien's *Erec et Enide* is clearly mirrored in this story.

First we have the idea that Dorigen is both the loved lady and the wife of Arveragus, just as Erec had in Enide both his wife and his *amie*. Moreover, like Erec, Arveragus pledged his service and his will to do his lady's bidding, except that he would retain his sovereignty. Dorigen was fully as loyal and obedient as Enide. Thus, with all the originality of Chaucer in his treatment of his subject, the differences effected by two centuries and the caustic practicability of the English poet's underlying nature, which could, sometimes, quip a little at chivalry, there is a noticeable similarity between this work and that of the French poet in whose tradition Chaucer is borne, as on the current of a great river that streams down through the centuries.

While Arveragus was winning glory in a distant land Dorigen went to the coast to live with a friend. The large and numerous rocks that covered the shore and extended out to sea, menacing the lives of sailors, disturbed her and were much in her mind. While she was there a man named Aurelius fell deeply in love with her. Restrained by the fear and hesitation caused by love he dared not express his love except in poetry where he complained of suffering that seemed destined to bear him to the grave. Finally he summoned courage enough to reveal the suffering he endured for this lady. She pitied him but told him firmly of her deep love for her husband and the impossibility of her ever being unfaithful to him. However, really in jest, she imprudently said that if he would perform the impossible task of removing all the rocks on the coast or sinking them underground so that they would no longer be a danger to the lives of men who sailed along that shore she would yield to his love. This was a promise intended to emphasize the impossibility of any weakening on the part of Dorigen. Nevertheless it was a promise. Such a promise was in line with the promise of Alexander's father to grant an unknown request before it was stated, or that of King Arthur to Kay, which led to the certain abduction of Guenevere in *Lancelot*. Promises were sacred and the idea gradually developed that nothing was so compelling as a promise. This was one element among the ideals in accordance with which Chrétien molded his knights, established the lofty conception of courtesy in its fullest sense, and set it in motion to roll on even into our own era.

Aurelius manages to get magical aid and the rocks are sunk by Venus beneath the bottom of the sea. He then demands the fulfillment of his promise. Dorigen weeps. She consults her husband. Arveragus decides that she is to keep her promise notwithstanding the grief and dismay but to keep the fact secret in order to protect him from public shame. Such nobility so moves Aurelius that he absolves Dorigen from her promise.

In the *Knight's Tale,* Theseus is made into a Medieval knight. He takes vengeance on Creon of Thebes like one of the great barons, leading his army of retainers, fighting in personal combat as in many a romance. It is interesting to note that Palamon and Arcite, those two great friends who lay wounded side by side, when taken to Athens and imprisoned in a tower by Theseus, should look down and feel a double wound from Love's arrows as Lancelot looked down in imitation of a passage in Ovid, Lavinia looked down in love on Eneas in imitation of Chrétien's passage to pass it on till it reaches Chaucer in an unbroken chain. The eyes of both young men are pierced by the same shafts that fly from Emily, sister of Ipolita, and so sister-in-law of Theseus. Thus a rivalry springs up between the two friends, to be settled by personal combat just as the struggle over Lavinia was settled between Aeneas and Turnus, which battle was a source of one already recorded between Cligès and the Duke of Saxony with Fenice as the prize. So the Arthurian romances and Chrétien gather strength of inspiration in Classical lore and pass it on to those who follow. The rich and pure stream that flowed from fountainheads like Virgil and Ovid disappeared in the deep valleys and swamps of the Dark Ages to rise again as a refreshing and vigorous spring in the works of Chrétien, to pour out inexhaustibly henceforth.

Arcite, released from prison at the behest of a friend but on condition that he remain forever outside the realm of Theseus, is in the prison of Love, that metaphorical prison where the victims of love weep, groan and suffer pangs that threaten to be mortal, in romances that copy Chrétien's works. Arcite's prison is so much worse that that of Palamon, who stayed behind in the tower, which seems like Paradise to Arcite. Meanwhile Palamon, in prison, thinks of Arcite as a man free in Thebes, who may attack Athens, capture the city and win Emily for his wife; and jealousy acting like love, for it is only an intensification of love, turns his features pale as ashes, dead and cold.

In Thebes Arcite suffers:

> When that Arcite to Thebes was come
> Full oft a day he swooned and said: "Alas!"
> For see his lady shall he nevermore.
> And, shortly to conclude all of his woe,
> So much sorrow had never a creature
> That is or shall be, while still the world endures.
> His sleep, his meat, his drink is him bereft,
> That lean he wax and dry as is a shaft;
> His eyes are hollow, and grisly to behold,
> His hue sallow, and pale as ashes cold,
> And solitary he was and ever alone,
> And wailing all the night, making his moan.
> - - - - -
> And in his manner for all the world he fared,
> And suffered the lover's malady.
> - - - - -
> Engendered of melancholy humor.

Awakened by Mercury from the slough of his despondence, he looked in the mirror and saw himself so disfigured by his disease that he thought he could live thus disguised and unknown in Athens. He was willing to take the risk of dying when he looked upon the loved lady.

After seven years Palamon escaped from prison intending to make his way to Thebes, there to raise an army and returning to Athens, to win Emily by force of arms or die.

Hidden in bushes not far away and waiting for darkness in order to avoid discovery, he saw Arcite approaching. Arcite had displayed such a fine and noble character and disposition at Theseus' court that he had become a great friend of the king and an officer in his household. Arcite sat down near the bush where Palamon was hidden and talking to himself told the story of his love and how he was living incognito and with an assumed name at the court.

In the characteristic manner of the lovers of the romances in the metaphors of Chrétien adapted to Chaucer's style, he declares that Love has thrust his fiery dart so burningly through his heart that it is killing him. Emily slays him with her eyes and is the cause of his imminent death. Then he fell in a trance; to be awakened, however, by the wrath of Palamon, who suddenly appeared and threatened to kill him unless he ceased to love Emily, whom, he claimed only he had the right to love.

In spite of fierce anger, Arcite, because of that chivalry established two centuries before, to flourish in the hearts of knights in literature and have its influence on men who lived in the world, Arcite promised to bring arms to Palamon and joust fairly with him for the right to love the fair Emily.

So it happened; and, by chance, Theseus himself came upon the knights and stopped the combat. When he learned that the contestants in this combat were his two deadly enemies, he, nevertheless, pardoned them on account of their love and its delightful folly. He decrees that a tournament shall be held with a hundred knights on each side and he who kills or defeats his opponent shall have Emily as his wife.

Preparations for the tournament are described in terms that recall the romances of Chrétien, the color and the lavish expenditure at the court of King Arthur.

Arcite who had solicited the aid of Mars won the tournament but Venus, to whom Palamon had prayed for help, was able to provide an accident so that Arcite, having removed his helmet and riding toward Emily, the prize of his valor, fell from his horse upon his head and was mortally wounded, so that Palamon finally had Emily's love. On his death-bed Arcite begged Emily to take Palamon as her husband if she should ever marry:

> "Naught may the woeful spirit in my heart
> Declare or tell of all my sorrow's smart
> To you, my lady, that I love most,
> But I bequeath the service of my ghost
> To you above every other creature,
> Since that my life now may no more endure.
> Alas the woe! Alas the pain so strong,
> That I for you have suffered and so long!
> Alas, the death! Alas, my Emily!
> Alas, departing of our company!
> Alas my heart's fair queen! Alas my wife!
> - - - - -
> I have here with my cousin Palamon
> Had strife and rancor many a day agone,
> For love of you, and for my jealousy,
> - - - - -
> As in this world right now know I none
> So worthy to be loved as Palamon,
> That will serve you and treat well all his life.
> And if that ever you shall be a wife,
> Forget not Palamon, the gentle man."

In *Troilus and Cressida,* Troilus like many characters in the romances is scornful of love; and Love takes vengeance on him, shooting him with an arrow from his bow. Then with one look at Cressida his heart caught fire. Dazed and sighing and groaning he complained of Love's cruel torment. The subtle beam from the eyes of Cressida was the dwelling place of cruel Love.

Communing with himself he asks why he feels such pain, if no love exists. If love is good he questions what causes his grief.

If it is evil, he marvels why all the suffering and torment seems so sweet to him. The more he drinks of love's elixir the thirstier he becomes. And why, if he burns on account of his own desire, whence comes his wailing and complaints. Why does he faint though not wearied. How could so much strange grief fill his heart unless he wills it himself. The sweet torture seems like a living death. What is this wondrous malady that seems to be killing him with heat in cold or cold in heat. He turned pale sixty times a day, though burning with love. Sleepless and without the power to eat, the sickness of love appeared in his face. He thought that a glimpse of the loved lady would cool his hot desire and give him comfort; but the nearer he came to her he loved the more he burned. If he could not win the lady's love he was sure he would die. All of this is most familiar.

Shakespeare, who like Molière took his material wherever he found it, garnered much from the Middle Ages. The romances bequeathed the love that appears in his poetry and his plays. In his use of the theme of Solomon's Wife, it is extremely interesting to compare *Romeo and Juliet* with Chrétien's *Cligès*. The role of Fenice's nurse, Thessala, is divided between Juliet's nurse, who is helpful in the love between hero and heroine and Friar Lawrence, who studies chemistry and has the knowledge of herbs, though not the magical powers of Thessala. He plans the simulated death of Juliet to save her from a second marriage to Paris after Romeo is banished following a quarrel between the two rival families of Capulets and Montagues, in which Romeo kills the loved Tybalt.

Friar Lawrence had secretly married Romeo and Juliet; and now, when her father insists that Juliet must marry Paris, and Juliet threatens to hurl herself from the high walls of the monastery, the Friar gives Juliet a potion that makes her appear to be dead; and she is buried in the family vault. Friar Lawrence's letter warning Romeo in his retreat is, accidentally, not delivered; but Romeo learns of Juliet's death. He returns before she awakes, opens her tomb to look upon her beauty; then takes poison and dies. When Juliet awakes and finds her lover dead she takes her life with

Romeo's sword. Thus love has its most powerful effect in the death of both lovers.

Love and jealousy cause death in *Othello*.

As You Like It is full of love theory. Silvius, who loves Phebe details much of this. Asked to tell what it means to be in love he says:

> It is to be all made of fantasy,
> All made of passion and all made of wishes,
> All adoration, duty, and observance,
> All humbleness, all patience, and impatience,
> All purity, all trial . . ."

A lover is described as having a "lean cheek, a sunken eye, a beard neglected, ungartered hose, shoe untied and careless desolation in all his appearance."

Silvius accuses Phebe of being as cruel as an executioner. Phebe discusses the wounds that eyes inflict upon a lover. She darts her glances with most murderous intent upon Silvius but they do not kill him. Silvius replies she may some day know the invisible wounds the keen arrows of love make.

In the *Midsummer-Night's Dream,* where dreaming is mingled with reality and fairies take a hand to make serious trouble with lovers, mixing their emotions in almost tragic manner, then correcting all and bringing harmony and pleasing solutions out of chaos, Hermia is willing to sacrifice her life for Lysander and nearly dies of grief when, influenced by a fairy charm, he abandons her temporarily. She takes the dangerous risk of eloping with him and spending a night in a forest.

When her father orders her to marry Demetrius and Theseus, King of Athens, decrees that she must either marry Demetrius or become a nun, her face turns pale and the roses fade from her cheeks. Nevertheless she recommends patience; for lovers have been ever crossed. Suffering is as surely "due to love as thoughts and dreams and sighs, wishes and tears."

CHAPTER XV

Seventeenth Century French Novels

The interminable and idealistic novels of the seventeenth century, five and ten volumes and many thousand pages long, are definitely in the tradition created by Chrétien de Troyes. Their authors followed a habit established by centuries of noble heroes, who mingled beauty, adventure, warlike combats, and love in romantic stories. They sought artistic instruction and inspiring models in Italy and Spain, and often turned to Virgil, Ovid, and other Classical authors, whose masterpieces Chrétien taught the Christian world how to use.

Honoré d'Urfé opened the floodgates of composition by prolific novelists. He furnished themes and suggestions, for forty years, to dramatic writers. And his fame in the seventeenth century was tremendous. La Fontaine read him with pleasure. Even Boileau, harsh critic and terror of many a writer, especially the novelists, gave some praises to d'Urfé's *Astrée,* describing it as lively and attractive, with most ingenious fictions, and characters intelligently imagined and developed. Worshipful admiration for him reached northward into Germany, where a group calling themselves the Academy of True Lovers took names out of *Astrée.* They wrote to d'Urfé and asked him, as an honorary member of their society, to take for himself the name of his hero, Céladon. Enthusiasm for *Astrée* continued into the middle of the eighteenth century; and it was read with lively pleasure by Prévost, the author of *Manon Lescaut.* Jean-Jacques Rousseau read it and wept over it with his over-indulgent father so far through the nights that often they heard the birds welcoming the dawn with their songs.

Amadis de Gaule continuing Spanish romances, the *Aminta* of Tasso, the passionate love poems of Petrarch, and the *Arcadia* of Sannajar were sources. Most important of all, in this remodeling of the pastoral romance was the influence of Georges de Montemayor's *Diana enamorata.*

In *Astrée,* as in all the idealistic novels of the period love service to ladies is the central theme. Devoted lovers, slaves of their loved ladies spend long years striving to win love and favor of ladies, whose pride demands repeated refusals of their love and interminable evidence of faithfulness on the part of the lover that must be proven by spotless loyalty, submission to every whim, and obedience to every command. This attitude was adopted in real life by those who frequented the *salons* of the time, social gatherings held in the homes of influential and, often, brilliant ladies, with the purpose of purifying both the language and the manners of their *précieux* society. A living example of love service emanating from Chrétien's *Lancelot* and imitated through the ages, exaggerated by the Provençal poets and carried to extremes in seventeenth century French novels, was furnished by the Marquis de Montausier who courted Julie d'Angennes, the daughter of Madame de Rambouillet, who held the first *salons* of the seventeenth century, during fourteen years before she granted him the full return of her affection.

Catherine de Vivonne, the Marquise de Rambouillet found in the elegant style of *Astrée,* in its idealism, in the polite manners and noble attitudes of the ladies and gentlemen, disguised as shepherds and shepherdesses, and the refined love of the story a literary expression of the hopes and ideals underlying her plan and conception of a purified social atmosphere and purified speech stripped of the vulgarity of manners and language and the crudity of lustful passions bred from long wars of religion and rebellion and protracted living in military camps.

All the novels of this type have almost perfect similarity, with the exception that the shepherds and shepherdesses become men and women of high society. The hero is perfect and handsome like Erec, Alexander, Cligès, Lancelot or Yvain. The ladies are beautiful and their portraits are drawn in the manner consecrated by Chrétien and still imitated in these novels. Each feature—or many features—was listed, the forehead gleaming like ivory or snow, the hair in golden curls, the eyes shining like stars, roses and lilies mingled in the complexion of the cheek. Red lips open to reveal rows of delicate ivory teeth, the bosom is snowy too, the arms and fingers long and graceful.

The loved lady, like Guenivere or Laudine, takes over the function of Love and torments the timid lover by trials that stretch out their monotonous and tragic torture through years that keep the sighing lover in unquenchable flames that burn in his heart. He is bound by the chains of love that hold him in sorrowful captivity, relieved only by valiant action in combats intended to win the approbation of the cruel lady, driven to the brink of death by despair, saved only by unexpected accidents or the intervention of gods.

The scene of *Astrée* is laid in the Forez on the banks of the beautiful Lignon. We shall overlook the absurdity of Knights and Nymphs mingling with Druids and Vestals in the fourth century of our Christian era and that of ladies and gentlemen seeking a quiet and leisurely life disguised as shepherds and shepherdesses, the ladies wearing silk and carrying golden crooks.

The hero of this story is Céladon, a shepherd, who has enjoyed a mutual and tender love with the shepherdess Astrée. One day he meets Astrée, as usual, while they pretend to watch their sheep. Astrée has been treacherously deceived and suspects that Céladon has been untrue to her. In anger she repulses him, and, like Laudine in Chrétien's *Yvain*, she banishes him forever from her presence. In despair, Céladon tries to drown himself in the Lignon. His attempted suicide is vain. He is rescued, revived, nursed and loved by the nymph Galatée, who falls passionately in love with him.

Filled with remorse, Astrée swoons and falls into the water herself to be rescued narrowly from death by other shepherds. Thus Astrée, relenting when her lover seems to have proven his love by the supreme sacrifice, like Guenivere, offering a variation of the Pyramus and Thisbe motive so frequently used by Chrétien and other authors of the romances, shows her own love for Céladon.

Otherwise she is like Guenivere and Laudine, jealous, capricious, haughty, imperious. It is natural for her to assume and maintain the absolute despotism of her beauty and the cruel and merciless power bestowed upon her by Love, her reputation, her pride (her *gloire* in the language of the day, a term made famous and immortal by Corneille, whose heroines, especially Chimène in *le Cid,* resemble Astrée). Corneille was strongly influenced by the novels of the century.

Céladon escapes from the Nymphs, in disguise, but like Yvain, he does not attempt to return to Astrée, since she has banished him from her presence. He awaits her pleasure and suffers obediently, alone in a cave in the woods. There, like Nicolete in the thirteenth century story of *Aucassin et Nicolete,* with a change of sex, Céladon builds a bower or temple of verdure. In the center of this structure, formed of interlaced branches, he erects a statue of his beloved Astrée. Upon it he engraves verses composed in her honor. On the altar he hangs, on branches of myrtle, the table of the Twelve Laws of Love, recalling the *De Amore* of Andreas Capellanus.

As one would expect, Astrée comes upon this temple built in her honor. There, she believes, is the spirit of Céladon. Overcome with emotion, she loses consciousness. In her sleep Céladon comes upon her, kisses her gently, and slips a note in her bosom. Astrée awakes, but dazzled by the sun, she thinks it is the spirit of her dead lover hovering above her and enveloped in a halo of supernatural light.

Aided by shepherds, nymphs, and vestals she builds a tomb for Céladon and all together they hold a burial ceremony with great pomp.

A druid decides to unite the two lovers and a nymph is sent to bring Céladon disguised as a nymph. He is given the name of Alexis and Astrée feels a deep friendship for her new friend. The two lovers feel delightful tremors of emotion inexplicable to Astrée and accompanied by some remorse on the part of Céladon, because of his deceitfulness.

Fighting breaks out and adds the element of combat at arms during which Alexis shows astounding courage.

Céladon, following the urging of a druid, reveals his identity to Astrée, whose anger overcomes her love when she recalls the intimacies that Céladon has snatched so deceitfully; and she commands him to go and die far away from her. The despairing Céladon obeys; and, repeating once more the familiar Pyramus and Thisbe motive both lovers contemplate suicide. However, a happy ending brings these two and several other pairs of lovers, whose stories have helped to lengthen the novel, together in marriage.

Céladon has several descendants among romantic heroes, especially René and Werther. Love sickness has cast over him its melancholy spell of patient suffering, bitter joy, and listlessness.

Silvandre, a secondary character wanders through a wood on a clear moonlight evening, dreaming of his love for Diane. He keeps stumbling against objects on account of his distraction. But whatever obstacle he encounters seems insignificant in comparison with the obstacles that thwart his passionate desires. The quivering of the leaves in the breeze seems slight in comparison with his own trembling with the fear evoked by love in the presence of the loved object. His absorption in thoughts of his love is so complete that he does not awake from his dreaming until he is caught almost inextricably in the tangled wood. This complete absorption is a frequent motive in the romances and is particularly emphasized in Chrétien's *Lancelot*.

The choleric Georges de Scudéry and his ardent sister Madeleine wrote *Artamène ou le Grand Cyrus* the most famous and most severely criticised of all the novels of the century. The brother is famous for his criticism of Corneille's *Cid;* and the sister held a *salon* called *samedis*. She was an ugly old maid but an intellectual and witty person. Their combined effort thrilled a wide public with legendary heroes who won great battles, captured towns and even empires, distinguishing themselves with mighty deeds of strength and valor. These fierce warriors submitted meekly to the beauty of their lady loves, became tender and languorous suitors in the drawing-room where witty and gallant conversation mirrored the *précieux* language of the *salons*. Here, too, just as in the *salons*, discussions of minute points in the code of love appear. Portraits that forecast the famous *Caractères* of La Bruyère abound and scarcely veil their living models among the great of the era.

In this novel that displays all the symptoms and effects of love of the romances, the young Cyrus falls in love with his fair prisoner Mandane. In a monologue typical of the consecrated love monologues for which Chrétien furnished the models, Cyrus debates with himself.

"What is this torment that I feel and whence comes this distress that worries me? What! because I have seen the most beautiful woman in the world, must I become the most unfortunate? Beautiful objects usually cause only joy; why is it then that the most beautiful object that will ever exist brings me only pain? I don't know whether what I suspect is love may not be something worse; for, after all, what do I want and what can I desire? But, alas! it is because I don't know what I want, nor what I could wish for that I am unhappy. I know very well, however, that if I follow my inclination, I shall love the beautiful Mandane, even though she is my enemy. But, alas! woe is me, have I not just learned that she is making sacrifices to thank the Gods for my death? And have I not just learned that Cyrus can never please her until he is in his grave where she now believes that he is buried?"

He thinks that this fact should be able to cure him of his budding passion. But suddenly hope, which alone keeps love alive and maintains the consuming fire which devours its victim, persuades him that since he is now disguised as Artamène and Mandane hates only Cyrus, the son of the Persian king, and he, as Artamène, need not be disturbed by words and acts directed against Cyrus, he can try to win her love. Wavering, however, as lovers waver, he thinks of his ardent desire to win glory in battle which, up to now, has always dominated his heart; and the ambition of a military conqueror struggles against his love for Mandane.

"What," he said, "could I abandon a mistress (war), who never fails to reward those who follow her and servitude to whom is so glorious that she gives nothing less than crowns and an immortal fame to those who are faithful to her! What has become of my powerful desire to be known throughout the world? . . . Have I left Persia only to become the lover of the Princess of Cappadocia (Mandane) and have I ceased to be Cyrus only to be the slave of a person who makes sacrifices of rejoicing over my death and who would push me back, perhaps with her own hand, into the tomb if she saw me issue from it? No, no, let me not be weak enough to yield so easily and let me not be cowardly enough to enchain myself. Remember, Artamène, how many times you were told in Persia that love was a dangerous passion: dispute with her then the entry into your heart, and do not allow her to triumph. But, alas, what am I saying and what am I doing? I speak of resistance and I am conquered: I speak of liberty and I am a slave: I speak of ambition and I have none except that of winning Mandane's love: I speak of glory and I wish to seek it only at the feet of my princess. In fact, I realize fully that I no longer belong to myself, and that my reason opposes my love in vain. My eyes have betrayed me, my heart has abandoned me (Chrétien wrote in Cligès, Alexander speaking: 'I thought I had three friends, my heart and my two eyes, but it seems they hate me . . . These three are my enemies and they are putting me to death.'), my will has followed Mandane; all my desires bear me toward that adorable person; all my thoughts are for her, I no longer care for life except in the sole hope of using it to serve her; and I feel that my reason, though it might well be in revolt against my heart, begins to argue for my princess. It tells me secretly that this beautiful passion is the noblest cause of all heroic actions; that it found a place in the heart of all the heroes; that the illustrious Perseus, the first king of my race, allowed himself to be conquered, valiant though he was, as soon as he had seen Andromeda . . . Finally, it tells me that Mandane, being the most beautiful

thing in the world, I am excusable for being in love with her . . .
Let me follow this love, then, which carries me away in spite of
myself and let me not resist any more an enemy that I could never
overcome and which I would even be sorry to have defeated."
This princess is abducted four different times, offering Cyrus
four opportunities to travel over great extents of country and accomplish many feats of valor to quadruple the rescue of Guenevere
by Lancelot in Chrétien's *Lancelot.*
At the end of this mammoth novel Artamène wins the love
of Mandane and marries her.

Clélie is a Roman story strung out through ten long volumes.
The real interest that this book has for the student of literary
history lies in the precepts and examples that furnish instruction
for a devotee of a *précieux salon,* the portraits of important people
of the epoch and a rather searching analysis of the intimate impulses and reactions of people in love. The course of the lover
courting his loved lady is laid out in a map called the *Carte de
Tendre.*

Tendre is a city or town, the goal of love. There are three of
these towns approached by three rivers. Tendre by Estime is
reached by passing through the various points of Great Wit,
Pretty Verses, Gallant Letters, Love Letters, Sincerity, Great Heart,
Generosity, Probity, Exactitude, Respect, and Kindness. This is a
long journey that may take many years. Tendre by Gratitude is
an easier route if one does not lose his way and pass through
Negligence into the Lake of Indifference or through Indiscretion
to Meanness and into the Sea of Enmity. Otherwise the villages
along the route are Complaisance, Submission, Small Attentions,
Assiduity, Eagerness, Obedience and a few others. The third
town is Tendre by Inclination. This is reached by a swift and easy
route, short and direct. One has only to take care not to be swept
on by a current of impetuousness into the Dangerous Sea and on
into the unknown territory of no return.

Later in the century there appeared a sort of psychological
novel entitled the *Princesse de Clèves.* A feature that was used
by Boccaccio in his *Fiammetta* reappears in this novel and again,

in the eighteenth century, in Rousseau's *Nouvelle Héloïse*. A married lady turns to her husband for help in preserving her virtue and marital faithfulness, and confesses to him her love for another man. In this novel, as well as in the other two, the husband forgives and does his best to protect his wife from her own emotions. In doing so Monsieur de Clèves suffers such unbearable pains of jealousy that he is completely stripped of his tranquility, his reason is threatened, and finally he suffers the ultimate effect of love in death.

This story is not without tournaments, nobility of character, the display of skill at arms. There are plenty of blushes, sighs, tears and severe distress caused by love.

Madame de Clèves loves the handsome and irresistible Duke de Nemours. Her rigor and the refusal of her favor is due to her strength of character and virtue. The struggle was a desperate one and her suffering was intense. While her husband still lived she seemed to need his support to save her from succumbing to her passion for her lover. After his death, however, her determination not to yield to a love that would have been sinful before and one that she thought had caused her husband's death became stronger and she refused his attentions.

The symptoms of love and its effects are present in violent form though not introduced in a detailed analysis. The Duke tells Madame de Clèves that he dares not speak to her or look upon her and he trembles whenever he approaches her. Often he cannot even speak. Madame de Clèves is so confused by his presence that she would gladly have died to avoid it.

There are love monologues. One of these occurs in the garden of the Clèves' home, where the Duke has entered at night. He sees the lovely woman of his dreams in a bower under a light and he worships her as a goddess. He sees her gaze at a painting of the Siege of Metz, in which he himself is represented. She looks lovingly on his picture. For him this is a scene that thrills him with hope and joy. He wishes she would come out into the garden. Since she stays, however, inside he contemplates entering the bower; but he trembles and hesistates for fear of changing that expression of sweetness on her face that so delights him into anger and resentment. Now his wavering thoughts constitute the consecrated love monologue.

Finally he attempts to enter; but as he tries to climb through a window, he awkwardly makes a slight noise; and Madame de Clèves withdraws into another room where there are other people. The Duke spends a large part of the night in the garden, hoping to see his dear lady again. He walks under the willows, lies down beside a rippling brook, his heart so full of the pain and joy of love that tears stream from his eyes.

Reviewing her rigor and cruelty in keeping him in banishment from her presence, he turns over thoughts of love and regret, hope and despair, yearning for an expression of her love for him, delighting in her beauty, wondering whether greater boldness would be more successful than timid respect.

There was a strong reaction against the idealistic novel in the seventeenth century, and just as Romanticism, in the nineteenth century was followed by Realism, so also in the seventeenth there was an attempt at realistic writing in a comic vein, as in Scarron's *Roman Comique,* with a satirical and burlesque type of protest most forcefully presented by Sorel in his *Francion* and the *Berger Extravagant.* In imitation of Rabelais' Panurge and of Lazarillo, Sorel wrote of thieves, pickpockets, peasants, gossips, dirty pedants, vagabonds, and wastrels. His Berger drives a small flock of mangy sheep, chooses a slattern for his lady love, whose portrait is a ridiculous caricature. A French and inferior Cervantes, he decries the idealistic novels in a parody that is an extreme travesty. The cleverest and most amusing passage is a parody on the *Metamorphoses* of Ovid, to whose works the novelists often had recourse following the example of the authors of romances from Chrétien down through the centuries.

The Berger, Lysis, was followed by Hircan, who walked softly behind him, snatched off his hat and threw it high up in a tree. Lysis climbed up to get his hat, slipped and fell inside the tree which was rotten and hollow. He disappeared within the tree so that only his head showed above the hole and his arms which he stretched out to seize the large branches. Finding himself thus engulfed he shouted to his squire, Carmelis:

"Fate willed that I should be changed into a tree. Ah! My Lord! I feel my legs grow longer and turn into roots that penetrate into the ground. Now my arms are branches and my fingers twigs. I can already see leaves budding and springing from them. My bones and my flesh are turning to wood, and my skin is growing hard and changing to bark. Oh ancient lovers, who have been changed by metamorphosis, henceforth I shall be of your number, and my memory will live eternally with yours in the works of poets. Oh you, my dear friends, who are here, receive my last farewells; I am no longer among the ranks of men."

"Ah!" said Carmelis, "you are mistaken, Master. Your face is just as handsome as it has always been. Just come out of there and you will see that you are still a man. There is your hat up there among the branches. I am going to knock it down with my crook. Don't you want me to put it on your head? It is getting chilled."

"Alas," replied Lysis, "What you take for a head is the end of my stem. It is not customary to cover it with a hat or a nightcap; for that would prevent its growing. I must be out in the open air now."

"Why do you think you no longer have a head?" replied Carmelis. "Don't I see your hair as curly as the wool of one of your sheep?"

"You are wrong," said Lysis, "it is no longer hair but moss."

In spite of this revery, which was meaningless to Carmelis, he knocked down the hat and put it on his master's head; but Lysis shook it off.

"You are very obstinate," said Carmelis. "Why don't you put on your hat even if you are a tree? You still have your doublet and trousers on, I think. I intend for you to put it on; and to prove that you are still Lysis, I do not need to give any other reason than that you are still dressed as a shepherd and that if you were a tree you ought to take off all your clothes."

"Ah!" said Lysis, "how absurd your reasons are . . . My clothes are a part of myself: They are nothing now but thick bark which has grown over my skin."

His friends tried to pull him out of the tree; but he clung to the branches so tightly in his frenzy that they were afraid of breaking his arms. The only way they could get him out of the tree was to have a woodsman cut it down.

The satire directed at the novels and the *précieux* was continued by Molière. His first attack is in the farce *Les Précieuses Ridicules*. Since all the rules of conduct for the *précieux* are explained at length in Mademoiselle de Scudéry's *Clélie*, Molière's satire is directed at that novel.

Préciosité had been a praiseworthy attempt at improvement in manners and language. The movement had a helpful effect on literature. Many literary works were read, before publication, in the *salons* and criticism there was frank and serious. Exaggeration, however, appears in the novels and in society to such an extent that affectation became ridiculous. The Map of the Land of Love (*Carte de Tendre*) is singled out particularly for ridicule.

Two young ladies are marriageable and the father of one, who is the uncle of the other, wishes to get them safely married and two young men have come to make proposals of marriage. The two young ladies, however, desire a courtship according to the conventions outlined especially in *Clélie*. So they spurn these downright characters who come straight to the point. They vex the young men and drive them away by yawning and repeatedly inquiring about the time of day. As the men leave the house one of them broaches a plan for vengeance. They will send their valets dressed in very fine clothes to make love in *précieux* style with comic exaggeration.

The young ladies express their objections to the bluntness of their suitors. Speaking to her father Magdelon says, with reference to *Artamène ou le Grand Cyrus:*

"My goodness, if everyone were like you how soon a novel would be finished. What a fine thing it would be if Cyrus married

Mandane at the very first and if Aronce married Clélie at once!"
She continues:

"My cousin will tell you that marriage must never occur until after the other adventures. A lover, in order to be acceptable, must know how to utter fine sentiments, sweet, tender, and passionate words; and his courting must be done in the proper style. In the first place, he should see, at church or on the boulevards or at a public ceremony, the person with whom he falls in love; or be taken with fatal result to her house by a relative or a friend, and leave in a dreamy and melancholy mood. For a time he conceals his passion from the loved object . . . Finally the day of his proposal arrives. The proposal should usually be made on a garden path somewhat removed from the rest of the company; and this proposal is followed by immediate anger, which appears in our blushes and which banishes the lover from our presence for a while. Finally he is able to appease us, to accustom us gradually to the declaration of his passion, and to draw from us the confession that causes us so much pain. After that comes the adventures, the rivals that cut through an established inclination, the persecution of parents, jealousy caused by false appearances, complaints, despair, abductions, and all that follows . . ."

Cathos, the niece says:

"I wager that they never have seen the Map of the Land of Love and that Love Letters, Small Attentions, Gallant Notes, and Pretty Verses are lands unknown to them.

The valets arrive and an ignorant servant girl announces their presence and desire to see the young ladies in commonplace terms.

Magdelon instructs her:

"Say: 'There is here an indispensable person who asks whether you are disposed to be visible.' "

And the servant girl replies that she doesn't understand Latin nor the philosophy of the *Grand Cyrus.*

This satire is continued in the *Femmes Savantes.* If one were to read no other literary work of the seventeenth century, one would note that the theory of love so highly developed by Chrétien de Troyes was still in vogue and that many of the terms that describe it were still commonplace in life and in literature. Clitandre is now enflamed with love for Henriette. For two years he had suffered the tortures and trials of love inflicted upon him by Henriette's older sister Armande. She is not a strong character nor naturally haughty and cruel. She has assumed the functions of Cupid as a tormentor of the male only because that is the fashion of the *précieux* society of the day. Clitandre tells us that Armande's beautiful eyes had conquered him and held him in the bonds of love. The flame that she lighted in his heart drew sighs from him. Their tyranny had made him suffer under their yoke. Burning with this flame he made loving sacrifices, showed eager attention, performed tasks and services with deep respect.

Now he has turned, in despair, to Henriette but a stronger flame still is burning in his heart and he receives such kind treatment now and such an assurance of a return of affection that his loyalty for his new love cannot be destroyed. Now Armande, too, late, is ready to yield. She explains that her reluctance to respond to Clitandre's loving advances was only a desire to purify his love, to eliminate the gross and bodily elements and retain only the ethereal delights of the soul; but if he insists on mingling the vulgar desires of the physical side of love she is willing to accept a union of their hearts and of their bodies and to yield now to his gross physical desires.

CHAPTER XVI

Corneille

The idealism of the novels, bravery, courtesy, adventure, and love also, characterize Corneille's dramas. All the devotion of the lovers of the romances and the novels for loved ladies persists, all the nobility of male characters in Chrétien's works and all of his efforts to create superior individuals, to improve social manners and similar efforts, though less happy in the results, that are to be found also in the idealistic novels of the century, are continued but with a more pronounced struggle between love and duty, love and honor or love and glory, with duty exalted above love, though love is more precious than life. The dramatic effect is produced in Corneille's plays by this perfection of character and the supreme adherence of his personages to their lofty ideals, which produce that admiration which is the essence of his dramatic appeal.

In the *Cid* love is still a burning flame. The pain of the Infanta's love redoubles because she must keep it secret. Love is a tyrant for her. The very name of Rodrigue makes her heart palpitate. Since love lives on hope, she will try to quench the fires of her love by giving Rodrigue to Chimène. She cherishes her reputation and pride (that is, her *gloire*) above her love but love will kill her in any event. She strives to cure her love by losing all hope of a marriage with Rodrigue, who is of a rank too low. Alone she prays to Heaven to put some limit on the distress that overwhelms her.

Rodrigue young, handsome, courageous, descends from a noble line of great warriors. His noble birth bestows valor and skill at arms upon him. Confident of his superiority and declaring that the maiden stroke of one of his race will be equal to his best, he challenges the greatest fighter of the realm, with the intent of avenging an insult to his father's honor and the honor of the family name. The offender is the father of the beautiful Chimène, whom he loves with ardent passion. This situation creates the struggle between love that is so powerful and duty characteristic of Corneille's manner. Confronted with a decision so difficult, Rodrigue communes with himself in the first love monologue of the play.

The strange pain of love that he suffers tears his heart. He expects to die on account of this suffering. He wavers. He thinks of allowing himself to be killed in the duel with Chimène's father. But on further reflection, it becomes clear to him, however great the agony in his loving heart, that he would be neither dutiful toward his father or his own honor nor even worthy of Chimène's love if he allowed himself to be defeated in battle. So he chides himself for momentary weakness and decides to win in the duel, which is to be a mortal combat. After killing Chimène's father, which, of course, will end his hope of winning Chimène, he will die.

Rodrigue's noble constancy and his great valor win the admiration of readers and audiences at the theater.

Chimène is now in the agony of a lost love. Her father defeated and killed in the duel, she feels no less love for Rodrigue, but her own honor demands that she seek punishment of her lover, who has smirched the family escutcheon. She appeals to the King; and the King defers his judgment.

The Infanta now has renewed hopes and with them the force of love dominates her completely. She admits that her reason is affected and she declares herself mad.

The first love scene occurs when Rodrigue comes to Chimène's house and begs her to take his life with the sword he wishes to place in her hands. She refuses; but her fortitude, finally shows weakness, the force of love asserts itself, and she admits that she still loves him. Nevertheless, she still intends to continue her prosecution, which honor demands. Rodrigue declares that his life will be a living death until such time as her prosecution will bring about his execution. And then she tells him that if she succeeds, her death will soon follow his. A second love scene occurs after Rodrigue has distinguished himself as the defender of the realm in a night battle against the Moors, who have made a surprise attack. The King has now allowed her to choose a champion who will fight in a duel against Rodrigue; but she must marry the victor. Weakness again permits her love to prevail, and she commands Rodrigue to win in the combat, though he had expressed his decision to allow himself to be killed so that Chimène may be avenged. She finally begs him to save her from Don Sanche.

Polyeucte mingles important military exploits, great deeds of valor, and high nobility of character with love. Sevère believes that his grand victories and his high station, achieved by outstanding courage and success in battle, have made him worthy of Pauline's love. When he learns that she has been recently married to Polyeucte, his grief is so deep that he implores fate to bring him death and desires to utter his last sigh in homage of the woman he loves so dearly. The love sickness with which he is stricken he has no wish to cure.

Pauline is bound to her husband by duty. Her heart is enflamed with love for Sevère, whom she had given up for dead when she married Polyeucte. Although she suffers grievously, she is determined to surmount all the pain of an illegitimate love and remain true to her husband. She admits that she suffers rigorous torment on account of her love for him; and deep sighs and streaming tears confirm her words. Sevère admires her great virtue, which, in her own opinion, she must maintain to keep herself worthy of the noble love of a great hero. In despair he expresses his intention of seeking death in battle as the only solace for his unendurable suffering.

This play has an element of epic grandeur since it mirrors the tremendous world conflict of Christianity and paganism and the martyrdom of early Christians. Polyeucte is converted; and his conversion and ardent faith arouse so much admiration that many others follow his example: and the great courage and the noble sacrifice of his life for his new faith finally win for him the love of Pauline.

CHAPTER XVII

Racine

It is not certain that passionate love would have held so high a place in literature if Chrétien de Troyes had not so firmly established all-powerful love to make it forever the grandest element in Christian literature. Friendship's affection might well have superseded it. There have been many reactions against it as an overwhelming force. Corneille placed will and duty above it. Spenser exalts friendship. Racine, however, restored all-powerful love to its preeminence. In his plays love dominates and masters the bravest and the noblest and brings tragedy into their lives. Its pain and torment destroy reason and life.

In *Andromaque,* Oreste is plunged into deep melancholy, which is Racine's term for love-sickness. His friend Pylade had long feared that Oreste's search for death would be cruelly seconded by fate. For many months the despairing lover had subjected himself to every possible danger to his life. Now he has come to Epirus on an embassy. Pyrrhus is holding Andromaque prisoner here. Her son Astyanax is with her. The Greeks fear that Astyanax may revive the military power of the Trojans when he comes of age and thus create a new menace for them. Oreste is to demand the surrender of Astyanax, who will be put to death as a measure of future security for the Greeks.

Oreste has won the honor of serving as the Greek Ambassador in the hope that Hermione whom he wishes to wed, will finally accept him as her lover. She has been promised to Pyrrhus and is waiting in anger and impatience at Pyrrhus' court, while he hesistates to marry her because he has fallen in love with his Trojan captive. Andromaque repulses him, choosing to remain faithful to the memory of Hector, her deceased husband. She wavers, however, because if she gives her love or promise of marriage to Pyrrhus he will protect her son.

The flames of love are burning in the hearts of Oreste, of Hermione, and of Pyrrhus. This fire has reached white heat after many months of suffering and torment. Oreste is still enslaved by love. Hermione is the haughty lady, who has the function of Love, the tormentor. Oreste has wavered between hope and hate. Enchained by love, he has wandered in senseless fury, dragging his sorrowing heart over many seas. Now he hopes that Pyrrhus will refuse to deliver Astyanax, that he will abandon Hermione for love of Andromaque, and that, then, Hermione will yield to his loving entreaties. His plan, now that the flames of his love have redoubled and now that love has taken complete control of his mind, is to persuade her to love him, to abduct her by force, or to die. The effects of love could not be more violent. His complaints against the cruelty of the woman he loves resemble the lyric cries of the Provençal troubadours.

Pyrrhus, in his turn, declares that all the suffering he has caused the Trojans are equalled by his own. Defeated by love, loaded with its chains, consumed by regret, he is burned by greater conflagrations, than those he kindled in the war against the Trojans. He is willing to cast aside all loyalty to his Greek allies and fight for the restoration of Troy. The madness of love could scarcely debase and tame a fierce and cruel warrior more.

Meanwhile Hermione is suffering bitter pangs of jealousy. Consumed by fury, she is ready to commit a terrible crime. She may yield to Oreste, but in leaving Epirus, she wishes to leave it in flames of destruction and Pyrrhus executed in punishment for his faithlessness. The mad fury of these three ends in death for all of them and Andromaque alone outlasts the fatal day.

In *Phèdre,* the heroine has reached the final day of long suffering. She is about to die. Love has wasted her strength and spread its palor on her face. She loves Hippolyte, her stepson. She has resisted this love and kept it hidden, even shown herself as a cruel stepmother in order to disguise her true feelings. Hippolyte secretly loves Aricie, a prisoner held by his father, Thésée, since she is the daughter and sister of enemies whose lives he wishes to exterminate. Hippolyte has, in the past, been scornful of love but now his heart is enflamed with a love that burns the hotter because he keeps it secret. His loyalty to his father forbids this love. Oenone reminds us of Thessala in Chrétien's *Cligès*. She tries to discover and persuade Phèdre to reveal the secret ill that so distresses her, just as Fenice's nurse begs her to confess her trouble.

Scarcely was Phèdre married when she blushed and grew pale at the sight of Hippolyte; but when his father brought him to *Trézène* where the scene of the play is located, Phèdre's wound was opened again and her love became "Vénus tout entière a sa proie attachée."

When a false report of Thésée's death reaches Phèdre, she confesses her love to Hippolyte. And when he spurns her she tries to take her life; but her *confidante* Oenone prevents her.

Thésée returns and being falsely informed by Oenone that Hippolyte has declared his love for Phèdre, he calls upon Neptune to avenge him; and Hippolyte is killed by what appears to be an accident, as he drives his chariot along the coast. Phèdre takes poison after giving Thésée a true report of her own guilty love and of Hippolyte's innocence.

In *Mithridate* the force of love is strong enough to bring three mighty warriors from three corners of the then known world to the scene of the action. Mithridate, King of Pontus and of many other eastern countries, holds Monime, who is already declared his Queen but not married, in a port on the Bosphorus. Defeated in battle and reported dead, he makes his way in disguise to the point where his loved Monime draws him with the tremendous magnetism of love. The death of their father seems to allow his two sons, ardently but secretly in love with Monime, to hasten to the scene of a powerful drama.

Talking to Xipharès, Mithridate's younger son, Monime complains of all her suffering, an orphan, without friends, held captive and filled with terror, now helpless, but, far worse than all the rest, annoyed and tyrannized by the older son, Pharnace, who means to compel her to marry him.

Xipharès promises to protect her and tells his love, which he says, has caused him far more pain, in concealing it, than all her suffering. He loved her before his father had seen her; and she loved him. Ever since distress and torment have assailed her, and keeping her love secret has caused greater pain.

Mithridate suddenly appears. He finds his two sons here, who should have stayed in the countries they govern, far from this spot; countries that they should defend. He learns from Arbate, Governor of the port, that Pharnace has declared his love to Monime and tried to force her to marry him. He has formed a grandiose plan to attempt an attack on Rome marching by a round about route, hoping to pick up reinforcements everywhere as he advances and turn his deplorable defeat into a glorious victory, reward of a project unequalled for courage and undaunted imagination; but first he intends to punish Pharnace. Meanwhile, trusting Xipharès, who has always been a dutiful son, he assigns to him the duty of guarding Monime. This command would place Monime and Xipharès in constant communication and intimate relations. Monime's reputation (her *gloire*) forbids such an arrangement. Her love for Xipharès would make it impossible for her to endure his presence. She could not restrain the strong attraction of her ardent love. She, therefore, orders Xipharès to find some pretext to avoid her, to depart and save her from a revelation of her love and its tragic consequences.

Mithridate reveals his grand project to his two sons and orders Pharnace to depart at once, to marry a Parthian princess, and defend Asia against the Romans. When Pharnace refuses and urges his father to ally himself with the Romans, with whom he has had secret understandings, Mithridate accuses him of political treachery and also of perfidy in becoming his rival in love. He calls the guard and has Pharnace arrested. At this point Pharnace reveals to his father the secret of Xipharès' love for Monime. Mithridate, however, pretends not to believe that his favorite son is guilty of this crime. Nevertheless he has his suspicions and summons Monime with the intention of setting a trap for her and of learning the true facts. Declaring that he no longer desires a marriage at his age, wishing to devote all his energy to his military ambitions, accusing Monime of a treacherous love for Pharnace, he expresses his intention of punishing her faithlessness by a marriage with the man she loves, the traitor Pharnace, friend of the Romans, who killed her father. Monime reveals her horror of such a fate and is led unfortunately to reveal her love for Xipharès and admit that she loved him even before she knew Mithridate. Now the rage of Mithridate is turned against the younger son. He resolves upon the death of both of his sons and sends poison to Monime. Pharnace places himself at the head of rebels and Romans and appears to have won a complete victory. The death of Xipharès is reported and Monime is about to take the poison with joy. Mithridate himself is wounded, defeated; and he plunges his own sword into his breast but, at the last moment, love wins over the cruelty of this warrior, which is unsurpassed in history, and he sends Arbate to save Monime's life. Xipharès distinguishes himself for bravery and defeats his brother. Mithridate dies.

In *Bérénice* we have a love monologue by Antiochus. He debates with himself whether he shall tell his love to Bérénice, who is supposed to marry Titus, before he leaves Rome in despair. For five years he has been doomed to silence or to exile by Bérénice after many attempts to speak through glances, tears, and sighs. Her rigor compelled him to promise obedience to her will; and he remained her dutiful and loyal friend. But now he can endure the agony of silence no more. He will leave Rome but he must declare his undying love. He will leave and seek speedy death.

On every side praises ring of Titus' virtue and valor and of Bérénice's beauty; but the laws of Rome forbid the marriage. He has loved her more than life. Many brave deeds and important victories in battle have seemed to him like love service but not enough to merit the love of Bérénice, whose beauty has dominated and vanquished his heart. But now after five years of sighs and tears and such cherished love completely won, Titus unwillingly will dismiss the unwilling Bérénice. A tragic decision; a repetition of the fate of Dido and Aeneas, saddest parting in a world of literature.

Twenty times Titus has tried to communicate this sad news to Bérénice, whose tender love could never imagine such an ending, and each time his tongue is frozen to silence in his mouth. Finally he must tell her the tragic news, how duty condemns their love. He hesitates and learns from her lips that the loss of his love would cause her death. He cannot utter the words that would seal her fate. Although duty wins over love, yet all his life will be a torment, grievous because of the lost love of Bérénice; and he hopes that death will soon end his agony.

Titus appoints Antiochus as the messenger who must inform Bérénice of the fateful decision. But Antiochus' noble nature makes him hesitate to give the message. He would have left Rome and disobeyed the new emperor. Moreover, he fears the punishment Bérénice is sure to accord him if he is the scapegoat who breaks her heart with such unwelcome news. His flight is interrupted by an encounter with Bérénice herself, who commands him to tell her what he wishes to withhold; and when, obeying her insistent command, he reveals to her the will of Titus, she banishes him in hatred forever from her sight. Thus for Antiochus she is still the tormentor; all the cruelty of Love is concentrated in her person. Still he fears and worries lest the pain of losing Titus' love will kill her.

Titus comes once more to see his loved Bérénice. Alone he waits for her to join him and breaks forth in a long love monologue. He questions whether he will have the fortitude to bid her farewell and banish her from Rome. Love is in her eyes and its shafts penetrate to his heart. He wavers in his decision and nearly fails to maintain his cruel determination. He senses a weakness that makes him cowardly and almost ready to yield the throne to a more courageous and stronger will.

Bérénice arrives and he states the sad fact. They must part. The laws of Rome compel them. She reproaches him for such cruelty.

Firm in his decision to respond to the demands of duty and glory, he declares that his future life without her will really be death, yet he chooses to reign. Soon, however, news of his death will convince her that he still loves her. She begs to stay near; though she may not be wedded to the Emperor, she still may see him.

The Emperor yields and consents that she may stay. Momentarily love rules his heart again. He weeps, sighs and trembles. In the end, however, he decides that Bérénice must go. In anger and despair, she threatens to leave, as enemies in his heart, her present grief, past love, and her blood that she means to shed in the palace.

Titus finally decides to solve the whole question by obeying the laws of Rome but by taking his own life. Bérénice now believes that he loves her as truly as ever; and with a noble strength of mind, she removes herself from the presence of both of her lovers and urges them to present an example, as she will too, of the most tender love the world has known and the most sorrowful.

CHAPTER XVIII

Manon Lescaut

Beautiful Manon is one of twelve girls being taken to the coast of France, thence to be sent to America, chained together at the waist, and conducted by six men.

The Chevalier des Grieux has followed Manon from Paris, trying to free her. He had arranged an attack; but his paid assistants ran away with the money without helping him. He bribed the six men to allow him to follow; but they collected money from him each time that he spoke to her, until his money was gone; and now they brutally prevent him from approaching her. He had to sell his horse and now is following on foot with the intention of continuing all the way to America. Such is his passionate love. His distress causes him to weep bitterly.

He had first met Manon at Amiens, where she had been sent to enter a convent against her will, accompanied by one of her father's male servants.

Des Grieux offered to risk his life to deliver Manon from the tyranny of her parents, who were forcing her to take the veil. He was astonished at his boldness; but it was the power of love that gave him courage.

Manon consented; and he was able to take her to an inn for supper, since she claimed that he was her cousin. This inn was owned by a man who had formerly been a coachman in the employ of Des Grieux' father, and who was loyally attached to the son.

Des Grieux' heart was flooded with a divine pleasure such as he had never experienced before. This delight was diffused throughout his whole being and so filled his mind and soul that he was deprived of the power of speech; and he wept copiously.

Melancholy often appears in Manon's face. Weeping, sighs, trembling, and loss of speech are the symptoms of the passionate love of these two young people.

They went to Paris and lived together, hoping that Des Grieux' father might consent to their marriage.

Meanwhile a rich nobleman won the favor of Manon because of her need for money. In order to be rid of Des Grieux, this man informed Des Grieux' father of his son's love intrigue. Servants accompanying Des Grieux' brother were sent to take him home and confine him there. As a result of this action, Des Grieux fell senseless to the floor. He resolved to die and he refused to eat; thus showing additional and familiar symptoms of the love disease.

For six months he remained in a state of hatred, of hope, and of despair. His thoughts during this period resemble a love monologue of the conventional type in vogue for so many centuries.

His friend Tiberge persuaded Des Grieux to enter the theological school of Saint Sulpice to study for the priesthood. For a while he was calm; and, taking delight in study, seemed to be cured of his love for Manon. But Manon finally found him. Sighs, tears, talk of death rekindled their love.

Manon's need for money and her constant dread of being without it led to repeated infidelities, shame, degradation, gambling, and even **thievery.**

Brief were their moments of joy and their miseries, of long duration.

They were both arrested. Des Grieux was put in the Saint Lazare prison. If he had known what had happened to Manon, he said he would have lost his senses and probably his life. She was shut in a narrow cell in solitary confinement, obliged to work each day, and had most unpalatable food.

Des Grieux is a man of high character and ideals, naturally honorable, of a pleasant and mild disposition but endowed with indomitable courage, ready to sacrifice comfort and life itself for a moral principle, for the sake of his honor or for love. This man of the finest type is as completely under the control of love as any hero of medieval romance; and he is so fascinated that he allows himself to be subjected to the deepest degradation, to suffer extreme hardship, to endure appalling shame, and even to commit criminal acts.

We have here only a curious form of love-service. This new form had to be substituted for love-service through knightly combat because the scene of the story is placed in a time contemporary with the author, who lived in the eighteenth century.

Adventures could scarcely be less probable than those of these two lovers. Des Grieux escaped from prison, killing a jailor; and he rescued Manon from her jail as well.

A final attempt on the part of Manon to obtain money and presents from another lover whom she proposed to rob and desert resulted in the imprisonment of both Manon and Des Grieux. Des Grieux was released through the influence of his father; but Manon was condemned to be transported to America. The result of the news of this sentence on Des Grieux was severe. He fell prostrate on the floor with palpitations of the heart that caused him to swoon; and even after he recovered he thought that he was dead. When complete consciousness and understanding returned to him, he intended to die; and he asked his father to kill him.

This story was supposedly told to Prevost by the hero, whom he had just met when he was following Manon to the point of embarcation for America.

In fact, Des Grieux accompanied Manon all the way to America. Riding along beside the van in which Manon was being taken to the seaport and gazing at her beauty now in distress, her clothes dirty and her face in tears, he nearly fell from his horse. We are reminded of the absorption of Lancelot in Chrétien's romance. Manon remained with her eyes closed until Des Grieux' sighs awoke her from her stupor.

They landed at New Orleans. At first Des Grieux was befriended by the governor and given a means of livelihood.

The governor's nephew was attracted by Manon; and when he discovered that the two lovers were not married, he obtained the consent of his uncle, who had absolute power over the destiny of the girls who had been shipped there, to take Manon as his wife. A duel ensued between Des Grieux and the nephew. Des Grieux thought that he had killed his opponent. Des Grieux was, himself, wounded in the arm. When Manon learned about this tragic occurrence she fainted in Des Grieux' arms and remained senseless for fifteen minutes.

The two lovers escaped together, fearing death from savages as they fled. Finally Manon died of weariness and exposure. Des Grieux buried Manon in the sandy soil; and he was found unconscious and nearly dead, lying on Manon's grave. He was sick for three months, until, finally, his friend Tiberge came over the sea to rescue him and take him back to France.

CHAPTER XIX

Rousseau

Rousseau resembles Chrétien de Troyes in an important way. He stands as a transmission agent at the extremely low point in the middle of the eighteenth century when the pseudo-classicism of France reached an ebb so low that insipidity and barren imitation characterized a period in which originality, vigor, and interest were lacking and lyricism had been absent from French literature for two centuries. The romances had yielded to pastorals and the uninspired and wearisome novels of the seventeenth century. Rousseau was a corrective force in morality, politics, and literature. He harps back to Tasso as a man of deep feelings and unhappiness. He was a complete misfit in his epoch, but an innovator, or more correctly, a revitalizer. Although he is not famous as a poet, he brought lyricism back through descriptions of nature, portrayal of love, outpouring of personal feeling, and the confessional type of personal expression that constitutes romanticism; thus motivating a tremendous revolution in art as well as in government. Like Chrétien de Troyes he fills a broad gap in the history of literature and in social regeneration. He gives a strong impetus to literary inspiration.

As a child he spent many hours reading the novels of the seventeenth century; and his conception of love is based largely on those novels, a fact which puts him directly in the romantic tradition that Chrétien inaugurated. In literature Rousseau is original only in the fullness of his confession and the extensive revelation of his own thoughts and actions. He had the example of Montaigne in autobiography. Montaigne professed to give a complete revelation of his own character, mental attitudes, and personal faults. Rousseau differs from Montaigne in the honesty of his self-analysis and in the limitation of his comments to his own personality in all simplicity. His description of love is new only in so far as it becomes extravagantly personal and sexual.

In the early stages of the love between Saint-Preux and Julie its ennobling quality is emphasized. This insistence reaches backward to Provençal love and that of the *Dolce stil nuovo* in Italy, where it is a distinguishing trait, and forward to the idea of love in the Romantic School and even to practice among the devotees of that school. It has an extreme example in Dumas' *Dame aux Camélias*, where a courtesan is rehabilitated by love.

The novel, full of tears, high-flown rhetoric and naive discoursing, is tremendously boring to the modern reader. Nevertheless, like the great Chrétien de Troyes of the twelfth century, this great genius of the eighteenth century presented in the *Nouvelle Héloïse* an important landmark in literary history. What Chrétien established in serenely eminent originality, in a period devoid of literary excellence, Rousseau revived in an era of artistic sterility. Romance and Romanticism is revived and a sparkling fountain of exuberant lyricism and idealistic art arises from the dark subsoil to burgeon forth in great streams of revivified art, tumbling and bubbling in the mighty current of nineteenth century literature that carries the novel to the summits of human achievement. Those divine waters flow from Classical times; and though buried for long periods under ignorance, barbarity, or regimentation, they never lost their power and refreshing vigor. Chrétien de Troyes realized what a great source of inspiration was provided by his two masters Virgil and Ovid and he fashioned their magnificent heritage into that form of literature that, after eight centuries, today stands preeminent.

A person living now can scarcely comprehend the joy and exhilaration of readers back in Chrétien's time, who could find in his stories a new world of brilliant beauty, the thrilling excitement of high adventure, a sublime vision of social perfection, noble ideals, and admirable courtesy. Chrétien told a clear-cut story. His invention was consummate art in his own day. Rousseau's novel was messy and lengthy; but many readers read it far into the night with an unaccustomed delight. People were weary of the old worn out precepts of pseudo-classicism. The horror of high mountains and deep dark valleys had lost its force. Nature in all its beauty and glory was revealed as a new world and a paradise of charm and delight; but most of all they were thrilled by the revelation of the passionate joy of love, its sweet torment reduced to personal terms; and what had been lasciviousness and the social habit of a decadent *Ancien Régime* became exalted ecstasy and an elevating inspiration. Love rose to a conception raised above laws and conventions. Idealized romance returned to overpower mediocre universality and barren objectivity.

Although we celebrate the rejuvenating and revivifying lyricism and the deep and quivering emotion that Rousseau restored to a dying art, we object vigorously to Mme. de Stael's statement that no one had dreamed before him that the "burning agitations of the human heart" might be expressed in literature. The literature of the world had been filled with just that for centuries; and even at the highest point in French Classicism represented in its grandest achievements, in the dramas of Racine, those burning agitations form the essence of several of his greatest masterpieces. Rousseau must have credit for elevating personal morality and the conscience of the individual above the immorality of a civilization that had only conventional and social standards of thought and action.

His lovers yield to an all-powerful love that brings sighs, trembling bodies, sleepless nights, burning pain, bitter sweet joy and floods of tears. The lover is banished, not by the lady, to be sure, but by a scandalized father. His wandering far from the loved lady creates within him all the sadness, longing, tears, unsettlement of the reason, and repeated contemplation of suicide that brings him to the brink of death, while Julie suffers similar torment at home.

The torture of love is continued in the latter part of the novel by two rather odd methods. Julie, now married, has formed a strong resolution to be virtuous and faithful to her husband. Secondly, her kind husband, who strongly resembles the husband in Madame de Lafayette's *Princess de Clèves,* relying on his wife's constancy and believing in it implicitly, pardons Saint-Preux and even goes so far, in a curious attitude, as to invite the former lover to come and live in intimate association with the loved lady in her own home. He even goes farther. He leaves them alone together while he takes a trip. Meanwhile the thrill of loving communion, even physical contacts, with the restraint of moral conviction, strains their trembling and sobbing hearts and bodies to the utmost. Agony saturates their beings and suicide is contemplated and barely evaded.

The melancholy love-sickness of Saint-Preux is mirrored again and again in later literature all over Europe. The deep feeling, the passion of the troubadour poet of Southern France was often frustrated by social conditions. The poet aspired to the love of a lady in a station of life far above him. Rousseau himself was, in like manner, frustrated because of low birth. He felt inferior and never ceased to deplore his lot. His hero, Saint-Preux, a modern Abelard, loved his Héloïse, a young lady of the nobility, and he, her tutor. The social barrier replaced the lady's rigor of the older romances and novels and banished the lover. Saint-Preux had a form of superiority in his intelligence, his high moral aspirations and lofty ambitions. He lacks the courage and determination of older heroes, but falls into a despair that those former heroes often experienced. For them, the result was insanity. Saint-Preux was also unbalanced mentally. He did not go completely over the brink of madness like Yvain or Orlando; but he also differed from them by the fact that he never recovered, as they did, from his despair. This condition or state of mind constituted a new sort of malady which became so infectious that it permeated the literature of Europe and received in France the name of *mal du siècle* because its virulence manifested itself at the turn of the century. Famous examples are Chateaubriand and Senancour. René is the archtype in France. Balzac's Lucien de Rubempré is another. Stendhal's Julien and Byron's Childe Harold are afflicted with this weariness and despair, people of lofty ambitions thwarted by society and thrown into despair—tearful and melancholy sufferers.

Lamartine's poetry is full of deep melancholy. His poem *Le Lac* echoes a passage in the *Nouvelle Héloïse*.

Saint-Preux and Mme. de Wolmar, who is the heroine, Julie, have taken an outing on a lake and they are driven by a storm to a point on the shore that is a scene of their earlier love. Memories of that earlier moment of happiness, so intimately associated with this scene, stir almost uncontrolable passion that floods their beings and nearly ends in tragic death for both of them. So Lamartine writes of a return to a lake where he knew great joy in company with Madame Charles. In Rousseau's passage the evenly measured sound of the oars leads to reminiscent dreaming. The lovers maintain a profound silence. He writes of the soft rays of the moonlight, the silvery shimmer of the water. The happy time of their love is over and has disappeared forever. It will never return.

These suggestions find the following expression in Lamartine's *Le Lac*:

Un soir, t'en souvient-il? nous voguions en silence;
On n'entendait au loin, sur l'onde et sous les cieux,
Que le bruit des rameurs qui frappaient en cadence
Tes flots harmonieux.

Temps jaloux, se peut-il que ces moments d'ivresse,
Où l'amour à longs flots nous verse le bonheur,
S'envolent loin de nous de la même vitesse
Que les jours de malheur?

Hé quoi! n'en pourrons-nous fixer au moins la trace?
Quoi! passés pour jamais! Quoi! tout entiers perdus!
Ce temps qui les donna, ce temps qui les efface,
Ne nous les rendra plus?

Qu'il (the memory of their love) soit dans le zéphyr
    qui frémit et qui passe,
Dans les bruits de tes bords par tes bords répétés,
Dans l'astre au front d'argent qui blanchit ta surface
De ses molles clartés!

CHAPTER XX

Sir Walter Scott

The novels of Sir Walter Scott are strongly influenced by the French romances of the Middle Ages. They are steeped in chivalry. Knights perform heroic deeds as love service to fair ladies. The heroes are modeled on those of the romances. They are paragons of bravery and honor, fierce in combat but gentle and chivalrous toward ladies. They assist the weak and defenseless. They are governed by the highest ideals of chivalry and by an all-powerful love for which they would gladly risk their lives.

In *Quentin Durward,* a Scotch youth, poor, but of noble blood ousted from his country, his family defeated and ruined, seeks service in France. He has an uncle who serves in the Scottish guard of Louis XI, and he is himself admitted to the same military unit.

Many are his adventures which demonstrate his great skill in combat and his indomitable courage.

In a boar hunt he is fortunate enough to save the life of King Louis. He is also wise enough to leave all the credit for killing the boar to the King, thus doubly winning the king's regard, he is selected to guard the King against the possible violence of the haughty Duke of Crèvecoeur, with whom he is supping for political purposes, unprotected except for Quentin, who stands hidden behind a piece of furniture, armed with a gun and instructed to kill the Duke instantly at a sign from the King. The Duke holds a high position in the service and councils of Charles of Burgundy, the powerful rival and foe of the King. He has come to Louis' court to bring strong protests and demands from his overlord. Among these demands is the restoration to the authority of Burgundy of

the person of the Countess Isabelle of Croye, whom the Duke of
Burgundy, since she is his vassal, has arrogantly promised in marriage to his favorite, the ugly Campo Basso. She is accompanied
by an older relative, Lady Hamelin de Croye, a lady who ardently
desires a husband and whose mind is full of tournaments in which
doughty knights fight for the love of fair ladies and in love-service
risk their bodies and their lives. She recalls one at which an ancestor
of hers was won in such a tournament by the bravest and strongest
knight—a tournament ever since famous in the annals of her family
and the country. She mentions with pride another tournament
fought in her own honor in which two adventurous knights were
killed, one backbone was fractured, one collarbone, three legs, and
two arms were broken, in addition to flesh wounds and bruises
uncounted. Thus have the ladies of the House of Croye always been
honored. The Knights of King Arthur are mentioned; and chivalry
and the romances are the whole source of the love story that runs
through this historical novel.

The Duke of Orleans, although affianced to Joan, daughter of
Louis XI, is deeply wounded by the shafts that dart from Isabelle's
lovely eyes and he flatters and courts her in the very presence of
his fiancée, who turns pale and almost swoons in jealous dismay.

Louis XI, his devious methods of diplomacy and desperate
efforts to maintain harmony and unity in France, in fact, the
Spider King and his era are the reason for the composition of
this fine historical novel. A love story, however, runs through it.

Joan is ugly and deformed. The Duke of Orleans feels only
repulsion for her. When Louis, influenced by the demands of *his*
great rival, the Duke of Burgundy, sends Isabelle away from his
court, under the escort of Quentin Durward, the Duke of Orleans,
accompanied by the best swordsman in France, the mighty Dunois,
attempts to abduct the lady who has stirred his heart so deeply.
He attacks Quentin but is unhorsed and badly hurt. Quentin nearly
defeats the powerful Dunois, but the King's guard suddenly arrives
and arrests both the Duke and Dunois. Quentin is allowed to
continue and carry out the King's commission.

The crafty Louis, however, has evolved a complicated scheme. He will ruthlessly sacrifice the highly favored Quentin Durward, whose death is nonchalantly taken for granted. He is only a pawn in Louis' diplomacy. In his plan to reduce the power of his formidable rival he is secretly stimulating insurrection in the town of Liege against the Bishop of Liege, vassal of the Duke of Burgundy. He also has taken as an ally the uncouth, glorified highway robber William de la Marck, called, on account of his ugly features and fierce and ruthless depredations, the Wild Boar of the Ardennes. Louis has informed the ignoble brute of the exact itinerary that he has laid down for Quentin Durward as he proceeds on his journey with the beautiful Isabelle and her wealthy aunt. The plan is for De la Marck to seize Isabelle at a designated spot along the route, marry her by force and lay claim to her large estates thus becoming a most uncomfortable thorn in the flesh of the King's rival. Quentin, however, is clever enough to discover the whole plot, to change his course, and to outwit De la Marck.

This is not the final solution, however. De la Marck with the aid of volunteers from the city of Liege captures the Bishop's castle and even kills the Bishop. Quentin, however, manages to rescue Isabelle and take her to the Duke of Burgundy. King Louis, in a tremendous display of bravery, rendered necessary for the strength and unity of his kingdom, comes with a meager escort into the very jaws of his rival at his court and is immediately thrown into prison. Diplomatic discussions follow, nevertheless. The dastardly and impious crime of De la Marck in murdering the Bishop of Liege arouses terrible wrath. In seething anger, the Duke of Burgundy demands the marriage of the Duke of Orleans to Isabelle to strengthen his own position politically. Isabelle refuses and the Duke of Orleans will not take her forcefully as his wife. In face of strong protests in the name of chivalry, the Duke resolves the whole problem by according Isabelle's hand and possessions to that person who will defeat the Wild Boar, murderer of the Bishop of Liege and bring his head to the Duke. This feat is accomplished by Quentin Durward whom Isabelle loves and who loves her passionately.

In this novel chivalry dominates the actions of the hero and of most of the noble personages. The Knights of King Arthur are mentioned and the love story follows the main outlines of the romances. There is a hero of exceedingly fine character, superior in his mastery of the art of military combat, clever in defense, courteous, and upright. There is a heroine of supreme beauty, and the two fall passionately in love. The various symptoms and effects of love are present: timidity, weeping, melancholy, trembling, sighing and weeping. The hero is often in despair; and he is willing to sacrifice his life and perform impossible feats of arms and of daring even when the rescuing of the loved lady seems impossible and the attempt inadvisedly futile. He is a perfect hero of romance; and he experiences difficult and dangerous adventures. There is even mention more than once of errantry by Isabelle who ventures on the highway under the protection of a knight in unconventional conduct shocking to staid members of higher society. The allusions to chivalry, knighthood, and the romances themselves are frequent.

The Middle Ages, knight-errantry, tournaments, mortal combats, ardent love all-powerful and even leading to folly, and all the pageantry of Chrétien's descriptions, learned from him and displayed in glowing color and the blazing light of gleaming arms and accoutrements in glorified manner by chroniclers appear in Scott's *Ivanhoe*. Noble heroes adept in the use of arms, winners of tournaments, courteous and kind in the protection of the weak and defenseless, perform great deeds of valor and pass through high adventures. This grand success in the field of literature, popular on publication and ever since, takes much of its inspiration from the romances directly and indirectly.

Courtly love and the courts of love are mirrored in conversation almost at the beginning of the novel. Sir Brian de Bois-Guilbert, the Templar, described as negligent of his vows, evidently had planned to sweep the beauteous Rowena off her feet in an amorous campaign without mercy. Comments by his companion the Pryor Aymer, also untramelled by the precepts of his holy office, in his worldly conduct, lead the Templar to remark that the Pryor is as proficient as a troubadour in all matters pertaining to the laws and judgments concerning love.

De Bracy is also passionately in love with Rowena and even abducts her. Speaking of his love for her he calls it a frenzy. Although she is really his captive he calls her his captor and declares that her lovely eyes can bestow upon him the doom that she fears from him.

Ivanhoe, or Wilfred, son of Cedric has been banished from his home because he has taken up Norman ways and learned the art of warlike combat at the Norman court, and also because he loves Rowena, Cedric's ward, whom Cedric wishes to marry to the Saxon Lord Athelstane.

Rowena's love for Ivanhoe is deep and constant. When he is wounded in a tournament she trembles and with the greatest difficulty restrains her tears and controls the expression on her face that might reveal far too clearly her great love for the hero.

Chivalry, love with its suffering even to frenzy, love-service displayed in warlike combat, tournaments, bravery unsurpassed and deterred by no danger or the weakness of one unarmed or sick, high ideals, great nobility of spirit and conduct, trial by battle, and the complete background laid in the century when Chrétien lived and put all of these grand and exciting elements into stories—all these characteristics, knights in armor, high adventure, love all-powerful driving its victims to courageous deeds, madness, grievous derangement and death constitute the texture of a novel inspired by romance in its most ideal and thrilling perfection and the fresh, sparkling charm of its pure, inspiring, and artistic beginning.

The lovely lady Rowena, daughter of a Saxon lord is loved by a paragon of knighthood so capable in armed combat that the most powerful knights fall beneath his lance and sword, so courageous that neither the weakness of sickness nor grievous wounds nor the weariness of long exhausting travel restrain him, so handsome that even Rebecca, a Jewess restrained by a great fortitude, prohibited by her religion and the despicable social position to which she is condemned by fanatic hatred of Christians, trembles with a deep love as she looks upon the still perfection of his beauty while she nurses him from the brink of death caused by wounds in a tournament. She gives away her jewels, which she will never wear again, relinquishing all hope of happiness, doomed to a life of sorrow and despair by a love deep and strong like the dauntless force of her noble character beneath the grace and loveliness of her beauty and the charm of gentleness and kindness in her manner and conduct.

The noble resignation of Rebecca is contrasted with the frenzy of Sir Brian de Bois-Guilbert, the Templar's love for Rebecca. He abducts her and makes every effort to compel her love. She stands on a parapet high up in the castle where he holds her a prisoner and threatens to leap to destruction far below if he approaches one step beyond the limit she prescribes. He, whose power and bravery have brought him to the verge and expectation of the highest honors in his order, would sacrifice the glory, which he values far above life, for her love. He would risk every danger and fly with her to distant lands there to carve out, by the force of his arms and the strength of his personality, a kingdom and great wealth all to be placed at her feet in passionate, devoted love. She refuses and suffers condemnation as a pagan magician. At her demand she is allowed a champion to defend her by ordeal of battle. In a scene reminiscent of that in Chrétien's *Yvain*, where Lunete is condemned to be burned and the pyre is made ready to consume her body in flames, while in terror she waits for Yvain, who almost fails to arrive in time, so Rebecca waits in agony and hope until finally Ivanhoe arrives. The Templar is to fight against him. They rush together. Ivanhoe is weak from his wounds; and he is thrown from his horse. Although his lance does not strike very hard on the Templar's shield, Sir Brian loses his stirrups and falls to the ground, dying from the terrible effect of love, which is in horrible conflict with his pride and ambition.

Ivanhoe's trials are due in large measure to his father's ideas and firm convictions. Cedric wishes to marry his ward, Rowena to the Saxon noble Athelstane and therefore is irritated with his son who is deeply in love with Rowena. His son also annoys him beyond endurance by apeing the ways of the Normans whom he hates and by living at the court and jousting in tournaments in the Norman manner. For these reasons Cedric has banished his son from his home. In the end however, Athelstane gives up all thought of marrying Rowena in favor of Ivanhoe; and the great hero's long love service and suffering end.

CHAPTER XXI

Victor Hugo

Victor Hugo, in his youth, was a disciple of Classicism. The old school of literature, that had outlived two centuries, still held the critical authority; and the young poet was definitely and completely under its sway. His most influential master, who did most to shape and perfect Hugo's artistic genius, was the Latin poet Virgil. With painstaking patience the ambitious youth strove to win the commendation of the older critics by observing the rules and conventions of the established school of literature. He wrote hundreds of odes in commendable style with uninspired facility. He won the praise of mature poets and the appellation of *enfant sublime*.

When he had achieved brilliant success and unstinted admiration and his leadership was accepted by a group of young writers, his courage and self-assurance were unbounded. He laid down the principles of a new school and an entirely new type of literature. Romanticism, whose real birth is to be found in the works of Chrétien de Troyes, who put love with all its joy and pain into the hearts of idealized personages of the noblest character and filled the lives of heroes with adventures that tested their courage and their strength, romanticism that was revived in the realm of feeling and passionate love by Rousseau, wells up again in the early nineteenth century with tremendous enthusiasm among a group of young writers, with the added element of lyricism poured out of their hearts in the expression of personal experiences joyful or sad, and glorified by the power of their great talents.

Among the precepts of the new school one was that of seeking inspiration, not in Greece or Rome, but in the native literature of the Middle Ages. Hugo himself drew such inspiration from the stories of the Middle Ages, to pour it out again in poetry, novels, and drama. He is one of the most important links in the tradition of idealized romance, whose charm and the pleasure it bears on its living and inexhaustible waters have endured from the twelfth to the twentieth century and will never disappear though the tremendous floods of its current may at times be reduced in volume.

The elements that characterize this strain in literary history appear earliest, in Victor Hugo's work, in the novel. It has a most exaggerated outburst in *Hans d'Islande* written in Hugo's earliest manhood. It presents wild adventure, tremendous feats of strength and bravery against forces that run even into the weirdly impossible.

The hero, Ordener, is a young man of the highest character. He resembles a knight in one of Chrétien's romances as much as a man living in a more modern age could. He has all the courage and skill at arms. He is generous and ready to protect helpless victims of cruelty and injustice. He loves as ardently as any lover of the days of chivalry and courtly love. He sacrifices his life in love service. Prince of the land, he loves the daughter of a man who was formerly high in government service, now in disgrace and held in a prison with his beautiful daughter, far in the north of Norway. Papers bearing evidence of her father's uprightness and of the evil and cruel plot against him have supposedly fallen into the possession of a hideous monster who equates the horrible and supposedly indomitable opponents that the olden knights defeated in superhuman encounters. This monster, Han d'Islande, has killed many men. No one is supposed to live after seeing this cruel scourge of the country. His hands look like the paws of a beast and they end in fearful, tearing claws. He lives on human blood, which he drinks out of the skull of his dead son, and sea-water. He has a pet bear to which he feeds the remnants of the human carcasses from which he has drained the blood. In extremity, he rides away on the back of the bear as it climbs down a precipice.

Ordener, to save the honor and to free from imprisonment the father of this lovely girl, for whom he sighs, journeys forth to find the monster and to attempt the impossible task of recovering the precious papers. He finally succeeds in his attempt.

The charming love story is buried in a setting of horror and evil sordidness, thus offering an early example of Victor Hugo's use of antithesis.

Notre-Dame de Paris is a masterful historical novel. It gives a marvelous picture of Paris in the late Middle Ages and of the Cathedral of Notre Dame, which we view from within and without under the direction of a glorified guide who knew and loved every stone, statue, and lacy tower. In this grand setting is placed a story of love's torment that costs the lives of three persons in ordeals as cruel as human imagination could present the effects of that passion.

Claude Frollo, a high church official, learned and conscientiously pious, falls in love with the beautiful gypsy girl Esmeralda who dances on the square before the Cathedral of Notre-Dame where the priest lives. His life is ruined. He loses mental control, suffers unendurable pain in the frenzy of his passionate love. Esmeralda's happy, carefree life is shattered by the consequences of her love for a handsome captain of the mounted police. Learning of her love and a rendez-vous with her lover, Claude Frollo follows her in mad jealousy and, at the moment when Esmeralda submits to the embrace of the rival, he stabs the young man. Esmeralda faints and she is found by the police, in the presence of the wounded police officer. She is arrested, but rescued by the powerful Quasi-Modo, the deaf, ugly and misshapen bell ringer of Notre-Dame and ward of Claude Frollo, and given sanctuary in the cathedral. There the dwarf protects and cares for her. Nevertheless Claude Frollo gets possession of her during a furious attack on the Cathedral and when she refuses to yield to his amorous advances turns her over to a recluse who lives in a hole in the underpinning of the church, that is covered by a grating. This woman, Dame Gudule, hates all gypsies because a band of them had stolen her child several years before. In a remarkable tragic climax Esmeralda and the recluse mutually recognize mother and daughter but it is too late. The police take Esmeralda. She is declared a witch, guilty of attempted murder, and sentenced to be hanged. The priest has the power to obtain her pardon and will do so if she yields to his love. She refuses. He is hateful and repulsive to her. Meanwhile she suffers such pain from the indifference of her loved Phoebus, the police captain, that she welcomes death gladly.

The agony of the priest is described in all its force. The raging heat of his emotion wastes his body and shows in red eyes and emaciated face. He descends to the damp prison cell where Esmerlda is confined and grovels in agony on the dirty floor pleading for her love and blazing with anger at her expressions of horror and repulsion.

From the top of one of the towers of Notre-Dame, Claude Frollo watches the execution of Esmeralda far away. Quasi-Modo, who had been his devoted slave for years, but now that he has caused the death of Esmeralda, whom he loved with a worship hardly to be expected of such a stupid and beast-like person, pushes the priest off into space; and he hurtles down to his death on the pavement below after agonizing moments while his cassock is caught on a lead pipe that gradually bends and turns downward, in a description ever since famous. Quasi-Modo goes to the charnel house where Esmerald's corpse is deposited and lies down to clasp the lovely body that he loves so desperately and vainly and to die there.

In *Les Misérables,* the most popular novel ever written, published simultaneously in ten great cities and read the world over, is a most highly idealized romance in which all the symptoms of love appear except madness and death. Great feats of strength, courage, and dangerous risk, even of life, are performed mainly by the hero Jean Valjean, who loves his ward Cosette as a father, but also jealously. Marius is a portrait of Victor Hugo himself. His love for Cosette is long and arduous, thwarted repeatedly.

No knight of the Middle Ages ever showed more nobility of character than Jean Valjean. None ever fought more skillfully or with more courage. None ever encountered greater danger. None ever defended the weak and defenseless more willingly and valiantly. None ever followed the path of duty and honor with greater self-sacrifice.

The appearance of *Erec and Enide* around 1150 marks the greatest date in the history of Christian literature. The novel was born. *Cligès* appearing around 1160 added the element of metaphorical style in the analysis and description of love in French literature. Nothing in our literature is comparable to these achievements in originality and invention. Most of what has followed has been developed out of Chrétien's tremendous inventions. Many other great achievements have been accomplished. The *Divine Comedy* of Dante, Cervantes' *Don Quijote*, Goethe's *Faust*, Shakespeare's dramatic works, and a great number of poets have excelled Chrétien in the excellence of their great masterpieces. That is something different. The originality and inventiveness of those great masters lie in the detailed artistry that their geniuses have put into forms of literature already created and established.

Victor Hugo's *Hernani*, intrinsically great on account of its lyric beauty, also marks a great date in literary history. It dealt the death blow to Classical tragedy entrenched behind more than two hundred years of authority and tyrannical dominance of the stage. It won a great victory for youth and enthusiasm. It freed the drama from restrictive rules and conventional attitudes; and it opened the way for all the progress of modern drama in France.

Melodrama had offered theater-goers a relief from the tedious tragedies. Hugo took advantage of the popularity of the melodrama that had proved so entertaining to the audiences of recent years and based his plays on this favorite form. Under the influence of Sir Walter Scott and his historical novels, Victor Hugo had become deeply interested in history and extremely well read in the field. He employed a historical background to give dignity to a form that would, otherwise, have been extremely trivial. Although the cloak could not cover or prevent the revelation of the underlying clap-trap and improbability, it shows how strong the influence of the lore of earlier centuries is and the vigorous vitality of medieval material.

The scene of the play except for one act is laid in Spain in the fifteenth century, when Charles the Fifth of Spain and Francis the First of France were rivals for the crown of the Emperor of the Holy Roman Empire.

Like the romances, the whole action of the play centers about the ambition or purpose of Hernani and his love for Doña Sol.

His purpose is to avenge his father, who was executed by order of Charles the Fifth's father, by killing the present king of Spain. He is the leader of a band of outlaws, many of whom have some similar wrong to avenge. Although he has sworn to carry out this purpose, although his honor demands it, and his whole life is dedicated to its accomplishment, love interferes and wrecks his plans, and finally is the cause of his death.

Hernani is one of three who love this beautiful and charming girl: the King himself, her guardian, the old grandee Don Ruy Gomez de Silva, and the outlaw Hernani. Ruy Gomez is immensely rich. As one might expect however, nobility, power, royalty all have little attraction for the lovely lady. In romantic fashion, she prefers the outcast and loves him with a passion and a faithful constance that mean far more to her than life. When it seems certain that she will be compelled to marry the old grandee, she intends to end her life with the thrust of a dagger. At the end of the play, when Hernani drinks poison in obedience to a solemn promise, she demands her share, drinks first and dies in an agony of pain.

For love of Doña Sol a king comes secretly and disguised to Silva's castle while the grandee is away, enters stealthily, by a trick, and means to risk his life in a duel with Hernani who follows close behind him. The duel is interrupted by the unexpected return of Silva. The all-powerful force of love is thus apparent. Its effects, even in causing death, are those with which we are familiar.

When Hernani arrives he has been wet by a cold rain. Doña Sol wishes to have his cloak dried, and, solicitous, asks whether he is not cold. He answers: "I burn when I am near you. Ah! when jealous love boils in our heads, when our hearts are swollen with tempests, what matters the storm of tempests and lightning that a cloud of the air may cast upon us as we pass."

He tells her of the hard life he leads and contrasts the discomfort and danger of living among outlaws hunted and in danger of the scaffold with the wealth and comfort she would enjoy in Silva's ducal palace. Would she dare to live among the rude mountaineers of his band among men like the demons of her bad dreams, sleeping on the ground, listening, while nursing a baby, to the whistle of bullets. Her answer is that she will follow him. She will elope with him at midnight the following night.

The King, hidden in most unkingly manner in a small broom closet, hears the arrangement and arrives beneath Doña Sol's window first. His attempt is in vain. Hernani's men surround him and Hernani holds the hated king in his power. In true romantic style he refuses to kill the King secretly in the dark. He desires a public vengeance and releases the King; but now he and his band will be hunted mercilessly. In the midst of such danger, risking his own life and the safety of his followers, he rashly and madly remains in the moonlight with the lovely Doña Sol to offer a most beautiful and lyric love interlude until the din of battle disturbs the scene and seals the doom of a whole band of outlaws. Hernani alone escapes slaughter or capture.

Now, with a price on his head, Hernani returns to see Doña Sol once more. He risks his life to visit Silva's palace. He has heard that Doña Sol is to marry the old duke. Mad with jealous rage he comes to reproach the woman so passionately loved. After listening to his fierce outburst, she calmly reaches into a jewel box and takes from its depths a dagger—the dagger that she had snatched from the King on the night when he tried to abduct the intrepid maiden, who would willingly share the outlaw's dangerous life. She intended to take her own life with that dagger if Hernani had not arrived to rescue her. Her intention is to kill herself before her marriage, which is forced upon her, is consummated.

A tender love scene follows. Hernani is determined to leave Doña Sol in peace. He is in too great danger now to take her with him. Hearing these words, Doña Sol replies that she will die. He sits beside her, declares that he is mad. In a frenzy of passionate love he begs her to kill him. At this moment the Duke arrives and finds his affianced bride in Hernani's arms. Though shocked at the scene he beholds, seeing himself deceived by his guest, for whom he has prepared the defenses of his castle, he, nevertheless, will obey the Castillian laws of hospitality. He hides Hernani in a secret recess until the King has gone. But in going, the King takes Doña Sol as a hostage. When Hernani is released from his hiding place, he is challenged to a duel by the weak old Duke. But Hernani persuades him to join forces with him in an attempt to kill the King and rescue Doña Sol. With other conspirators they await the announcement of the election of Charles V as Emperor, in the catacombs in Aix-la-Chapelle, where the King has come to enter the tomb of Charlemagne with a mystic desire to commune with the spirit of his great predecessor. The conspirators are caught but Hernani and Silva are pardoned in a grand gesture of clemency by a man raised to the noble stature of Emperor.

Hernani had promised to give his life to Silva whenever he should demand it. Doña Sol is accorded to him as his bride. On his wedding night, in a tragic ending to a beautful scene of love, the old Duke arrives and demands the promised life of Hernani, in a jealous rage, which has reduced his flesh to the sharp features of a spectre.

Previously, the love of this old man is displayed in moving words. He has lost control of himself, haughty Spanish nobleman filled with pride in his high lineage and of a naturally dominating spirit and will, he feels the fear of love for a beautiful young woman. His heart is flaming with the intoxicating fire of love. Now at the end he presents the phial of poison to Hernani. Doña Sol snatches it from him, drinks her share first. She returns the poison to her husband and lover. He drinks the rest and they die in each other's arms.

In *Ruy Blas* love confers great power and ability on a man of low birth, in the court of Spain, at the moment of Spain's decadence. Love service by this man makes him risk his life repeatedly and finally, lose it. He suffers all the torment of love. He is thrown into adventures perilous, intensely exciting, arduous, and highly improbable. He meets the challenge of tremendous opposition, of the gravest danger and of honor with the fortitude of a noble character and courage bolstered by love. All these qualities of the hero, all-powerful love, love service, folly verging on madness, agonizing torment bodily and mental, ending in death, are the typical elements of the romances and of Romanticism reborn. Ruy Blas begins as a lackey in the service of a powerful though despicable noble. Secretly he loves the Queen. He, a lackey, is jealous of the King. In his breast he bears a hydra with teeth of flame that crushes his heart in its toils. The pain of secret love is horrible, strange, and senseless, worse than a frightful poison. Like a madman he waits every day for the Queen to pass. She loves a flower that she knew in her native Germany before she came to Spain. And every day he journeys a league into the country where he finds this blue flower. At midnight, like a thief in the night, he scales the lofty palace wall crowned with cruel spikes to place a bunch of these flowers on a seat in the palace park, at the risk of losing his flesh and entrails on the spikes or of being run through by the pike of a guardsman.

Not only is this Ruy Blas consumed by the despair of a hopeless love, he feels the shame of wearing livery. He watches young nobles dressed in splendid clothing enter the palace and even talk to the Queen. To be able to join this group of fortunate people, he would sell his soul to the devil. His blood boils in his veins; and he loves the Queen madly.

The Queen has banished the great lord who is Ruy Blas' master. He has vexed her unendurably by trying to seduce one of her German handmaidens. Don Salluste, the great and powerful lord, plans vengeance. He has been the head of the national police and he still has power, even in disgrace. He hears Ruy Blas speaking of his love for the Queen to a cousin of his, named Don César, but now disguised and living as a bandit. Don César had squandered all of his wealth; but he retains some sense of chivalry and nobility buried under his ragged costume. Don Salluste had intended to use Don César as a tool to take vengeance on the Queen. Don César learns only that he is to take vengeance against a woman; and he refuses. Then Don Salluste turns to Ruy

Blas. He employs the lackey in a plan which he does not reveal. He makes Ruy Blas sign two documents: one is a declaration of his condition as a lackey to Don Salluste and a promise to serve him obediently; the other is a love letter in which a lady is urgently requested to come to Don Salluste's house secretly and at night. The first, Ruy Blas signs with his own name. The second he is required to sign: "César." Don Salluste states that it is a name that he uses in his love affairs. These documents form a trap for Ruy Blas, into which he will unknowingly fall later in the play. Don Salluste dresses his lackey in fine clothes and presents him at court as his cousin who has been absent for years. This lackey whom Don Salluste has heard confessing his love for the Queen, whom he saw, exhausted and pale, fall in a swoon on an armchair, is told to court the Queen and win her love.

He is entered into the service of the King and brings the Queen a letter from the King. He is to be transferred to the service of the Queen. When the Queen looks at the letter she sees that the handwriting is the same as she had found on a note left with the blue flowers that had been left for her on a bench in the palace park.

She had kept this letter and reread it many times; and she carries it on her person. The letter reads as follows:

"Madame, under your feet, in the darkness, a man is there
Who loves you, hidden in the night which veils him;
Who suffers, an earthworm in love with a star;
Who would give his soul for you, if it were needed;
And who dies below while you shine above."

The Queen had also found a bit of lace torn away and stained with blood. Ruy Blas had wounded himself on a spike at the top of the wall. The Queen also carries this bit of lace over her heart. And the letter and the lace burn her like fire—a symptom of love.

The long ride to bring the letter, the loss of blood on account of his wound cause him to swoon. The Queen comes to his aid; and the small piece of lace that had been torn from his cuff slips far enough out of the bosom of her dress so that Ruy Blas sees it.

Then the shafts of love that pass from eye to eye enter the hearts of both. Ruy Blas prays to Heaven that he may not be driven insane by his love.

Ruy Blas rises high in the service of the Queen. He has become her Prime Minister. Under his guidance great improvements have been made in the government. He conducts a meeting of the chief men of the state so cleverly that the Queen, who has heard all from a secret observation post, steps out and congratulates him. Then she confesses her love to him.

Don Salluste returns to carry out his plan of vengeance. Ruy Blas is compelled to submit to his master,—otherwise his true status will be revealed to the Queen. To protect her from shame and public disgrace he obeys for a while.

The letter written by Ruy Blas under the dictation of his master and signed "César," which is the name by which he is known to the Queen, is sent to her. She comes to Don Salluste's house, where he has ordered Ruy Blas to remain, in spite of careful measures that Ruy Blas has taken to prevent her, but which have not been successful. When she arrives she encounters both Ruy Blas and Don Salluste, the cruel grandee whose scheme has been successful. A duel ensues in which Don Salluste is killed. The Queen's honor is saved. Ruy Blas drinks a poison that kills him.

CHAPTER XXII

Alexandre Dumas

Alexandre Dumas takes a place in the Romantic tradition by virtue of a strong influence from Sir Walter Scott and Cervantes, both important transmitters of the chief elements of the old romance, and from the *Roman de la Rose,* in which all the art of love is enclosed in allegory. All the dauntless courage, constant fighting and high adventure, all the love and love service, with all the tremors, the fears and the trials of love that characterize the idealized romance constructed and set up by Chrétien de Troyes to constitute models for future ages appear and stamp the *Three Musketeers* as a descendant of the arch-type.

The musketeers of Louis Thirteenth's guard take no insult, avoid no combat, shrink from no danger. They have the arrogance and the bravery of the Gascon, who, like d'Artagnan will carry on a fight even when so exhausted that he swoons in the midst of his challenge to impossible battle. These musketeers will play a game in which one will attempt to prevent three others from mounting a staircase all four with sharp-pointed swords. When d'Artagnan leaves home to take service in Paris with the Musketeers his parents give him a potent recipe to cure innumerable wounds that are considered inevitable. Like Chrétien's knights the Gascon musketeers have proficiency in the handling of arms by birth. The young d'Artagnan wins victories in dueling over several of the best swordsmen of the day and he is the hero of two serious conflicts between the King's guards and the Cardinal's.

Loyalty of four friends to each other, firmness in keeping pledges, the spirit of *noblesse oblige* that grows out of chivalry, and honor above everything characterize this novel. Athos goes to jail, mistaken for d'Artagnan, in order to leave d'Artagnan free to operate according to their plan.

He falls in love with Madame Bonacieux, the wife of his landlord and a handmaiden and confidante of the Queen. His love gives evidence of itself through sighs, the first symptoms. Love is warfare, so says Dumas.

The handsome Duke of Buckingham loves the Queen and his acts and his speeches are in the style of the romances. The greatest courage, the most extravagant adventures, the most ardent love service carried to the excess of madness, so admitted, characterize his thoughts and acts, at the risk of his life or of the lives of thousands, to prove his love or to gain a few moments in the company of the person he loves, to touch her hair, to hold her hand, to bask in her beauty, to see a smile in her lovely eyes, or to receive from her some trifle that she has worn, a ribbon or a jewel, or to kiss the hem of her dress. He visits France, invited by a letter, purportedly from the Queen, but sent as a trick by the Cardinal to ruin him. The stratagem is detected. The Duke is advised; but he refuses to leave France without seeing the Queen. Several people's lives, including that of the Duke, are placed in jeopardy to permit and arrange this interview.

In the presence of the Queen, he accuses her of cruelty, of coldness toward his love. He admits the madness of his love. He describes all his labor of love. He tells how meager response she has made to his love, what joy the slightest contact with her has given him. He threatens to bring about a war between England and France so that in the end he may come to France as an ambassador just to be in the presence of the Queen for a few moments and gaze on her fair face. This plan of the Duke is compared to the exploits performed by the knights of the romances for the sake of love. The Queen, though veiled and protected by the dignity of her high station, allows her love to shine through.

Aramis is secretly in love and fears that the loved woman has been faithless to him. D'Artagnan shrewdly suspects this love when he sees that his friend is suffering from some unspoken emotion. To comfort his friend he tries to probe the secret. Aramis says that his questions will soon pump tears just as flies extract the blood from a wounded deer. D'Artagnan is no less grieved because Madame Bonacieux, whom he loves, has been abducted. Madame Bonacieux is the Queen's confidential messenger to the Duke of Buckingham. She brings him to the royal palace and guides him through secret passages into the presence of the Queen and is thus subjected to great danger. The Cardinal and his spies learn of her activities and take her into their own custody. The danger that she incurs in her terrifying adventures causes deep grief, sighs and tears to d'Artagnan. The arrival of a letter for Aramis from the lady of his heart brings such joyful news, however, that his sorrow changes to a delirium of ecstasy.

D'Artagnan is still full of grief because of the abduction of Madame Bonacieux. This abduction reminds us of similar motives in the romances, where the heroes search ardently, encountering many adventures, fearful dangers, and fierce combats during long love service, over wide extents of territory. D'Artagnan declares that he would search for his loved lady to the ends of the earth.

D'Artagnan suspected that the Conte de Wardes had abducted Madame Bonacieux; and since de Wardes, agent of the Cardinal, worked with Madame de Winter and there was a love affair between them, d'Artagnan thought he could find his loved lady through Madame de Winter. He courted her therefore; and, somewhat faithless toward Madame Bonacieux, he fell in love with Madame de Winter. Our author now uses the device, common in the old romances, of trying to win the lady with the help of her waiting-maid. So the unscrupulous lover sets to work to win the confidence of Ketty—he already has her love without a conquest. She is madly in love and reveals it by deep sighs. Although d'Artagnan learns of the perfidy of this monstrously wicked woman, his love for her affects his reason, one of the most serious effects of love since the beginning of this type of love in French literature. Ketty sobbed, wept and stayed awake all night because of her love and jealousy. Ketty carried letters sent by his mistress to de Wardes but she delivered them to d'Artagnan, who sent a most insulting reply which Madame de Winter thought de Wardes had sent her.

This apparent spurning of her love had the usual effects of love unrequited and a fever wasted her being. D'Artagnan finally revealed the trick he had played on her and she turns into a fury, tries to kill d'Artagnan, and when he escapes her, she faints—terrible effects of love and anger.

Madame de Winter goes to England with the intention of finding some person whom she can persuade to murder the Duke of Buckingham. Although seized by her brother-in-law and held imprisoned, she succeeds in so fascinating her chief jailer that, driven to madness by love of her, his reason overcome by false statements of cruelty inflicted upon her by the Duke, he stabs and kills the Duke in a frenzy of love. Thus love caused the Queen of France great suffering and caused the death of Buckingham. It was not only the love of Felton, Buckingham's jailer, but his own love for the Queen of France that is the cause of his death. On account of that love and in order to see the Queen, he armed England for war against France. To prevent the invasion of France the cardinal arranged for Buckingham to be killed.

Finally Madame de Winter succeeded in poisoning Madame Bonacieux as vengeance against d'Artagnan. Madame Bonacieux' death was thus, in fact, due to her love for d'Artagnan.

CHAPTER XXIII

Théophile Gautier

In his *Capitaine Fracasse* Théophile Gautier, influenced by the *Roman Comique* by Scarron, represents a company of actors barnstorming in the manner of Molière's troupe through France to arrive in Paris. This company plays masked comedies (*commedias del arte*) in which the characters play set parts. The Capitaine Fracasse is the braggadocio captain, whose sword is decorated with a spider's web, suggestive of the fact that, in reality, it is never drawn from its scabbard.

This company comes, at nightfall, upon the Château de Misère, the dilapidated ruin that is the home of the penniless Baron de Sigognac.

A young lady named Isabelle plays the part of the ingenue. Sigognac falls in love at first sight of this charming young lady born of an actress and a nobleman and thus committed by birth to this occupation. After a night spent in this tumbledown dwelling, the troupe started out with the actors and the scenery in an ox-cart. Sigognac went along as the poet of the company, since their author had received an inheritance and, in consequence, had abandoned his ill-paid employment with the strolling company. He made a sorry sight clad in the old-fashioned clothes of his father that, too big for him, hung on his body like the ludicrous attire of a scare-crow. He had scarcely slept at all during the night. His mind was full of thoughts of Isabelle, the light of whose eyes dispelled the natural color of his face, produced an obvious palor followed by a flush of scarlet. The timidity of the stricken lover, his sighs, his trembling voice, the glitter of his flaming eyes enhanced by pallor and emaciation, the mental absorption that continually distracted his attention clearly revealed his infatuation to the young lady, whom pity for the awkward but noble-minded youth had already inclined to love. Meanwhile Sigognac's mind was filled with dreams of terrible adventures and deeds of extreme bravery that might constitute the love-service of a hero comparable to that of the stalwart knights of romances that he had read—adventures and dangers surmounted that might grant him courage to utter the confession that seemed to strangle his throat and swell his heart with burning agony.

His first adventure comes at dawn, when the first rays of the sun glistened on the barrel of a musket placed in the grasp of one of several dummies stuffed with straw to simulate a band of highway robbers partially hidden in a thicket along the way. A single desperate brigand with a revolver and a Spanish knife had set up this staging with which he often so terrified travelers that he was able to extract from the timid a pitiful booty. Sigognac was too courageous and too good a swordsman for the unfortunate Agostin, whose only companion was a little girl named Chiquita. The troupe was so amused at the clever masquerade that, after disarming the brigand, they inflicted no punishment and, so, gained his good will and that of the little Spanish girl with a present.

Sigognac basked in the praise of Isabelle, who compared him to a hero of romance. This is one of several references by Gautier to the romances and seventeenth century novels that imitated the romances. Among other references there is the mention of *Amadis* and *l'Astrée*. Sigognac thinks of the tremendous exploits of the knights of the romance of chivalry contending with giants and uncounted opponents and hopes for dangerous encounters to prove his love.

The troupe is invited to give a performance at the Château of the Marquis de Bruyère. In commenting on the play she is going to see and the actors, the Marquise speaks in terms that recall the love displayed by the romances saying that she likes the fine sentiments and gallant compliments that the heroes utter while swooning with love at the feet of inhuman mistresses, blazing and burning like volcanoes of love, drawing their swords with the intention of taking their own lives, in despair over the heartless cruelty of the ladies they love so madly. The rigor of the loved lady often irritates her and in her impatience over long servitude and extreme suffering she inflicts to try her lover, the Marquise would like to see the lady experience a like torture.

We have a gentle love scene between the timid lover and the beautiful Isabelle, in the moonlight. The trembling of the lovers' voices, their emotional tones, sighs, silences, and the confidential manner in which they communicate ` vague and insignificant thoughts reveal the deep love in their hearts.

Sigognac's athletic neighbor, Yolande, disdainful of his love as so many heroines in the romances were, noticed the young lovers beneath her window and she was vexed because she could not endure the thought that Sigognac should not waste away, languish, and die a slave to hopeless love for her.

The braggadocio captain of the troupe succumbed to the hardships of the trip, which became severe with the arrival of cold weather. Sigognac smothered his nobleman's pride and took over the role, giving himself the name of Capitaine Fracasse. On the stage he played the role of a bragging coward; but, in fact, he was a superior swordsman extremely well trained. This virtuosity in fencing was of great advantage to him; for a rich and powerful noble fell in love with Isabelle and fought Sigognac to snatch from him his loved lady. He was attacked by a hired ruffian celebrated for his strength and dexterity at arms. Sigognac had many adventures in the protection of his own life and the struggles to defeat his rival. In fact, Gautier's novel has all the characteristics of the romances except for the absence of knights in armor and the unreality of giants, magicians, and otherworld personages.

CHAPTER XXIV

Honore de Balzac

Although Balzac has often been called the leader of the Realistic School of French writers, romantic elements persist in his novels. One of his shorter works entitled the *Duchess of Longeais* is highly romantic. Balzac had great admiration for Sir Walter Scott, whose influence appears in this story, particularly in the feat of entering a convent on a rocky island, overcoming the supposedly insurmountable difficulty of scaling a cliff that rises sheer and high above the water of the Mediterranean Sea.

In the long series of romantic and idealized romances and novels reaching from Chrétien's twelfth century to the nineteenth, one might be interested to point out differences more than similarities. Nevertheless there are elements first introduced into Christian literature by Chrétien that are the real essence of Balzac's story.

The hero is an extremely courageous and noble-minded person. He suffers the all-powerful force of love and its effects. He trembles, sighs, weeps, lies awake at night. He suffers pain and sorrow. The loved lady inflicts such torment that he even thinks of giving up his life. She becomes an all-powerful and a sacred force. His heart burns with love.

The divergence of this story from the romances of the Middle Ages lies in the method and incidents that must be used to create a situation in which the loved lady can exercise her function as tormentor, in which the lover can suffer while performing love service and in which he can accomplish great deeds of an adventurous nature, winning an apparently impossible victory in an almost superhuman attempt, with a long search for the loved lady, who has been removed from his presence and his world and hidden away so secretly and successfully that the hero finds her only after five years of constant seeking.

The Duchess is left to lead her own life by a husband living at the court in complete neglect of his wife. This noble lady has the pride of race and the intention of maintaining a reputation for virtue in the world of high society while amusing herself by subjecting numerous male admirers to the heartless tyranny of her beauty and attractive personality. Thus she becomes the haughty mistress of the General, Armand de Montriveau, armed with Cupid's function of tormenting, refusing to yield to his love while holding him in complete subjection and loving slavery, hope constantly alternating with despair in his flaming heart. He is nearly driven out of his senses and contemplates death. Using the Ovidian metaphor of love as warfare, the Duchess erects, as she says, several redoubts for the lover to reduce with increasing but vain hopes of victory.

In final exasperation, believing that the lady loves him but will yield only to force, which, in spite of his strong character, his famous determination, and invincible courage, he, rendered timid by his love, hesitates to use, nevertheless, announces to her his intention to subdue her. She defies his power to accomplish his design. Playing continuously with fire, escaping narrowly from the impetuousness of her lover by ringing for her maid or by rising abruptly and rushing to her piano to play music that tells her love but secures for her an interlude of safety and a moment of recovery from weakness, she drives her maddened lover to the extreme of kidnapping her. He takes her to his own apartment, tied hand and foot. He attempts to strike terror into her heart by threatening to brand her with the mark of a criminal on her forehead.

He is here following the Ovidian precept which declares that a woman will yield to force and likes to be dominated. This statement appears in Chrétien's *Perceval* and in Ariosto's *Rolando Furioso*.

Forceful treatment is successful in Balzac's story. The Duchess is willing to be branded and to be publicly proclaimed the property of the General. Her love pierces her rigorous exterior and displays itself in passionate submission.

To increase and prolong the torments and trials of love the General returns the lady to her friends unharmed; but, in vengeance refuses to see the loved lady for days. She writes him and he leaves her letters unopened. She comes to his apartment but he is absent. Finally she comes and stands on his doorstep at an appointed time. Employing a surprisingly weak device, the author has the General unintentionally return to his apartment too late. In despair, the Duchess departs and enters a Spanish Convent on an island in the Mediterranean. Filled with remorse and sorrow but full of courageous determination, the General searches for five years until he finds his loved lady, now a nun in a convent of the' strictest rule. In the church, he hears her play the organ. She mingles strains of French music with her playing and the beauty of the music and the fervor of her execution proclaim both her love and her despair, the hopelessness of her situation but the joy of knowing his love. Then he hears her voice in song and recognizes it.

Now he determines to enter the convent and rescue the loved lady. His plans require many days, superhuman courage, and great ingenuity. With loyal friends he climbs the precipitous and lofty rock and penetrates to her cell but there he finds her lying dead on her bed. He takes the body away and gives it burial in the waters of the Mediterranean.

CHAPTER XXV

Tennyson

The stories of Arthur and his knights interest several of the modern poets. Among them are Tennyson whose *Idylls of the King* give important recognition to lore that shows its influence in modern art, poetry, painting, sculpture, and music. There are also Wadsworth, Morris, Swinburne and Arnold.

Tennyson's source is Malory. For *Geraint and Enid* he used the Welsh translation of Chrétien's poems. There is no direct influence from Chrétien—all is indirect. The story of *Geraint and Enid* is much like Chrétien's *Erec and Enide* though shortened.

A moral tone permeates the poems and his later versions are excessively allegorical.

Elaine is perhaps the most charming of these poems. This pure but passionate girl, innocent and timid, though called willful, loves Lancelot when first she lifts her eyes to scan his war-scarred face. She looked and loved him, with that love that was her doom. So love is the cause of death. Love, too, has marred the hero's face and love of Guinevere has caused him torment and pain.

> His mood was often like a fiend, and rose
> And drove him into wastes and solitudes
> For agony, who was yet a living soul.

> When the smile faded from his face and
> Died from his lips, across him came a cloud
>   of melancholy (i.e. love sickness)

> Sleepless all night long Elaine lay
> And all night long his face before her lived.

232

Elaine persuaded Lancelot to wear her favor in the tournament where he was to fight incognito, at the suggestion of Guinevere, for love of whom he had at first refused to go to battle. She, however, overruled him; and since he had given a recent wound as an excuse to the King, she suggested that he could pretend that his name alone gave him too great an advantage in a fight and that he wished to test his valor when he appeared as an unknown contender. He accepted Elaine's favor and wore it in the tournament. When Guinevere heard of this action on the part of her lover she shed wild tears in jealousy; and when Elaine heard of the wound he had received she nearly swooned.

A large diamond was the prize of victory won by Lancelot. The King learned the truth from Guinevere and sent Gawain with the diamond to find Lancelot and give him the prize. He found Elaine and gave the diamond to her. Now, escorted by her brother she found the hero and gave him the diamond. Her face was near him as he lay; and he kissed her, whereupon she fainted from the emotion it caused her. She nursed him and cured him; but when he was well he left her and she died heartbroken.

CHAPTER XXVI

Rostand

The character of Cyrano in Rostand's *Cyrano de Bergerac* will never cease to delight the public. This heroic figure can never be forgotten, and this fact will keep the name of Rostand alive as long as our Christian civilization endures. Rostand is a late Romanticist, not unimportant in our romantic tradition that we have followed through the centuries of Christian literature.

All the elements of the old romances are present. The hero is deeply in love; and he suffers love's pangs. The consecrated symptoms of love appear. Two heroes are exalted by courage and very great skill in the use of arms. Protection of the weak and defenseless is present in a pronounced degree. There is plenty of fighting and plenty of love service.

Cyrano rivals the exploits of the old knights by defeating a hundred opponents. Love adds to his strength and courage. He loves the beautiful Roxane. Since the scene is laid in the seventeenth century with a considerable amount of local color, Roxane is a *précieuse*. This fact, in itself, provides an influence from the novels of the seventeenth century, the *salon* of that time and consequently from the romanticism and the love that developed directly out of courtly love and the old romances. Roxane thinks in terms of love service and the arguments and debates on the theory of love as it was developed and imitated from courtly love. Such discussions and the land of love as it was represented in Mademoiselle de Scudery's *Clélie* are mentioned and form an important part of the background of the play.

Early in the play Christian de Neuvillette reveals his love for Roxane too, saying that he is dying of love for her. Christian is a man of fine character. He learns that one hundred men are to be posted by a nobleman to waylay and murder the drunken poet Lignière, who has lampooned him. Christian is shocked by this cowardly action and filled with pity for the helpless poet. He searches for him to warn him of the danger.

He leaves with regret; for he has learned that a powerful noble, named De Guiche, himself married, plans to use his great influence to force the marriage of Roxane to a man named Valvert, who will be an entirely complaisant husband so far as De Guiche is concerned. If it were not for the need to hurry away in search of Lignière, he would challenge Valvert to a duel.

Christian shows his courage again by braving the first swordsman of the day, Cyrano. Cyrano's face is disfigured by an extremely large and ugly nose. This feature causes him so much annoyance and embarrassment that he picks a quarrel with anyone whom he suspects of an intention to mock him or an inclination to find his nose amusing or repulsive. The boastful assumption of superior courage and prowess on the part of the Gascon soldiers, in whose company he has been enrolled, annoys Christian. They also ignore him. In order to prove his own courage he makes repeated use of the word "nose" in frequent interruptions while Cyrano is telling the story of his attack on one hundred ruffians, who had been set upon Lignière by De Guiche, the commander of the regiment of which Cyrano's company forms a part.

To the amazement of all of his friends Cyrano, though angered almost beyond control, does not attack the insulting young man. His cousin, Roxane, has confessed her love for the handsome recruit and has asked Cyrano to protect Christian from his ferocious comrades. Apparently driven to extreme rage by Christian's interruptions, Cyrano orders everyone to leave the room. They all think that Cyrano will give the young man a terrible punishment. Quite the contrary. He immediately embraces Christian and reveals to him the wonderful news that Roxane loves him. Christian, nevertheless, despairs of winning Roxane. She is a *précieuse*, fond of wit and fine speeches. Although Christian has a ready wit when in a warlike or quarrelsome mood, he is usually rather tonguetied.

He cannot make gallant compliments nor write love letters. He is a remarkably handsome man, intelligent in appearance. Cyrano knows that Roxane has only friendship for himself and no love. Thus in despair of his own cause, he conceives the brilliant idea of combining forces with Christian. With Christian's beauty and Cyrano's superior literary talents, for he is a poet, they will, together, make an ideal lover. From this point on Cyrano courts Roxane by proxy and rises to a great height of exultation by his success in winning Roxane for his friend Christian, even though he suffers sorrowful pangs in secret.

Christian is killed in battle; and Roxane, in mourning, retires to a convent, to weep all her life for Christian, who she believes wrote her many wonderful letters, especially the last one, found on his dead body. We know that Cyrano wrote all of the letters that she admired and the fine speeches that Christian learned by heart. That is a part of his love service, all unknown to Roxane. He drove the fat actor Montfleury from the stage because he allowed his lascivious glance to fall on the woman he loved. His fight against one hundred ruffians is to be included in this love service. For years he visited Roxane in the convent to bring her news of the world and to entertain her by reciting it in witty verse.

The suffering that love causes Cyrano is intense. His ugliness banishes him from the whole map and realm of love. He is condemned to watch Roxane's love for Christian grow. Although Christian's success is really his own, because Roxane delights in fine language, bitterness and sorrow rule his inner thoughts and feelings.

The trials of love get a sort of initial impulse in the action of the play when Cyrano receives a letter from Roxane asking for a rendezvous at Ragneau's bakeshop. He feels a tremendous uplift. His hopes are raised and his courage is so elevated that he cannot find foes enough to combat. The hundred ruffians who are to attack Lignière seem like a small force, absurdly few compared to the strength with which love has endowed him. How great is his disappointment and grief when he learns that Roxane loves

Christian and meets him only to ask his protection for the man she really loves! His love sighs run to tears.

Christian and Cyrano come beneath Roxane's balcony at night to court her with gallant phrases composed by Cyrano. Along the wall where they stand, Christian in front, Cyrano hidden, ivy and jasmine mount and encircle the balcony. A bench stands below. The ascent to the balcony is easy.

Cyrano says that a cruel word dropped by her, from above, on his heart would kill him. Christian speaks at first, prompted by Cyrano, but Christian is slow in transmitting the words that Cyrano suggests and so Cyrano decides to talk directly to Roxane. He explains the halting speech by saying that whoever meets her lovely glance trembles in dizzy consternation. His timidity, which lovers naturally feel, is lessened by the darkness and he speaks more freely. Speaking to her now, declaring his love in lyric ecstasy, he would like to die of joy because she trembles as he speaks and, in poetic fancy, the trembling of her hand descends to him along the jasmine vine. Roxane answers: "Yes, I tremble, I weep, and I love." "Then let death come." cries Cyrano.

Christian mounts to the balcony to take the kiss and the love of Roxane. He has the joy; Cyrano, the grief.

Years later, on the day of his death, Cyrano asks Roxane to let him read Christian's last letter. It tells of a love that even death will not destroy. He reads it in the courtyard of the convent among the golden leaves of autumn that fall steadily from the trees. He reads until the light fails in the late afternoon; and he cannot see. Now Roxane knows that Cyrano is reciting the letter from memory, that he composed it himself. She has worn it over her heart for years; and her love was more for the elegant sentiments expressed by this and other letters than for the beauty of Christian. Now she knows that it was the soul of Cyrano that she loved; and never knew it.

Rostand's interest in the love poetry of the Middle Ages appears in his play entitled *The Distant Princess,* where he portrays the highly romantic figure of the Troubadour, Jeffrey Rudel, who loved an Eastern princess, whom he had never seen, but whose great beauty was reported by pilgrims returning from the Holy Land. The poet is supposed to have travelled to the country of the distant princess, exalted and impelled by an ardent and irresistible love that wasted his being in a consuming fever, but drove him on until he reached the loved lady's land but took his life in the harbor of his dreams.

Chantecler mingles a great ambition and confidence in the destiny and the important role of the hero with a great love, in the form of an allegory wherein animals play all the parts and portray the emotions and reactions of human beings. This great play is too difficult to be staged profitably and audiences of sufficient size to support the cost of presentation, endowed with the necessary poetic appreciation, the ability to transport themselves mentally into an unaccustomed atmosphere and to accept a strange and, to many, a silly medium of expression cannot be mustered frequently enough to keep the play on the stage of any theater.

The play shows the interest of the author in the lore of the Middle Ages because it is influenced by the beast epic of that period which, under the title of the *Roman de Renard,* gave to various animals the traits of human character.

Chantecler, who rules the barnyard flock and defends it from its natural enemies loves the beautiful pheasant hen who has appropriated the handsome feathers of the male. His great role in life, his duty and his great destiny is, in his noble and ambitious though deluded mind, to make the sun rise by crowing in the twilight of the early morning. This attitude and belief in the importance of one's work is intended to be symbolical of human ambitions that fill men's minds with the ardor that glorifies their striving to accomplish great things, exalts their souls with high hopes and makes life tremendously worth living. When Chantecler's delusion is revealed by the female, who is jealous of his ambitions and his devotion to his work in life and wishes to hold the first place in his heart and mind herself, he still persists in his duty and treasures, deep within himself, a desperate hope that great things may be accomplished by sticking to his labor and working with all the other individuals throughout the world who are making a similar attempt and that finally darkness may be dispelled from the world. Thus nobility of character, courage in battle, for he fights the hawk and the game cock, the most ardent love service and suffering characterize this highly romantic play.

Conclusion

Today the novel stands preeminent. It lends its vigor, its art, its very substance to other forms of literature. Nine centuries have been its life-span. Then, as now, but far more, it towered above all other forms. It sprang forth full-formed, at the middle of the twelfth century, a spontaneous creation of one of the world's great geniuses. With an amazing vision and creative understanding, Chrétien de Troyes saw a tremendous gold mine of literary treasure gleaming in the works of Virgil and Ovid. He knew how to take it and shape it to his own needs and to the taste of his age. The enthusiasm with which this great invention of the novel was received and its models were imitated was like the Great California Gold Rush. The durability of the form and its high value then, now, and probably forever, stamp it as the purest and the finest of literary gold; indestructible, brilliant, satisfying, delightful, valued.

The importance of this invention cannot be exaggerated. Thousands of people in Chrétien's own day were suddenly transported from boredom to exciting joy. In dark castles all over Europe the golden light of Chrétien's masterpieces brought a refulgence that flooded those dismal interiors like the gleam of magic jewels so often described in the romances of the Middle Ages.

Noble characters appear like the gods and goddesses of Classical mythology, men of high resolve, dedicated to the glory of their names, handsome, attractive, irresistible in their manly strength and valor, welcoming and seeking adventure and danger, courteous, helpful, protective, generous, models of chivalry, setting ideals for the twelfth century and all Christendom ever since. The glamor of loveliness and charm resides in his feminine characters with youth, beauty, the light of love in their eyes, the gilding of love over the perfection of their forms, inciting to great deeds in service to their charms desired far above life. People read about such paragons with ardent admiration and took their example into their hearts to cherish it as the light and hope for which civilization should strive, a goal, distant as the stars but thrilling and attractive as a summit in the imagination of a world moving ever toward higher spheres of social improvement.

Delving into the rich quarries that Virgil and Ovid offered, Chrétien extracted great masses of gold to form the framework of his novels, nuggets to build episodes, and glittering dust to sprinkle all through and decorate his shining poems.

When he had created these noble forms, rapacious imitators plunged into them to find materials and artistic models that might bring them reflected glory from the great master, who was revered for two centuries. Provençal poets reached into the treasure bag of his works to imitate the new style he had perfected. Centuries of romancers in verse and in prose in France, Italy, Spain, Germany, England, and Scandinavia, authors of lyrics, epics and drama exploited the love he described and continued the analysis and theorizing he began. Down to the fourteenth century Chrétien was copied directly, notably by the Provençal *Flammenca,* Ariosto's *Orlando Furioso,* and even by Dante. Many times the exaggerations of his followers through the ages led to reactions and satire, but never did the idealistic novel cease to maintain its vigor and its interest for a world of grateful readers.

In brief and rapid form the course of this great tradition launched by an astounding, creative genius has been traced through representative works in French, Provençal, Italian, Spanish and English literature in the hope of restoring to Chrétien de Troyes the glory that is his by right.

Index

. . A . .

Achilles, 50
Adonis, 72
Aeneas, 50, 63, 76, 90, 92, 93, 98, 100, 120, 122, 165, 193
Aeneid, 2, 10, 11, 17, 18, 26, 37, 39, 53, 69, 70, 73, 75, 76, 77, 78, 84, 85, 90, 92, 93, 94, 95, 96, 98, 100, 119, 120, 121, 122, 159, 165
Aesacus, 98
Alexander the Great, 7
Amadis de Gaule, 172, 227
Amata, 18, 76
Aminta of Tasso, 172
Amores of Ovid, 26, 34, 43, 50, 64, 73, 83, 156
Anchises, 53
Andreas Capellanus, 45, 108, 136, 138
Androcles and the lion, 90, 102
Andromaque, 188-189
Angennes Julie d', 172
Apollo, 25, 26, 44, 63, 81, 97, 98
Apuleius, 74
Arabic literature, 124
Arato, 163
Argonauts, 63
Ariosto, 149-153, 159, 202, 230, 241
Art of Love, 23, 27, 42, 44, 45, 46, 63, 77, 84, 85, 87, 90, 95, 104, 111, 113, 117, 124, 125, 134, 156
Art of Poetry, 12, 20
Artamène ou le Grand Cyrus, 175, 182
Ascanius, 70, 93
Astrée, 7, 171, 172, 173, 227
As You Like It, 170
Atlanta, 44
Atropos, 46
Aucassin et Nicolete, 141-143

. . B . .

Balzac, Honoré de, 202, 229, 231
Benoît de Sainte-More, 22, 124, 162
Berger Extravagant, 180-182
Bernard de Chartres, 6

Boccaccio, 155-159, 162, 163, 178
Boetius, 103, 147
Book of the Duchess, 162
Born, Bertran de, 125
Briseis, 50
Brut of Wace, 22
Byblis, 51, 78
Byron, 159, 202

. . C . .

Canterbury Tales, 163
Capitaine Fracasse, 226-228
Caractères, 176
Cardigan, 20, 21, 24, 27
Carthage, 63
Cato, 25
Cavalcanti, 137
Celtic Hypothesis, 19
Celtic stories, 55-59, 80
Cemetery of the Innocents, 53
Cercamon, 124
Cervantes, 129, 161, 180, 215
Cestes, battle of the, 76, 84
Chantecler, 238-239
Character portrayal, 32-33
Charlemagne, 5
Charles d'Orléans, 163
Chartier, Alain, 163
Chateaubriand, 175, 202
Chaucer, 162-169
Chivalry, 6, 7
Chrétien Legouais, 46, 52, 163
Chronology, 21, 22, 118, 119-122, 123
Cid, le, 175, 185, 187
Circe, 72
Clélie, 7, 178, 182, 234
Cligès, 10, 19, 22, 26, 43, 45, 47, 49, 62, 78, 79, 117, 118, 119, 120, 121, 127, 129, 134, 137, 145, 147, 154, 155, 157, 158, 164, 165, 169, 172, 177, 215
Consolation of Philosophy of Boetius, 103, 141
Corneille, 129, 175, 185-187
Court of Love by Chaucer, 162, 163
Courtly love, 21, 88, 123-125, 134

Crusades, 5, 6
Cupid, 22, 43, 44, 64, 65, 68, 69, 85,
    97, 121, 122, 135, 143
Cure for Love of Ovid, 44, 51, 67, 156
Cyniras, 72
Cypassis, 73
Cyrano de Bergerac, 150, 234, 237

.. D ..

Dance of Death, 53
Dante, 45, 129, 133, 137, 154-155, 215,
    241
Daphne, 26, 97, 98
Dares, 76
De Amore, 45, 108, 136
Demophoon, 50, 90, 95
Descartes, 41
Deschamps, Eustache, 46, 163
Desconfiado, el of Lope de Vega, 161
Diana, 93
Diana Enamorata of Montemayor, 172
Dido, 18, 28, 38, 50, 53, 69, 90, 92, 93,
    95, 102, 119, 193
Dipsas, 73
Distant Princess by Rostand, 237-238
Dit de la Fontaine Amoureuse, 162
Divine Comedy, 154, 215
dolce stil nuovo, 45, 88, 129, 137, 200
Don Quijote, 160, 215
Duchesse de Longeais by Balzac, 229-231
Dumas, Alexandre, 222-225

.. E ..

Echo, 72
Egeria, 96
Eleanor of Aquitania, 1, 2, 43
Eneas, 22, 48, 119-122, 165
Entellus, 76
Epics, 5, 6
Epistles of Ovid, 50, 101, 117
Eracle of Gautier d'arras, 22
Erec and Enide, 10, 17-40, 41, 42, 43,
    45, 53, 79, 80, 89, 90, 92, 118, 121,
    124, 127, 128, 130, 131, 164, 173, 215,
    232
Escoufle, l', 145-146
Eteocles, 74
Euryalus, 70

.. F ..

Fasti, 96, 156
Faust, 215
Femmes Savantes, 183
Fiammetta, 155-159, 178
Flamenca, 127-131, 159, 241
Floire et Blancheflor, 139-140, 141
Foerster, Wendlin, 92
Francion, 180
Froissart, 163
Furies, 46, 47

.. G ..

Galeron de Bretagne, 143-145
Gautier, Théophile, 226-228
Gautier d'Arras, 22
Gerusalemme Liberata, 154, 159
Goethe, 175, 215
Golden Ass, 79
Golden Fleece, 59
Great Fool, 115
Griselda, 30
Guido delle Colonna, 162
Guillaume de Lorris, 148, 163
Guillaume de Palerme, 146-147
Guinicelli, 129, 131
Gyges' ring, 11, 90, 99

.. H ..

Hans d'Islande, 212-213
Hector, 70
Heine, 159
Helen of Troy, 50, 79
Henry I of Champagne, 7
Henry II of England, 43
Hercules, 44, 95
Hermione, 51
Hernani, 130, 215, 218
Heroides of Ovid, 34, 43, 50, 51, 91, 162
Hesperia, 98
Hippodamia, 83
Hippolytus of Seneca, 159
Historia Regum Britanniae, 8, 37, 64,
    78, 79, 103, 104
Holbein, 53
Holy Grail, 10, 111, 112, 114, 115
Homer, 25
Horace, 11, 12, 14, 20, 53, 63, 64, 74, 90,
    136

Hugo, Victor, 36, 130, 211, 221
Hyppolytus, 51
Hypsipyle of Lemnos, 50

. . I . .

Idylls of the King, 232
Ille et Galeron of Gautier d'Arras, 22
Ivanhoe, 207-210

. . J . .

Jason, 50, 59, 63, 67
Jean de Meung, 148
John of Salibury, 6
Jupiter, 96

. . K . .

Keats, 159
Knight's Tale, 164, 165

. . L . .

La Bruyère, 176
Labyrinth of Crete, 40
La Fayette, Madame de, 7, 156, 158, 178, 180, 201
Lai de l'Ombre, 148
Lais of Marie de France, 22
Lamartine, 203
Lancelot, 22, 37, 76, 79, 88, 120, 121, 122, 130, 131, 134, 137, 145, 164, 165, 172, 173, 175, 178
Latinus, 19, 77
Lavinia, 18, 19, 26, 76, 102, 165
Leander, 101
Les Misérables, 214
Libro de Buen Amor, 160
Lope de Vega, 161
Louis VII, 1

. . M . .

Macabrun, 124
Machaut, 162, 163
Manon Lescaut, 171, 195-198
Man sorely tried by fate, 12
Map of Love, 8, 178, 182
Marie de France, 22, 147, 148
Medea, 49, 59, 65, 67, 77
Mercury, 28, 93, 95

Metamorphoses, 14, 25, 26, 35, 43, 46, 49, 51, 60, 65, 72, 78, 82, 84, 86, 91, 97, 98, 117, 122, 137, 141, 156, 162, 163, 180
Mezentius, 38
Midsummer-Night's Dream, 170
Milanion, 44
Minos of Crete, 80, 82, 95
Minotaur, 40, 59, 80, 106
Mithridate, 190-192
Mnemonides, 82
Molière, 130, 169, 182, 183, 226
Monmouth, Geoffrey of, 8, 37, 64, 78, 79, 103, 104, 115
Monologues, 34-35, 49, 50, 136
Montaigne, 199
Montausier, 172
Montemayor, George de, 172
Mordred, 79
Mont Saint-Michel, 37, 103
Munchhausen, Baron, 109
Myrrha, 49, 72, 73, 77

. . N . .

Nape, 73
Narcissus, 26, 65, 66, 147
Neptune, 83, 97
Nisus, 70
Notre-Dame de Paris, 213-214
Nouvelle Héloïse, 200-203
Numa, 96

. . O . .

Odes of Horace, 20
Oedipus, 47, 117
Oenone, 50, 51
Orlando Furioso, 149-153, 159, 202, 230, 241
Orpheus, 59, 80, 147
Othello, 170
Ovid, 14, 21, 23, 26, 34, 41, 42, 43, 44, 45, 50, 51, 60, 61, 62, 64, 65, 66, 72, 73, 77, 78, 81, 82, 83, 84, 85, 87, 88, 89, 90, 91, 95, 96, 97, 98, 99, 100, 101, 104, 111, 113, 114, 116, 117, 119, 120, 122, 123, 124, 125, 129, 134, 135, 136, 137, 141, 152, 156, 158, 159, 160, 161, 162, 163, 171, 180, 200, 230, 240, 241
Ovide Moralizé, 46, 163

.. P ..

Pallas, 70, 73, 121
Pamphilus de Amore, 160
Pandarus, 37, 38
Paris, 50
Parliament of Fowls, 162
Parsifal of Wagner, 115
Pèlerinage de Charlemagne à Jérusalem, 31
Pelops, 45, 83
Penelope, 50
Perceval, 10, 22, 35, 36, 111-115, 230
Personal portraits, 25-27
Peter of Blois, 6
Petronius, 92
Phaeton, 63, 81
Phèdre, 189-190
Philomena, 22, 25, 26, 46-54, 117, 137
Phyllis, 50, 91
Picus, 72
Pisan, Christine de, 163
Plato, 25
Pluto, 47, 80
Poe, Edgar Allen, 89
Pola, Gaspar Gil, 160
Polyeucte, 187
Polynices, 74
Polyphemus, 37, 103
Pomona, 65
Portraits, 163
Précieuses Ridicules, 130, 182
Prévost, 171, 195-198
Priam, 70, 71, 76
Princesse de Clèves, 6, 7, 158, 178-180, 201-202
Proserpine, 80
Provençal poetry,21, 82, 88, 116, 117, 123, 135, 241
Psyche, 79
Pyramus and Thisbe, 37, 38, 47, 65, 82, 85, 96, 102, 147, 173
Pyreneus, 82

.. Q ..

Quentin Durward, 204-207

.. R ..

Rabelais, 150, 180
Racine, 129, 188-194

Rambouillet, Marquise de, 172
Rash boon, 81
Rinaldo by Tasso, 159
Roman Comique, 7, 180, 226
Roman de la Rose, 116, 148, 163, 222
Roman de Renard, 238
Romances of Antiquity, 116-122
Romantic School, 33
Romeo and Juliet, 77, 169
Rostand, 234-239
Rousseau, 159, 171, 179, 199-203
Rudel, Jaufré, 124
Ruiz, Juan, 160
Ruy Blas, 218-221

.. S ..

Saint Augustine, 115
Sainte Eustache, Legend of, 12
Salmoneus, 96
Salons, 45, 88, 130, 136, 172, 175, 176, 234
Satires of Horace, 14, 63
Scarron, 7, 180, 226
Scott, Sir Walter, 204-210, 215, 222
Scudéry, Madeleine de, 7, 175, 182, 234
Scylla, 82
Senancour, 159, 202
Seneca, 159
Shakespeare, 36, 77, 169, 215
Shoulder Bite of Chrétien, 45, 117
Sir Orfeo, 80
Solomon's wife, 11, 77, 169, 170
Song of Roland, 5
Sorel, 180-182
Spenser, 129
Stael, Madame de, 201
Statius, 10, 11, 47, 63, 72, 74, 75, 76, 100, 117, 118
Stendhal, 202
Swift, 36
Sychaeus, 92

.. T ..

Tantalus, 14
Tasso, 154, 159, 172, 193
Tennyson, 232-233
Thebaid, 10, 47, 63, 72, 74, 75, 100, 117, 118
Thèbes, Roman de, 10, 22, 47, 71, 72, 100

Theseida, 163
Theseus, 59, 60, 61, 80, 90, 95, 106
Thibaut de Champagne, 7
Three-Day Tournament, 11
Three Muskateers, 222-225
Tisiphone, 46, 47
Toilers of the Sea, 130
Tristan and Isolt, 55-61, 75, 78, 87
Tristan of Chrétien, 22, 45, 137
Tristia 14 note, 101, 156
Troie, Roman de, 10, 22, 45, 122, 162
Troilus and Cressida, 168
Troyes, 7
Turnus, 19, 37, 70, 75, 76, 165
Tydeus, 74, 75, 76

. . U . .

Ulysses, 37, 50
Urfé, Honoré d', 7, 71

. . V . .

Ventadour, Bernard de, 125
Venus, 72, 93

Virgil, 2, 3, 10, 11, 17, 18, 26, 37, 39,
41, 63, 69, 70, 73, 75, 76, 77, 78, 84,
85, 86, 90, 92, 93, 94, 95, 96, 98, 100,
119, 120, 121, 122, 159, 165, 171, 193,
200, 240, 241

. . W . .

Wace, 22
Wagner, 115
Walls of Jericho, 40
White Stag, 20
Widow of Ephesus, 92
William IX of Aquitania, 1, 123
William of England, 12, 16, 17, 22, 45
Windsor Castle, 69, 70, 71, 73, 76

. . Y . .

Yvain, 11, 22, 37, 48, 79, 80, 89-110,
117, 131, 137, 141, 151, 172, 202, 209